These views are of the front of the Burial Grounds, and are taken from the opposite side of the City Road. In the top one are two numbers, which indicate (1) the tomb of JOHN GUYSE (see page 57), and (2) the grave of DAVID DENHAM (see page 59).

BUNHILL FIELDS

WRITTEN IN HONOUR AND TO THE
MEMORY OF THE MANY SAINTS
OF GOD WHOSE BODIES REST
IN THIS OLD LONDON CEMETERY

BY

ALFRED W. LIGHT.

———

WITH CHART OF THE GROUND AND MANY
ILLUSTRATIONS.

———

LONDON:
C. J. FARNCOMBE & SONS, LTD.,
30 IMPERIAL BUILDINGS, E.C.
1913

Give me the wings of faith to rise
  Within the veil, and see
The saints above, how great their joys,
  How bright their glories be.

Once they were mourning here below,
  And wet their couch with tears ;
They wrestled hard, as we do now,
  With sins, and doubts, and fears.

I ask them whence their victory came,
  They, with united breath,
Ascribe their conquest to the Lamb,
  Their triumph to His death.

They mark'd the footsteps that He trod
  (His zeal inspired their breast ;)
And, following their incarnate God,
  Possess the promised rest.

Our glorious Leader claims our praise
  For His own pattern given ;
While the long cloud of witnesses
  Shows the same path to heaven.

ISAAC WATTS.

PREFACE.

THE need for a new work on "Bunhill Fields" has long been apparent, not only to me, but to all who have taken any interest in this wonderful "God's Acre." There are only two books extant dealing exclusively with it, viz.: "Bunhill Memorials," by John Andrew Jones, and "The Official Guide," published by the City Corporation. The former is, however, now very rare, and as Mr. Jones wrote chiefly of Ministers, he did not entirely meet the needs of the ordinary visitor. The names, too, he gave in alphabetical order, which makes the book somewhat confusing to use as a guide, although the numbered intersection of each grave is given. It should also be noted that, as "Bunhill Memorials" was published in 1849, many of the tombs, head-stones and inscriptions which Mr. Jones described have entirely disappeared, whilst, on the other hand, new monuments have been erected and epitaphs re-cut. The Ground, too, has been altered, so that the positions of some, as given by Mr. Jones, are now inaccurate. The official publication is a very small, incomplete and perplexing guide, and is really of little use for this purpose, except in a few special cases.

I have found persons from well-nigh all parts of the civilized world wandering about the grounds in dismay, therefore I hope that, by means of the chart and the instructions given, much difficulty and disappointment will be avoided, and a tour through Bunhill will be made both instructive and interesting. I venture to think also, that many who are not privileged to visit this sacred spot in person, may now be able to obtain some idea of it.

Practically every grave which is mentioned has either a sketch or photograph of the tomb or head-stone, and this feature will be particularly valuable to visitors, because many inscriptions are undecipherable, so that some special mark of indentification is really necessary.

I have to thank many friends for kind encouragement, and some for much valued help.

The four illustrations which have been loaned to me by Mrs. Fuller, of Aylesbury Lodge, Bedford, were sketched by the skilful hand of her late much lamented husband. They are Elstow Church, The Village Green at Elstow, Bunyan's Den, and Bunyan's Cottage.   Mr. J. E. Hazelton also kindly lent four illustrations.

For all the other sketches and most of the illustrations I am indebted to Miss F. Bertha Buggs, of Church Farm, Capel, nr. Tonbridge, and Mr. Arthur Wood, of Church Road, Paddock Wood.   I had a great desire that the book should be brought within the reach of all, and particularly that Sunday Schools might obtain it at a special price, and if I had been compelled to employ a professional artist and a photographer, the cost would have been considerable, so that a much higher price would have been put upon the book.   I feel therefore, that, not only my thanks, but also those of all who obtain it, are due to the kind friends who have given willingly of their time and skill.   Their united work in sketching will rescue many tombs from oblivion, and Mr. Wood's camera has produced some most pleasing results.

The City Surveyor, S. Perks, Esq., obtained special permission for my friends to sketch and photograph, and also placed the records, of which he is the custodian, at my disposal.

I must also thank Miss Alice Alexander, of Salusbury Road, Brondesbury, for valuable help in reading, for correction, many of the accounts.   In reply to my oft-repeated query, " What advice give ye ? " (2 Chron. x. 9), I received, " Herein I give my advice " (2 Cor. viii. 10), and this was invariably what could be accepted and which made for accuracy.

The lines by the gifted poetess, Mrs. Chaplin, of Galleywood, Chelmsford, enrich the book, and I most sincerely thank this friend for so graciously acceding to my request for a suitable poem.

The extracts, which were specially chosen by some whom I count it an honour to call my friends, will, I am sure, be appreciated and prove a special feature of the book.

I must thank my wife for her unremitting patience in carefully reading " proofs " and for general assistance.   I hope her little poem will not pass unnoticed, but that it will meet with at least a measure of appreciation.

I must also express my deep indebtedness to the printers and publishers, Messrs. C. J. Farncombe & Sons, Ltd.   They knew what my wishes were with respect to the price of the book, and were cordially in agreement with me.   They were equally desirous that a new reward for Sunday Schools should be obtainable, and they have been almost prodigal in supplying blocks for illustrations.   The book is larger than was intended, but it is only just to say that they have acceded to all requests in this direction in a most generous way.

ALFRED W. LIGHT.

NOTES.

THE reader must not conclude hastily that all spelling and grammatical errors are the fault of the author or printers. The extracts, inscriptions, &c., have been given as nearly as possible to the originals, so that they should appear in their old-world form.

Many visitors to " Bunhill Fields " are under the impression that the grave of George Fox, the Quaker, is here. This, however, is not so, but the small head-stone on which the name of Fox is inscribed stands in the Friends' Burial Ground in Roscoe Street, and may be seen easily through the railings. It is about three minutes' walk from the entrance gate at the west end of " Bunhill."

Some confusion has arisen owing to there having been a " New Bunhill Burial Ground." This was in Islington, and amongst others, Henry Fowler, the preacher and hymn-writer, was buried there. This Ground has long been built upon, and now there is nothing to show for what purpose it was once used.

Neither John nor Charles Wesley is buried in Bunhill. The former's tomb is at the back of his old chapel, opposite Bunhill, and the latter's at Marylebone Parish Church.

The epitaphs given without illustrations or positions appeared on tombs and headstones which have now disappeared.

The easiest way to Bunhill from the south, east or west of London, is to get to the Bank of England and then take one of the several lines of 'buses that pass the gates. The numbers of these are 21, 43, 43a, 60 and 76. From the northern districts a L.C.C. tramcar going to Moorgate Street will pass along the front.

On entering the Ground, the left-hand pillar of the Gateway bears the following inscription :—

BUNHILL FIELDS.

This burial ground of the Nonconformists, known anciently as Bunhill in the Fields, was enclosed with a brick wall, at the sole charge of the City of London, in the Mayoralty of Sir John Lawrence, Knight, Anno Domini 1665 and afterwards, the gates hereof were built and finished in the Mayoralty of Sir Thomas Bludworth, Knight, Anno Domini 1666.

On the right-hand pillar there is the following inscription:—

BUNHILL FIELDS.

At the time of the closing of this Ground, in 1852,* more than 120,000 bodies had been interred therein. In the year 1867 it was committed by Act of Parliament to the care of the Corporation of London, and having by them been planted and restored for public resort, it was opened by the Right Hon. James Clarke Lawrence, M.P., Lord Mayor, on the 14th of October, 1869.

CHARLES REED, Esq., M.P.
Chairman of the Preservation Committee.

* This is a strange error, as according to the records the last interment took place on Jan. 5th, 1854. The name of the person then buried was Elizabeth Howell Oliver, who was 15 years and six months old.

CONTENTS.

BUNHILL FIELDS.

WHAT *is* there, in a child of God, which makes a place like *this*
So good to think upon,—so full of hallowed memories?
A sense of dear companionship with those whose dust lies there;
A fellow feeling with the things which made their lives so rare.

The Lord aye has His messengers with special gifts inspired;
And every age has had the men its special needs required;
David, with equal skill, could touch the Psalter or the sword;
Our Goodwin spent his days to shew the fulness of the Word.

God loved them, called them, used them, crowned their labours with
    success;
Lives there a "Zion's pilgrim" now who has not learned to bless,
And link with childhood's treasures, and their life's more sacred
    spots,
The Pilgrimage of Bunyan, and the hymns of Dr. Watts?

Long as God has a living Church on earth their names shall live;
And we who from their bypast thought such luxuries receive,
May surely breathe our quota of appreciative words,
Though the faint melody be drowned in their sublimer chords.

As we grow older,—we who love the old theology,—
A weightier meaning fills the words,—life, death, eternity;
And hope steals wistfully about the deathbeds of the past,
So faith may find a vantage ground to stand on at the last.

And reverent love, while lingering here, lays natural fears aside,
Seeing how Christ has loved to bless His people's eventide;
As He *has* been, so He *will* be; as *they* were, so are *we*;
Timid believers, with a love to all His family.

Oh, pilgrims of the past, we take fresh courage as we learn
Of *your* triumphant passage to the home for which we yearn.
Gladly we pass your records on, God give them living power
To quiet the foreboding thoughts about a dying hour.

   Galleywood.   M. A. CHAPLIN.

   Tread softly! sure the foot's on hallowed ground,
      For many a saint of God is resting here;
   The busy hum of City life's outside—
      Within the railings lies the dust that's dear.

   Some that were mourned by loved ones who were left;
      Some for whom countless tears were often shed;
   For they live on in many hearts to-day—
      In prose, in poem, whether sung or read.

We see the wondrous Bard of Bedford's tomb ;
　Here rests the precious dust of Joseph Hart ;
Dear Isaac Watts, not very far to seek—
　Quite close, within the sound of busy mart.

John Owen lies within these sacred walls ;
　And Gill is here, and many more the same ;
Old Andrew Gifford, Rosewell, Goodwin, too,
　All spoke the truths the Bible teaches plain.

Macgowan's lines will surely reach the heart,
　A hidden chord be touched as on we read ;
For " sinner saved by grace " is here the strain—
　Such minds, so taught, are on this point agreed.

But when we reach the plains above we'll know
　That Jesus Christ has everything done well ;
And with dear Swain we'll laud His wondrous love,
　Who plucked us " as a burning brand from hell."

There Samuel Stennett's "raptured eyes shall see
　The Saviour's lovely face " he sang of here ;
And Burder's " warmer heart in brighter world "
　Shall "shout that God is love" in accents clear.

But Bunhill Fields is *full* of wondrous tales,
　And true ones, too, of favoured saints of old
Who served their Master spite of pain and loss ;
　Cared not for glory, but for truth were bold.

The sovereign grace of God—that sweetest sound
　To man who's taught his sinful heart to know—
Was striven for at mighty cost by those
　Whose bones lie mingled with the dust below.

What wondrous sight 'twill be on that great day
　When Jesus, coming down the parted skies—
The resurrection morn—to meet the saints,
　Will call His blessed ones and with them rise !

Good Lady Erskine, Rippon, Cromwells, too,
　And many more the pen would fail to name ;
The spots are given where all of these are laid ;
　Go, search—your quest were surely not in vain.

Descriptions some you'll find within this book,
　Entrancing stories, witching tales are here ;
There's Fleetwood's famous name and old De Foe's,
　And Lady Page, whose sufferings are clear.

And when you've read the tales that here are told—
　A few culled from the page of history's lore—
The writer will be very well repaid
　If Bunhill Fields you love a little more.　　　　M. J. L.

BUNHILL FIELDS.

To the mere passer-by, this sacred plot in the City Road, London, is just an ordinary disused burying ground. To the tired factory girl and weary mechanic it is a place in which to rest during the dinner hour. To the builder it presents itself as a splendid site for factories and offices. To crowds of people it is a short cut from the busy City Road to the quieter Bunhill Row. To popish clerics it is almost as a plague spot that should be carefully avoided. To a lover of liberty of conscience, of freedom of thought, of an open Bible and of spiritual religion it is, however, hallowed ground, for beneath its turf there are resting thousands of brave men and women who counted not their lives dear unto them, but who "contended earnestly for the faith once delivered to the saints." The principles of Scriptural Dissent are here magnified, whilst thoughts of cruel and wicked persecutions by spiritually ignorant clerics, magistrates, and evil princes crowd into the mind. Here are buried some 120,000 persons. Many of these died in poverty and distress, some even within prison walls, whilst had they been willing to comply with the regulations, and to accept blindly the teachings of such popish bishops as Laud, many would have occupied positions of national distinction.

The following account is chiefly compiled from two publications of the City Corporation, viz., "Bunhill Fields Burial Ground; Proceedings in reference to its Preservation," and the Official Guide. The former, which contains very important correspondence between the City Fathers and the Ecclesiastical Commissioners, was published in 1867, and is now somewhat rare; the latter can still be obtained of the keepers at the Grounds.

The history here given is of great importance, and there is true cause for thankfulness that the Ecclesiastical Commissioners, into whose hands the valuable Finsbury estate, of which Bunhill Fields is a portion, fell in 1867, had a wealthy and powerful body to contend against. Amongst the City Fathers during the critical period there were Sir Charles Reed and others who boldly championed the cause of righteousness and justice.

In the old days, at the original entrance, there was a stone with the following inscription: " This churchyard was inclosed with a brick wall, at the sole charge of the City of London, in the Mayoralty of Sir John Lawrence, Kt., A.D. 1665; and afterwards the gates hereof were built and finished in the Mayoralty of Sir Thomas Bludworth, Kt., A.D. 1666." Strangely enough it has been completely lost.

This takes us back to the days of the Great Plague and Fire of London, although it is probable that centuries before there was a Saxon burying place at Bon-hill or Bone-hill Fields.

The whole district was swampy, and at various spots archers, apprentices, and the soldiers practised with their bows, staves, and other weapons. From this place many had in the past gone to fight the French at Cressy, Poitiers and other famous battles; and here the City train-bands brought themselves to a state of proficiency by zealously and constantly engaging in their more peaceful combats.

The land itself was originally part of a great church property, but in the fifteenth century the Corporation took it over at a yearly rent of twenty shillings. For this sum the Lord Mayor was granted " for himself and for his successors all his right and claim " to the property, which was considered to be a grant of the land in perpetuity. There must have been, however, some flaw in the provisions, as in 1553 the Corporation obtained a lease for ninety years at a rental of £29 13s. 4d.

In 1561 a most terrible thunderstorm and tempest burst over London, and in every quarter houses were wrecked, whilst the lightning struck and seriously damaged St. Paul's Cathedral. Indeed a portion of the

Cathedral was actually destroyed whilst the terrified citizens for the most part gazed helplessly on. To repair the noble structure and to re-lead the roof was a great undertaking, towards which the Corporation provided about twenty tons of lead. In return for this two further leases of seventy years each were granted, which gave the City possession for 215 years, and this was naturally considered to be very little short of a freehold.

During the Commonwealth, when the church lands were sold, the Corporation bought the Finsbury estate and thus became Lords of the Manor. As such they paid no rents, but when some ten years later the Stuart family in the person of Charles II. regained the throne of England, all the properties returned to the Church. It was quite in keeping with the character of the new king and of the ecclesiastical authorities that there was no repayment of the purchase money, so the City suffered the loss of their money and property. The land was now put to some use in order to produce income, and De Foe is of opinion that the Great Plague Pit was at or near this spot. The city burying places were soon filled, for persons were dying at the rate of eight or ten thousand every week.

It is stated in " Maitland's Survey " (1739) concerning this land that " Part whereof at present denominated Tindal's or the Dissenters' burial-ground, was by the Mayor and Corporation of London, in the year 1665, set apart and consecrated as a common cemetery for the interment of such corpses as could not have room in the burial-grounds in the dreadful year of the pestilence. However, it not being made use of on that occasion, the said Tindal took a lease thereof, and converted it into a burial-ground."

The ground is marked for a time on the maps by the name of Tindal instead of the Bon-hill Fields. As the books of the City were destroyed by fire there is no record of it earlier than 1698, but a stone was found on which was the name of Debora Warr, the date being November 10th, 1623. It is thought probable that this is the date of the woman's death, but that the body was reinterred. There was another, however, of " Joannes

Seaman, natus 6 Feb. 1665, ob Jul. 23, 1665," and this is most likely to be the more ancient. In turn, Bunhill Fields was in the possession of a James Browne, and a certain Elizabeth Fetherstonhaugh, but about 1741 the Corporation took sole charge once again, and by this time the revenue was very considerable.

Special attention was drawn to the Finsbury Estate in the Parliament of 1766, and there were proposals to make some use of the lands " now the resort of idle and disorderly persons." These arrangements were far reaching, but in all the plans it is clearly shown that the burying-ground was to remain untouched. Merchants' houses and homes for professional men were to be erected, and the city authorities entered without delay into negotiations with Prebendary Wilson. The official committee reported to the Common Council that they had " agreed with the Prebendary to join in an application to Parliament for an Act to enable the Prebendary and his successors to grant a lease to the City of the Prebendal Estate, from Christmas last, for a term of ninety-nine years, renewable at the expiration of seventy-three years, by adding fourteen years, to make up a term of forty years, and afterwards every fourteen years in like manner for ever." In some extraordinary way a clause to this effect (although in the Bill) was omitted from the Act, but it has not been discovered how this unfortunate accident occurred. It is obvious that the renewal of the lease every fourteen years for ever was to be a vital point in the agreement, but at the appointed time no renewal did take place or was ever allowed to do so. The result ultimately was that an immense and most valuable property fell into the hands of the Ecclesiastical Commissioners, and thus from henceforth the enormous income was to be used for Church of England purposes. The spirit of the voluntary agreement was absolutely ignored by the clerical party, and the Corporation had to suffer this second great loss by the absolute letter of the Act being maintained.

There is ample evidence that in addition to the City authorities, the public and also the church party believed that the property was to be held in public trust practi-

cally till the end of time, and that because of this there
was a conviction that the stones and resting-places of
the noble dead in Bunhill Fields would never be disturbed. Any other supposition is impossible, for certainly
Dissenters would not have purchased graves and erected
monuments if these afterwards were to be placed at the
mercy of a priestly caste. When it became known to
the public that Bunhill had changed hands, a Committee
made application that the burial ground should be held
sacred for ever. Considering that hitherto this portion of
the estate had been always omitted for valuation purposes, the reply of the Commissioners was very strange.
They stated that the ground was considered to be worth
£100,000—presumably for building purposes—but that
they were willing under the circumstances to receive
£10,000 by way of compensation. This led to a memorial
being presented to the Corporation, at which an appeal
was made that authority should be obtained from Parliament to prevent secular use being made of this sacred
spot.

On the 16th November, 1865, at the Court of Common
Council, the following special resolution was passed :—

"Resolved unanimously—That this Court learns with regret that in the communications with the Ecclesiastical Commissioners, the Committee have not found any disposition to
concur in an arrangement for the preservation of the Bunhill
Fields' Burial Ground, except upon terms of sale and purchase.

"That having regard to the antiquity of this spot as a place
of extramural sepulture, that it has been held by this Corporation for more than five hundred years, that it has been set
apart and used for centuries as a place of interment ; that a
public pledge has been given by the conjoint authorization of
the Ecclesiastical authorities and the Corporation—' That the
ground should at all times hereafter remain for the purposes of
burials only,' and that up to the year 1832, upon these conditions and assurances, vaults have been sold : this Court
protests against this ground or any part thereof being applied
to secular uses. That, considering the high historic interest
attaching to the Bunhill Fields Burial Ground, in consequence
of the interment of so many distinguished and honoured men
of all creeds and parties, this Court is willing to accept
the care and preservation of the ground on behalf of the

public, and to assist in promoting any well-advised scheme for
securing against molestation and disturbance the final resting-
place of so many thousands of their fellow-citizens.

"Ordered: That a copy of the foregoing Resolutions be
transmitted to the Ecclesiastical Commissioners."

In a remarkably short time a Bill was prepared and
became an Act, one of the clauses being:—" The Burial
Ground shall from time to time, and at all times . . .
be held, used, and enjoyed, as an open space, accessible
to the public at such times and under such regulations as
the Corporation shall from time to time think proper
and expedient . . . and no house or other building,
whether for the purpose of residence or trade, or for any
other purpose, shall, from henceforth and for ever hereafter, be built or erected upon the burial ground or any
part thereof."

Immediately after the Act was obtained a special
Committee was appointed by the City authorities to
make alterations and to restore and improve the ground
generally, the place being opened to the public in October,
1869, after two years labour. A statement was made to
the Corporation by the Chairman of the Committee in
the following words:—

" In the presence of representatives of families whose dead
were buried here, and of the delegates of churches and societies
whose pastors and founders rest in this ground, I desire to say
that in all the reparations and alterations carried on within
this enclosure, not a fragment of stone has been taken away,
nor has any portion of the soil been removed. Tombs have
been raised from beneath the ground, stones have been set
straight, illegible inscriptions have been deciphered and re-cut,
hundreds of decayed tombs have been restored, paths have
been laid and avenues planted: and in all the sacred rights of
sepulture scrupulously respected. An accurate copy of all the
principal inscriptions exists; a complete register of all in-
terments is preserved; an exact plan of the entire ground has
been taken; and it is now hoped that the Corporation of London having voluntarily done so much, the families owning
graves here may come forward to do the rest. Within a few
weeks the Committee will have discharged a trust readily
undertaken in the public interest. They have considered
themselves as fulfilling a sacred duty while renewing to pos-

terity the emblems of the zeal and the suffering of their fore-
fathers, and thereby, in the language of one buried here,
' trimming, as it were, the beacon-light left to warn future
generations to defend their religion, even unto their blood.' It
only remains that I should ask your lordship* to declare this
ground open, under the conditions of the Act of Parliament
which gives to the people this their prized and rightful
inheritance."

The appeal that " the families owning graves here may
come forward and do the rest " met with some response,
and certain monuments were erected by public subscription.

It is full time, however, that more interest and love
should be shown for the tombs of such noble men and
women. The decaying hand of time is to be seen upon
almost every stone ; some are broken in two, others
have sunk into the ground, and many more are now
practically unreadable. Unless something is done it will
be quite impossible to locate the stones of some of the
most famous and godly persons, and this will be a disgrace to the public in general, but to Dissenters in
particular.

At different times since the opening various alterations
have been made. There is now a new entrance and a
path running through from the City Road to Bunhill
Row, but the old gateway may still be seen with its row
of fierce, cruel-looking spikes which were placed there to
prevent the body-snatchers doing their gruesome work.
Trees have also been planted, especially the planes with
their strange " moulting " trunks, and the ground has
been re-turfed, flowers planted, and seats provided. In
addition to the official keeper there is also a gardener
employed, so that for the most part this " God's Acre " is
in a fair condition. But one look at the stones in their
decaying state is a sad, sad sight, and the expense of pre-
serving the main ones would be but a small matter to the
great Dissenting bodies, whilst in addition, surely there are
many others who love the honour of these men and the
truth of God sufficiently to subscribe in order that the last

* The Right Honourable the Lord Mayor, Sir James Clarke Lawrence,
Bart., M.P.

resting-places of some of England's noblest children may not sink entirely into obscurity.

The writer of the Official Guide makes a most moving appeal in the following words: " Shall no friendly hand clear away those dank weeds which hide the lowly stones? Shall none appear to cleanse the soiled and weather-worn slab, so that its record may be traced? Shall none be found to lift up the headstones fallen slantwise to the earth, or to renew the masonry of the altar tombs, lying now in shapeless and pitiable ruin? Is there none to chisel out the faded inscription, and with pious hand to grave still more deeply the time-honoured memorials? Nonconformists! is there no 'Old Mortality' amongst you, who, out of love for these sainted ones and for their Lord and Master, would live awhile amongst the tombs, and make it impossible that the names of our illustrious dead—confessors, historians, pastors, poets—and their dying witness to His love, should evermore be hidden from our view?"

AN EPITAPH.

Here lyes embalmed in careful Parents Tears,
A Virgin Branch, cropt in its tender Years:
Reader, as in a Glass, thou perfectly may'st see
How all things here below vain and uncertain be.
Dear Virgin Child, Farewel! thy Mother's Tears
Cannot advance thy memory (who wears
A Crown above the Stars), yet I must mourn
And show the World mine Offerings at thy Urn.
'Tis not (Dear Child!) a stone can deck your Herse,
Or can your Worth lodge in a narrow Verse.
No, no, blest Virgin! this engraven Breath
Is not to speak your Life, but weep your Death.
This Herse is only layed by th' careful Trust
Of a sad Mother, in Honour of your Dust.

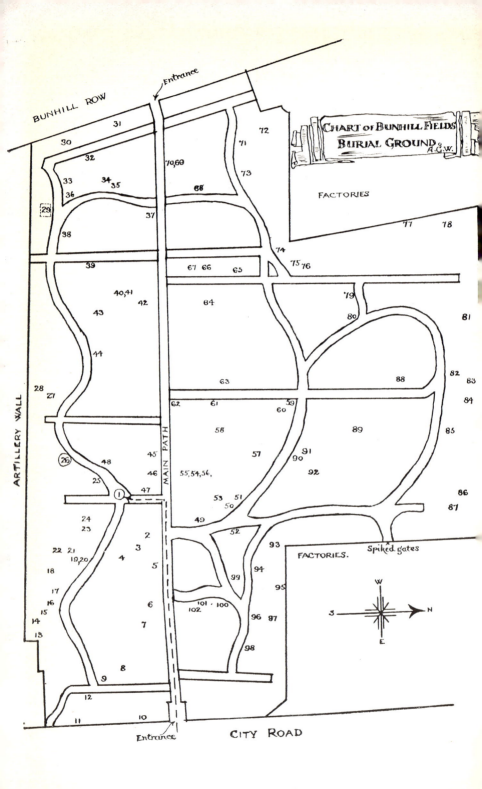

KEY TO CHART.

SOUTH SECTION.

1. Bunyan.
2. Rosewell.
3. Rowe.
4. Gale.
5. James.
6. Wavel.
7. Goodwin.
8. Jenkyn.
9. Stafford.
10. Guyse.
11. Denham.
12. Morley.
13. Chandler.
14. Fleetwood.
15. Gifford.
16. Ross.

17. Chin.
18. Hopkins.
19. Hayward.
20. Nicholson.
21. Owen.
22. Pomfret.
23. Brand.
24. Bragge.
25. Button.
26. Cromwells.
27. Williams.
28. Hume.
29. "Sunken Tomb."
30. Rippon.
31. Nasmith.
32. Ivimey.

33. Anderson.
34. Gill.
35. Burford.
36. Hutchings.
37. Burder.
38. Palmer.
39. Nicol.
40. Powell.
41. Tutt.
42. Ford.
43. Aldridge.
44. Mrs. Wesley.
45. Pennyman.
46. Buck.
47. Stockell.
48. Bland.

NORTH SECTION.

49. Cartwright.
50. Crow.
51. Daniel De Foe.
52. Franklin.
53. Rosewell.
54. Brine.
55. Reynolds.
56. Reynolds.
57. Skepp.
58. Hughes.
59. Wilks.
60. Fauntleroy.
61. Neal.
62. Hyatt.
63. Gibbons.
64. Taylor.
65. Jenkins.
66. Dame Mary Page.

67. Oldfield.
68. Stennett.
69. Bradbury.
70. Winter.
71. Langford.
72. Jones.
73. Davis.
74. Waugh.
75. Priestley.
76. Hart.
77. Shrubsole (1).
78. Erskine.
79. Powell.
80. Durrant.
81. Shrubsole (2).
82. Bradberry.
83. Crole.
84. Terry.

85. Bennett.
86. Johnson.
87. Ashlin.
88. Conder.
89. Martin.
90. Macgowan.
91. Stevens.
92. Swain.
93. Lilburn.
94. Lilley.
95. Wilkinson.
96. Williams.
97. Grosvenor.
98. Dowars.
99. Watts.
100. Say.
101. Eames.
102. Cruden.

BUNYAN'S COTTAGE, ELSTOW. (See page 14.)

THE OLD PRISON AT BEDFORD. BUNYAN'S DEN. (See page 20.)

THE ACT OF UNIFORMITY.

As frequent reference must be made in these pages to this infamous Act, it is desirable that some little account should be given of it.

At the death of Cromwell on the 3rd of September, 1658, the future king of England (Charles II.) was an exile at Breda, in Holland, and seizing a favourable opportunity to return as king he, on April 14th, 1660, issued a declaration which was purposely drawn up to catch the unwary. Amongst other things he stated although " the passion and uncharitableness of the times have produced several opinions in religion " he did " declare a liberty to tender consciences ; and that no more shall be disquieted or called in question for differences of opinion in matters of religion which do not disturb the peace of the kingdom, and that we shall be ready to consent to such an Act of Parliament as upon mature deliberation shall be offered to us for the full granting that indulgence." Much joy was caused in England by this apparently frank statement, for after the dreadful persecutions of the past the people were particularly anxious as to their religious liberty. So satisfied were the Puritans that several of them made special journey to Breda to return thanks to Charles and also to make clear some other points. The false Prince* received them graciously, and strove with much success to impress upon his visitors a sense of his godliness. One of the chief things mentioned was the fact that the Book of Common Prayer was so very little used that in many parts the people had never seen or heard it ; " and therefore they besought him that he would not use it so entirely and formally, and have some parts

---

* One writer has stated that Charles " superseded the reign of saints by the reign of strumpets : who was crowned in his youth with the Covenant in his hand and died with the Host sticking in his throat."

only of it read, with mixture of other prayers which the
Chaplains might use." This point was also insisted upon
after the Restoration at a Conference with the King in
London, where they presented a document which had been
drawn up at the invitation of Charles himself. Some of the
bishops made reply, and whilst a controversy was proceeding the monarch issued another declaration dated the
25th October, 1660, in which he clearly and definitely promised many reforms. The year passed away without
anything being accomplished, but on January 10th, 1661,
a most disheartening declaration was published.* This
was a prohibition of conventicle services, and several sects
were definitely mentioned with a view to suppression.
The only places where services could be held were "in
some parochial church or chapel in this realm or in
private houses by the persons there inhabiting." The
value of the reference to "tender consciences" and the
promises so lavishly made were now seen in measure, but
very few seemed to apprehend the real dangers which
were ahead. There were naturally many disputations,
and Charles appears to have been weary of it all, and, in
order to bring the matter to a conclusion, issued a

---

* A study of the Corporation Act by means of which all persons who
refused on principle to conform to the Episcopal Church were expelled
and excluded from the magistracy and from all public offices, and the
other persecuting Acts passed in the early days of the reign of Charles II.,
is most instructive. By the statute against the Quakers more than
4,000 persons were cast into prison, whilst the Conventicle Act decreed
that all persons who refused to attend the public services of the Established Church should for the first and second offence be imprisoned and
fined, whilst for the third offence transportation was the sentence, and if
the sufferer ever returned to the homeland death was the penalty. This
abominable Act was passed in 1664, but it in measure broke down during
the great Plague when after the Clergy had through fear left their
churches and flocks the non-conforming divines returned to the metropolis, which was virtually a death trap, and preached to their old congregations once again. The King and Court were safely housed at Oxford, but a
new penal law was passed to deal with the case, and in 1670 the Conventicle
Act was enforced with even harsher terms. No trial by jury of these
godly men could now take place, their persons could be seized on any and
every occasion, whilst no exception could be taken to the warrants even
though these were irregularly and incorrectly drawn. It has been
recorded that one notable ecclesiastic, the Bishop of Peterborough,
declared that, "It hath done its business against all fanatics except the
Quakers! but when the Parliament sits again, a stronger law will be
made, not only to take away their lands and goods, but also to sell them
for bond slaves." What a kind and good shepherd!

warrant dated March 25th, 1661, convening the Savoy Conference. On each side were to be twelve men—the Establishment sending one archbishop and twelve bishops; whilst Reynolds, Bishop of Norwich, appeared on the other side with eleven Puritan divines. The instructions of Charles were to the effect that the Prayer Book was to be considered, and whilst as few alterations as possible were to be made, due notice should be taken of real objections. The first session was held on April 15th, 1661, but it was soon evident that the Conference would be utterly fruitless as the Bishops absolutely refused to make even the slightest concession. In vain did Baxter, Reynolds and the others plead for relaxation on eight several points, viz., using the sign of the cross in baptism, the compulsory wearing of a surplice, the forcing of people to receive the bread and wine kneeling, the obligation to pronounce all baptized persons regenerated by the Holy Spirit, the admitting of evil persons to the table, the absolution in definite expressions of unfit persons, the giving of thanks to God for all whom they buried, and the solemn declaration " that there is nothing in the Common Prayer Book, Book of Ordination and the Thirty-nine Articles, contrary to the Word of God."

The arguments of the Puritans were unanswerable, but the Bishops were determined not to give way, and the Conference broke up on July 25th, without arriving at any agreement. It is true that a revision of the Prayer Book shortly afterwards took place, but although the alterations were numerous they were of comparatively small importance, and everything to which the Puritans objected was carefully retained. Following this the Act of Uniformity was passed, and on the 19th of May, 1662, the Royal Assent was given. The object was to force every beneficed clergyman to use and to declare his " unfeigned assent and consent to all and everything contained and prescribed in and by the book intituled The Book of Common Prayer ! " The day appointed was Michaelmas, but it was altered to St. Bartholomew's, August 24th. Why this change ? In giving an answer it is impossible to avoid charging the officials of the Establishment with a particularly mean and cruel action.

On Michaelmas Day the tithes became due, and it was then that the clergy paid their accounts for the year and generally straightened out their financial matters. By altering the date to August 24th, the non-conforming ministers would be compelled to leave their benefices without means to discharge their debts and without any money to help them through a very trying period. But such refined cruelty could after all only be expected from such men, and they certainly were not disappointed at the result of their efforts. It was generally known that an Act of Uniformity had been passed, but as this was by no means the first, very terrible results were not expected. When, however, the terms of the Act were made public there was great consternation, for it was clear that there was no middle course, but that it was either conforming or non-conforming. A study of this period and of the correspondence between the Puritans is most instructive and touching.

The ill-fated day drew on apace. In the reign of Elizabeth it had been celebrated by the French King and priests in a great massacre of unresisting and innocent Huguenots, and now England under the guidance of Charles the false, and godless Bishops, was to sin against light and knowledge. There was little, if any, drawing back amongst the Puritans, and a most noble spirit was manifested. One clergyman, Mr. Lawrence of Baschurch, alluding to his wife and ten children said, " I have eleven arguments for conformity, but Christ has said, ' Whoso loveth wife or children more than Me is not worthy of Me.' " Old Richard Baxter wrote:

> " Must I be driven from my books ?
>   From house, and goods, and dearest friends ?
> One of Thy sweet and gracious smiles,
>   For more than this will make amends.
> My Lord hath taught me how to want
>   A place wherein to lay my head ;
> While He is mine I'll be content
>   To beg or lack my daily bread."

Some two thousand noble men, with brave wives and children, left their dear homesteads, and " took cheerfully the spoiling of their goods " that they might " keep a conscience void of offence towards God and towards man." Was there ever an occasion quite like this, or a fact equal to this fact? Think of it! Two thousand godly, educated, tender, intelligent men severed friendships, cast aside all hope of earthly prosperity, gave up their homes, their daily bread, their treasured libraries, with all their comforts, and went forth into the wilderness—many to perish of want and privation, some to be harried like hares, others to die in prison, and all because they could not sully their consciences by making a false oath and by declaring their agreement with doctrines and ritual which they believed were contrary to the Word of the living God. Well might the Act of Uniformity be called the Act of Ejection!

In roaming through Bunhill Fields it is not easy to avoid a contemplation of this subject, and without some knowledge of the facts here briefly recorded, it is quite impossible to understand the reason why so many men who believed in Episcopacy, in set forms of worship, and who had no objection to a State church, are resting in a Non-conformists' burying ground.

AN EPITAPH.

Here lyes interred the Body of Mr.
Thomas Holmes, Citizen and Haberdasher
of London, and Son of Mr. Thomas Holmes,
of Wigston, in the County of Leicester, who
yielded to Nature the 4th day of December,
1694, in the 38th Year of his Age.

Dear Holmes hath found
A Home among the Blest,
His weary body for to rest:
For no where can his Flesh
True Slumber have;
But in this Trust Home on Homely Grave,
His Soul in Heavenly Tunes doth sing,
Hell, where's thy Triumph?
Death, where is thy Sting?

JOHN BUNYAN.

PASSING from the City Road, through the main gates into the middle path and through the first gate on the left into the southern section of the ground, immediately ahead the visitor will see the massive railed tomb of John Bunyan. On the top of it is his recumbent figure, and in the north panel a representation of the pilgrim with his burden on his back, leaning wearily on his staff. In the west panel it is recorded that the tomb was "Restored by public subscription under the presidency of the Right Honorable the Earl of Shaftesbury, May, 1862." In the south panel the pilgrim is again seen, now at the cross with the burden rolling from his back, whilst in the east panel the inscription is as follows :—

JOHN BUNYAN, Author of the "Pilgrim's Progress." *Obt.* 31st. August, 1688, *Æt.* 60.

The "immortal tinker" and "glorious dreamer" was born in the village of Elstow, near Bedford, in the year 1628. He was thus contemporary with some of the greatest men whom England has ever known. At the time of his birth Richard Baxter, John Milton, Thomas Goodwin, Lord Chief Justice Hale, John Owen, Archbishop Ussher, and Bishop Hall were all alive, and this cluster of names strikingly indicates the great richness of the age both in godliness and in ability. Bunyan was different from all these in that he was denied the advantages of an early education, but none of them was so strikingly original, or had such a marvellous command of language.

Almost the only books he ever read were the Bible, "Foxe's Book of Martyrs," "Luther on the Galatians," and the two volumes: "The Plain Man's Pathway to Heaven" and "The Practice of Piety," which formed his wife's wedding portion. According to Bunyan's own description he was of " a low, inconsiderable generation ; my father's house," says he, " being of that rank which is most despised of all the families in the land." It is definitely understood that he was trained to be a brazier and worked as a journeyman in Bedford, for according to his own account he was of a generation of tinkers, his ancestors having been bred and born to that calling. In his early days, when cursing and swearing more than his companions, he had qualms of conscience, often being afflicted even whilst asleep with dire apprehensions. When nine or ten years of age he was so distressed in his soul that he often wished "either there be no hell, or that I had been a devil, supposing they were only tormentors."

As he grew into manhood Bunyan became a leader in profligacy, but he could not take any real pleasure in the wild and sinful habits of his companions, and it always shocked him to see persons walk and act in a manner unworthy of their religious profession. There were many remarkable providential circumstances connected with Bunyan's early days. On one occasion he fell into a creek of the sea, and on another, out of a boat into the river Ouse; each time being saved from drowning. Again, when passing from Elstow to Bedford, an adder crossed his path, he stunned it with his stick, forced open its mouth, and with his fingers plucked out its tongue, which he supposed to be the sting. Of this he says, "By which act, had not God been merciful unto me, I might by my desperateness have brought myself to my end !" As the Civil war was now raging, he, being a soldier in the Parliamentary Army, was drawn to go to the siege of Leicester. Just when he was ready to start one offered to go in his stead : "To which," says Bunyan, " when I had consented, he took my place ; and coming to the siege, as he stood sentinel, he was shot in the head with a musket ball and died." Bunyan at this time was 17 years of age, and referring to the circumstance afterwards, he said, " Here were judgments and mercy, but neither of them did awaken my soul to righteousness, wherefore I sinned still and grew more and more rebellious against God and careless of my own salvation."

Two or three years after this Bunyan was married, his age at the time probably being 19 or 20. His wife was a godly young woman, and they "came together as poor as might be, not having so much household stuff as a dish or a spoon betwixt them both." Her dowry, as has already been noticed, consisted of the two books: "The Plain Man's Pathway to Heaven" and "The Practice of Piety." The two would read these together, and the young wife would make mention of her father's godly conversation, and walk in the hope that her profane husband would be made ashamed of his words and conduct. It must not be supposed that Bunyan ever lived an openly immoral life, for in after years he defended himself in remarkably plain language on this point. He said, "If all fornicators and adulterers in England were hanged up by the neck until they be dead, John Bunyan, the object of their *end*, would be still alive and well." He had a great reverence for the Established Church, which indeed amounted to superstition, and amongst other things he thought it a wonderful act of righteousness to ring the bells, although as soon as the service was over, and he with the others had performed their duties, he would go off to play the then popular game of "cat." One day, however, the minister preached what appears to have been a faithful and outspoken sermon on the sanctity of the Sabbath and the great evil of desecrating it. This made his conscience very uneasy, but after he had been home to his dinner he managed to drive away his depressing thoughts, and again entered into his games with great delight and zest.

Whilst playing, and as he was about to strike the "cat" from a hole, it seemed as if a voice from heaven spoke to him and said, "Wilt thou leave thy sins and go to heaven, or have thy sins and go to hell?" "At this," he said, "I was put to an exceeding maze, wherefore leaving my 'cat' upon the ground I looked up to Heaven, and was as if I had, with the eyes of my understanding, seen the Lord Jesus looking down upon me, as being very hotly displeased with me, and as if He did severely threaten me with some grievous punishment for these and other ungodly practices." The effect was

ELSTOW CHURCH. (See page 16.)

THE VILLAGE GREEN AT ELSTOW. (See page 16.)

BUNYAN'S TOMB.

THOMAS ROSEWELL
NONCONFORMIST MINISTER
ROTHERHITHE
DIED 1692
TRIED FOR HIGH TREASON
UNDER THE INFAMOUS JEFFRIES
SEE STATE TRIALS 1684

(See page 30.)

marvellous and he came to the awful conclusion that it was too late for him to turn from his wickedness, for Christ would not forgive him. " My state," he moaned, " is surely miserable; miserable if I leave my sins, and but miserable if I follow them. I can but be damned, and, if I must be so, I had as good be damned for many sins as be damned for a few." There he stood among his thoughtless, ungodly companions, who were all quite unaware of the great exercises of his mind and the depression of his spirits. He said nothing to them, but went to his sport again, desiring to take his fill of sin, and hoping that he might taste some sweetness from it before he should die. Afterwards in relating the circumstance he said, " In these things I protest before God I lie not; neither do I frame this sort of speech; these were really, strongly, and with all my heart, my desires. The good Lord, whose mercy is unsearchable, forgive me my transgressions!" His language was now so terrifying and profane that even wicked people were shocked and astonished at him. In fact one who was herself an evil woman advised his companions to quit his company or he would make them as bad as himself. She said " that he was the ungodliest fellow for swearing that ever she heard in all her life, and that by thus doing, he was able to spoil all the youth of the whole town, if they came in his company." He hung his head in silence, " wishing," as he says, " in my heart that I might be a little child again that my father might learn me to speak without this wicked way of swearing."

It was not long after this when he met a poor man who had some conversation with him concerning the Scriptures which was the means of leading him to the Bible. For the first time he took pleasure in reading it, being especially interested in the historical parts, but the Epistles he says, " I could not away with, being as yet ignorant both of the corruption of our nature; and of the want and worth of Christ to save us." A considerable outward change took place in him which caused his neighbours much amazement, and they now began to speak well of him both to his face and behind his back. " Now I was, as they said, becoming godly; now I was

C

becoming a right honest man; but oh, when I understood these were their words and opinion of me it pleased me well, for although as yet I was nothing but a poor painted hypocrite, yet I loved to be talked of as one that was truly godly. I was proud of my godliness, and indeed I did all that I did either to be seen of or to be well spoken of by men; and thus I continued for about twelve months, or more. . . . I knew not Christ, nor grace, nor faith, nor hope, for as I have well seen since, had I then died my state had been most fearful."

One of his great delights had been bell ringing, but this he now abandoned as a " vain practice." He however frequently crept to the tower in order to look at the ringers, but there came upon him a great fear that one of the bells might fall. This caused him to move to the steeple door, but now he dreaded the steeple itself might come down; and these things brought him into a very nervous state physically. One of his greatest amusements had hitherto been dancing, and it was quite a full year before he could leave this. When he at last managed to do so he thought, " No man in England could please God better than I, poor wretch as I was. I was all this while ignorant of Jesus Christ, going about to establish my own righteousness, and had perished therein had not God in mercy shewed me more of my state by nature."

Bunyan continued in his self-righteous condition until one memorable day when, as he was attending to his tinkering business in Bedford, he overheard three or four poor women as they conversed about their own spiritual state. He presently joined in their conversation, as he was " a brisk talker in the matter of religion," but he soon found that these persons had a knowledge which he lacked. It was indeed a case of " Then they that feared the Lord spake often one to another," for their talk was about regeneration or the new birth, conviction of sin, the revelation of Christ to their souls, the promises which had been applied, the conflicts they had endured, the temptations with which they had been beset, and the persecutions they had suffered—their own awful unbelief, wretchedness of heart, and the great lack of any creature righteousness that could please God.

They quoted much Scripture, and it was clear to Bunyan that he was quite out of their secret. He made as frequent journeys as possible to Bedford to hold conversation with the women, and found that they were members of a little Baptist congregation, the pastor of which was John Gifford. The more he talked with them, the more did he read his Bible, and he was now assailed by two great doubts—as to whether he was elected, and whether his day of grace had been passed. As he stated his feelings to the women, they told Mr. Gifford of him, and the worthy minister invited the distressed tinker to his house and had some speech with him. It was while Mr. Gifford was one day preaching that comfort first came to Bunyan. The text was, "Behold, thou art fair, My love; behold, thou art fair," and the preacher based his remarks chiefly upon the words, " My love." The words of Gifford were, " If it be so, that a saved soul is Christ's love when under temptation and destruction, then poor tempted soul, when thou art assaulted and afflicted with temptations, and the hidings of God's face, yet think on these words, ' My love,' still." At times the darkness of Bunyan was gross and deep; still he continued to sit under the ministry of " holy Mr. Gifford," and through the preaching of this faithful man he received real and eternal good. His experience now was most trying, for whilst he was sometimes blessed with faith and hope, at most seasons he was in the depths of despondency. After about two and a half years of this almost constant wretchedness there came to him one day, when he was in a field, the words, " Thy righteousness is in heaven," and he also declares, " I saw with the eyes of my soul Jesus Christ at God's right hand—there, I say, is my righteousness, and to-day, and for ever."

Bunyan was now an intense student of the Bible, and here we arrive at the secret of the purity of his English, both in speech and writing. It has been a source of wonderment how an illiterate man could have acquired a style which for elegance, purity, simplicity, and strength, has never been excelled by the greatest masters of English literature. He also read very closely Luther's " Commentary on the Galatians," whilst " John Foxe's Book of

Martyrs " afforded increasing delight to his mind. After the death of John Gifford, in 1656, the Baptist church chose for its minister John Burton, and Bunyan was employed as an itinerating preacher in the villages. His doings were soon noised abroad, and as he now began to write, his name became familiar to many people. In the year 1657 he was brought into serious trouble, as an indictment was conferred against him for preaching at Eton. This was the more surprising as it was in the days of the Commonwealth, but the effort to silence Bunyan entirely failed. His greatest afflictions came after the Restoration and, as might have been expected, Bunyan was one of the first to suffer for his Dissenting principles. A warrant was issued against him, and he was arrested at a small place called Samsell, in Bedfordshire, where he was preaching in a private house. He could doubtless have escaped, but he resolved " to see the utmost to what they could say or do to him." He was indicted because, " as a man he devilishly and perniciously abstained from going to church to hear divine service, and he was a common upholder of unlawful meetings and conventicles, to the great disturbance and distraction of the good subjects of the kingdom." His defence was most able, and when pressed with respect to the Book of Common Prayer he said, " Show me the place in the Epistles from where the Common Prayer is written, or one text of Scripture that commands me to read it, and I will use it." The judgment of the magistrate was that he should be put back to prison for three months, and then if he did not submit to go to church and leave his preaching, he should be banished from the realm. He was also told that " If after such a day shall be appointed you be gone, you shall be found in this realm or be found to come over again without special licence of the king, you must stretch by the neck for it; I tell you plainly." The answer of Bunyan was what might have been anticipated, that if he was out of prison to-day, he would preach the gospel again to-morrow, by the help of God. He was taken back to " durance vile," and there kept for twelve years. His wife pleaded with fervent eloquence with Sir Matthew Hale and other judges, but all to no purpose.

One passage in Bunyan's experience at this time shows what he had to break from and leave, and what the difficulties and dangers were in going to prison. "I found myself a man encompassed with infirmities. The parting with my wife and children hath often been to me in this place as the pulling the flesh from my bones; and that not only because I am somewhat too fond of these mercies, but also because I should have brought to my mind the many hardships, miseries, and wants that my poor family was likewise to meet with, especially my poor blind child, who lay nearer to my heart than all I had beside. Oh, the thought of the hardships I thought my blind one might go under would break my heart to pieces! Poor child, thought I, what sorrow art thou like to have for thy portion in this world! Thou must be beaten, must beg, suffer hunger, cold, nakedness, and a thousand calamities, though I cannot now endure that the wind shall blow upon thee! But yet recalling myself, thought I, I must venture you all with God, though it goeth to the quick to leave you. Oh, I saw in this condition I was as a man who was pulling down his house upon the head of his wife and children, yet, thought I, I must do it, I must do it. And now I thought on those two milch kine, that were to carry the Ark of God into another country, to leave their calves behind them."

Bunyan was the first person in the reign of Charles II. who was persecuted for nonconformity, but though his experience was so painful and bitter, yet it was in the prison-house of Bedford that he wrote "The Pilgrim's Progress," which has been the delight of children, the joy of men and women, and the comfort of dying saints ever since it was first published.* There were shut up with him sixty other Dissenters, some being ministers and some laymen; the former were confined for preaching, and the latter for hearing, the gospel outside buildings belonging to the Established Church. The old prison-

* It must be noted that Dr. Brown, the celebrated Bunyan Biographer, has concluded that the "Pilgrim's Progress" was not written in prison, but after its author had obtained his release. But even if this view should be correct, it may be safely affirmed that the work was composed in the mind whilst Bunyan was in his lone cell, though it were afterwards placed upon paper.

house of Bedford stood on the bridge, and its condition
was generally very damp and dreadful. There was no
place either for exercise or for out-door work, there being
only stone walls, iron bars, a bridge, and a river; his cell
having but a grated window, he could not look very far
through it, but he could see a little of the sunlight, the
generally placid river, the green meadow and cornfields,
and the clouds in the heavens. Some of his gaolers were
very cruel and oppressive, but others were kind to him.
Under any circumstances twelve years' imprisonment
would be hard to bear, and it seems quite certain that
during the first six or seven years of these he was never
allowed to set his foot outside the rocky fortress. He
did what work he could in making tagged thread laces, so
that he might support his wife and the four children who
were dependent upon him, and who were sometimes
allowed to visit him. His poor blind Mary lay very near
his heart, and to his joy she was at times allowed to stay
by his side and be a companion to him. In the prison
cell there were three books, namely, the Bible, a Concordance, and his much loved copy of the "Book of
Martyrs." The latter part of his incarceration was by
no means so oppressive as the former, for he was often
allowed to leave his dungeon and preach to congregations
in and around Bedford. He was also permitted by a kind
gaoler to sleep occasionally at his own home. One night
when he was there he was so restless that slumber would
not come to his eyelids, so he told his wife that he must
return immediately to the prison. He received much
blame from the gaoler for coming in at so unseasonable
an hour. It appears, however, that some of the clerical
authorities had received news that Bunyan's confinement
was not so close and rigorous as they thought it should
be, and they had despatched a special officer to Bedford
to find out how matters really stood. He was to arrive
in the middle of the night, and when he reached the
prison his first question was, "Are all the prisoners
safe?" "Yes," was the reply. "Is John Bunyan
safe?" "Yes." "Let me see him," was the demand,
and Bunyan was called. After the officer had left, the
gaoler said to his famous prisoner, "Well, you may go

out again when you think proper, for you know when to return better than I can tell you."

It should be remembered that Bunyan could have obtained his liberty at any time had he expressed his willingness to conform to the Church of England and cease from his preaching. His release from prison took place in the year 1672, or early part of 1673, he having been befriended by Dr. Barlow, who was afterwards Bishop of Lincoln. His actual liberation, however, is now said to have been obtained by Whitehead the Quaker, but it is probable that they both used their influence, and thus effected the release of the man who had for no just reason been imprisoned twelve long weary years.

He now had built for him a regular meeting house in Bedford, and large congregations were gathered together. Indeed, it was before he came out of prison that he was chosen pastor by the church, his ordination taking place in the year 1671. For the rest of his life he continued writing, preaching, and visiting in Bedford and the adjacent villages ; he also frequently visited London. When the people in the metropolis had notice of his coming there were often as many as 3,000 gathered together to hear what the released prisoner had to say. His fame reached Charles II., and the King, ridiculing John Owen on one occasion for hearing an illiterate tinker prate, received from the learned and eloquent Puritan the reply, "May it please your Majesty, could I possess that tinker's ability for preaching, I would most gladly relinquish all my learning."

Bunyan now became engaged in many controversies, the one upon Strict Communion between himself, Kiffen, Jessey, and other Baptists being the most notable. Whatever may be thought of his opinion, it is certain that Bunyan showed a Christian spirit, and carefully refrained from using words that would wound and cause scandal.

There is not much known of his later days, but it is clear that he plainly foresaw the crafty designs of King James to favour Popery, and he "advised the brethren to avail themselves of the sunshine by deliberately endeavouring to spread the gospel, and to prepare for the approaching storm by fasting and prayer."

Amongst other places that he now visited was Reading, and he travelled there for a dual object, namely, to preach the gospel and to make peace between a father and son who had become alienated. The meeting-house here was on the bank of a branch of the river Kennett, and a bridge was thrown over the water so that the worshippers could easily escape in case of an alarm. It was in this place that Bunyan contracted the disease which brought about his death. After he had made peace between father and son, he returned to London on horseback through a very heavy tempest and much rain. He was seized with a mortal fever, and the end came ten days after, while he was the guest of his friend, Mr. Strudwick, who was at Snow Hill. The earliest biographer of Bunyan records that "He comforted those that wept about him, exhorting them to trust in God, and pray to Him for mercy and forgiveness of their sins, telling them what a glorious exchange it would be to leave their troubles and cares of a wretched mortality to live with Christ for ever, with peace and joy inexpressible, expounding to them the comfortable Scriptures, by which they were to hope and assuredly come into a blessed resurrection in the last day. He desired some to pray with him, and he joined with them in prayer; and his last words, after he had struggled with a languishing disease, were these, ' Weep not for me, but for yourselves; I go to the Father of our Lord Jesus Christ, who will, through the mediation of His blessed Son, receive me, though a sinner, where I hope we ere long shall meet to sing the new song and remain everlastingly happy, world without end.'" Such a death was what he would himself have wished, and which indeed he had so often dwelt upon. His own description of Christian may be aptly applied to himself: "I saw in my dream that this man went in at the gate; and lo! as he entered he was transfigured, and he had raiment put on him that shone like gold. There were also that met him with harps and crowns, and gave unto him the harps to praise withal, and the crowns in token of honour. Then I heard in my dream that all the bells in the city rang again for joy; and that it was said unto him,

'ENTER THOU INTO THE JOY OF OUR LORD.'
I also heard the man himself sing with a loud voice, saying, 'Blessing and honour, and glory and power, be unto
Him that sitteth upon the throne and unto the Lamb for
ever and ever.'"

The number of books that Bunyan wrote is said to be
sixty, and he died when he was sixty years of age. His
body was taken to Bunhill, and placed in a tomb where
several others have been buried, and where, in 1697, the
body of John Strudwick was also placed. Bunyan died
a poor man, for his widow, who was his second wife,
issued an advertisement in which she stated "that she
was unable to print the writing which he had left unpub-
lished." Three children also survived, but it was a great
mercy that blind Mary died before him. The poet Cow-
per's apostrophe to Bunyan is as follows :—

> " O thou whom, borne on fancy's eager wing,
> Back to the season of life's happy spring,
> I pleased remember, and while memory yet
> Holds fast her office here, can ne'er forget—
> Ingenious dreamer ! in whose well told tale
> Sweet fiction and sweet truth alike prevail ;
> Whose humourous vein, strong sense, and simple style,
> May teach the gayest, make the gravest smile ;
> Witty and well employed, and like thy Lord,
> Speaking in parable His slighted word ;
> I name thee not, lest so despised a name
> Should move a sneer at thy deservéd fame.
> Yet e'en in transitory life's late day,
> That mingles all my brown with sober gray,
> Revere the man, whose Pilgrim marks the road,
> And guides the Progress of the soul to God ;
> 'Twere well with most, if books that could engage
> Their childhood, pleased them at a riper age ;
> The man approving what had charmed the boy,
> Would die at last in comfort, peace, and joy ;
> And not with curses on his heart who stole
> The gem of truth from his unguarded soul."

By this we gather that a century ago "The Pilgrim's
Progress," "The Holy War," "Grace Abounding," with
the other works of the now world-famous tinker, were
little known or read. In recent years he has, however,
been acknowledged in a national sense, and amongst
other things a stained-glass window has been placed in

Westminster Abbey to his memory. It is to be feared that, in spite of these things, the doctrines which Bunyan loved so dearly are despised and hated, even by those who give lip homage to him.

In writing his own rhymes Bunyan scorned to make any attempt at elegance; they are full of a rugged and simple beauty all their own. His ballad on " The Child and the Bird " is undoubtedly one of the sweetest and most natural things in the language.

THE CHILD AND THE BIRD.

My little bird, how canst thou sit
   And sing amidst so many thorns ?
Let me but hold upon thee get,
   My love with honour thee adorns.
Thou art at present little worth,
   Five farthings none will give for thee;
But prithee, little bird, come forth,
   Thou of more value art to me.

'Tis true, it is sunshine to-day,
   To-morrow birds will have a storm :
My pretty one, come thou away,
   My bosom then shall keep thee warm.
Thou subject art to cold o' nights,
   When darkness is thy covering.
At day thy danger's great by kites,
   How canst thou then sit there and sing ?

Thy food is scarce and scanty too,
   'Tis worms and trash which thou dost eat;
Thy present state I pity do,
   Come, I'll provide thee better meat.
I'll feed thee with white bread and milk,
   And sugar-plums, if thou them crave;
I'll cover thee with finest silk,
   That from the cold I may thee save.

My father's palace shall be thine,
   Yea, in it thou shalt sit and sing;
My little bird, if thou'lt be mine,
   The whole year round shall be thy spring.
I'll teach thee all the notes at court,
   Unthought of music thou shalt play;
And all that thither do resort
   Shall praise thee for it every day.

I'll keep thee safe from cat and cur,
   No manner o' harm shall come to thee;
Yea, I will be thy succourer,
   My bosom shall thy cabin be.
But lo, behold, the bird is gone!
   These charmings would not make her yield;
The child's left at the bush alone,
   The bird flies yonder o'er the field.

COMPARISON.

The child of Christ an emblem is;
   The bird to sinners I compare;
The thorns are like those sins of theirs
   Which do surround them everywhere.
Her songs, her food, her sunshine day,
   Are emblems of those foolish toys,
Which to destruction leads the way—
   The fruit of worldly, empty toys.

The arguments this child doth choose
   To draw to him a bird thus wild,
Shows Christ familiar speech doth use
   To make the sinner reconciled.
The bird in that she takes her wing
   To speed her from him after all,
Shows us vain man loves anything
   Much better than the heavenly call.

———

At the request of the Author, Mr. J. E. HAZELTON, the well-known Secretary of the Aged Pilgrims' Friend Society and minister, chose the following extract from the writings of John Bunyan, prefacing them with a few remarks:—

"Bunyan's theological merits rank very high; we cannot fail to perceive how minutely he had studied, and how deeply he had pondered the Word of God, under the guidance of the Holy Spirit. The doctrine of justification, free, instant, and entire, by the imputed righteousness of Christ, none, even of the Puritans, could state with more Luther-like boldness than he. Here, in illustration, is an extract from 'Grace Abounding,' that we might call A Song of Deliverance:—

"'But one day, as I was passing in the field, and that too with some dashes on my conscience, fearing lest yet all was not right, suddenly, this sentence fell upon my soul, "Thy righteousness is in heaven," and methought withal I saw, with the eyes of my soul, Jesus Christ at God's right hand: there, I say, as my righteousness; so that wherever I was, or whatever I was doing, God could not say of me, He wants my righteousness, for that was just before Him. I also saw, moreover, that it was not my good frame of heart that made my righteousness better, nor yet my bad frame that made my righteousness worse; for my righteousness was Jesus Christ Himself, the same yesterday, and to-day, and for ever.

"'Now did my chains fall off my legs indeed; I was loosed from my affliction and irons, my temptations also fled away; so that from that time those dreadful Scriptures of God left off to trouble me; now went I also home rejoicing for the grace and love of God. So when I came home, I looked to see if I could find that sentence, "Thy righteousness is in heaven," but could not find such a saying; wherefore my heart began to sink again, only that was brought to my remembrance, He "of God is made unto us wisdom, and righteousness, and sanctification, and redemption;" by this word I saw the other sentence true.

"'For by this Scripture I saw that the Man Christ Jesus, as He is distinct from us as touching His bodily presence, so He is our righteousness and sanctification before God. Here therefore I lived for some time, very sweetly at peace with God through Christ. O, methought, Christ! Christ! there was nothing but Christ that was before my eyes; I was not now only for looking upon this and the other benefits of Christ apart, as of His blood, burial, or resurrection, but considered Him as a whole Christ! Oh, I saw my gold was in my trunk at home! in Christ my Lord and Saviour!'"

ROBERT BRAGGE, JUNR.

THE original inscription was :—

Near this Place lyeth interr'd the Body of the Reverend Mr. ROBERT BRAGGE, who departed this Life April the 14th, 1704. Under this Tomb lieth interred the Body of Mr. JOHN BRAGGE, Eldest Son of Mr. Robert Bragge, who by his Will caused this Monument to be erected, in Memory of his Father and himself. He departed this life August 19th, 1711, in the 55th Year of his Age.

The tomb is the same as that in which Bunyan is resting, although there is now no notice of the interment of the several other persons whose remains were deposited here.

Mr. Bragge's life appears to have been a somewhat uneventful one, but for some time he was evening lecturer at Salter's Hall, and upon the death of Mr. Nathanial Mather he became pastor of the Congregational Church in Pave Alley, Lime Street, London. He remained with the church almost forty years, and in addition to his pastorate he was also one of the Merchant Lecturers at Pinner's Hill.

The other persons buried in this tomb are Mrs. Phœbe Bragge, Mr. Theophilus Bragge, Dr. Robert Bragge, Miss Ann Jennion, Mrs. Sarah Poole, Mrs. Anne Holyhead, Mrs. Elizabeth Jennings, Mr. John Long, Ensign Joseph Jennings Poole, and also Mr. Strudwick, in whose house Bunyan died.

AN EPITAPH.

The Body's here, the Soul is fled
　　To Regions which are pure and bright,
And tho' the meaner Part lies dead,
　　The noblest's gone to Heavenly Light.
She did request that she might be
　　To her blest Saviour's Bosom ta'en,
And now she dwells where she doth see
　　What does exceed Reports of Fame.

THOMAS ROSEWELL.

TURNING the back on Bunyan's tomb, and leaving the path to the left, the visitor will see, about five rows of stones ahead but nearer the railings, the now "double" headstone of Thomas Rosewell. On the original stone there was a Latin inscription, of which the translation is given as follows :—

> Here lieth the body of that celebrated divine, THOMAS ROSEWELL, M.A. A man not more eminent for his learning than for his piety and modesty; a preacher distinguished for judgment, eloquence, and study; a most diligent and skilful interpreter of the sacred volume. Who after many labours, and through the iniquities of the times, and many bitter sufferings, which for the sake of Christ he bore with the greatest fortitude, calmly departed this life at Rotherhithe, February 15th, in the 62nd year of his age, and of Christ, 1692.

There is now this inscription :—

> THOMAS ROSEWELL, Nonconformist Minister, Rotherhithe. Died 1692. Tried for High Treason under the infamous Jefferies. See "State Trials," 1684.

Mr. Rosewell was born at Dunkerton near Bath on May 3rd, 1630, and his mother and father both died before he was ten years old. He and his sister had a considerable fortune bequeathed to them, but this was dissipated whilst living with an uncle during their minority. When about 16 years of age he began to sit under the ministry of Mr. Matthew Haviland, and to his preaching Rosewell always confessed that he owed his conversion. After spending some time under a tutor in London, he removed in March, 1674, to Pembroke College, Oxford, where he prosecuted his studies under Dr. Langley. He entered the ministry of the Church of England, and was presented to the rectory at Rhode in Somersetshire, in 1653, and in 1657 to Sutton Mandeville in Wilts.

He was vicar here in 1662 when the Act of Uniformity
came into force, and was one of the noble men who
suffered ejectment then. He now became tutor to the
son of Lady Hungerford, but in 1674 he was elected
minister of the Presbyterian congregation meeting at
Rotherhithe. In spite of much persecution he continued
preaching, but he was tried for high treason in 1685.
Daniel Neal gives an account of this in his history as
follows :—

"Jefferies, now Lord Chief Justice of England, who was
scandalously vicious, and drunk every day, besides a drunken-
ness of fury in his temper that looked like madness, was prepared for any dirty work the court should put him upon.
September 23rd, Mr. Thomas Rosewell, the Dissenting minister at Rotherhithe, was imprisoned in the Gate House,
Westminster, for high treason ; and a Bill was found against
him at the Quarter Sessions, upon which he was tried on
November 8th at the King's Bench Bar, by a Surrey jury,
before Lord Chief Justice Jefferies, and his brethren (viz.)
Withins, Holloway, and Walcot. He was indicted for the
following expressions in his sermon of September 14th : ' That
the King could not cure the King's evil, but that priests and
prophets by their prayers could heal the griefs of the people ;
that we had had two wicked Kings (meaning the present King
and his father), whom we can resemble to no other person but
to the most wicked Jeroboam ; and that if they (meaning his
hearers), would stand to their principles, he did not doubt, but
they should overcome their enemies (meaning the King), as in
former times, with rams' horns, broken platters, and a stone in
a sling.' The witnesses were three infamous women, who
swore to the words without the innuendoes ; they were laden
with the guilt of many perjuries already, and such of them as
could be found afterwards, were convicted, and the chief of
them pilloried before the Exchange. The trial lasted seven
hours, and Mr. Rosewell behaved with all the decency and
respect to the Court that could be expected, and made a
defence that was applauded by most of the hearers. He said
it was impossible the witnesses should remember, and be able
to pronounce so long a period, when they could not so much as
tell the text, nor anything else in the sermon, besides the
words they had sworn. Several who heard the sermon and
writ it in shorthand, declared they heard no such words. Mr.
Rosewell offered his own notes to prove it, but no regard was
had to them. The women could not prove (says Burnet), by

any one circumstance, that they were at the meeting; or that any person saw them there on that day; the words they swore were so gross, that it was not to be imagined that any man in his wits would express himself so, before a mixed assembly; yet Jefferies urged the matter with his usual vehemence. He laid it for a foundation, that all preaching at conventicles was treasonable, and that this ought to dispose the jury to believe any evidence upon that head, so the jury brought him in guilty; upon which (says the bishop), there was a shameful rejoicing; and it was now thought, all conventicles must be suppressed, when such evidence could be received against such a defence. But when the words came to be examined by men learned in the law, they were found not to be treason by any Statute. So Mr. Rosewell moved in arrest of judgment, and though it was doubtful, whether the motion was proper on this foundation after the verdict, yet the King was so out of countenance at the accounts he heard of the witnesses, that he gave orders to yield to it; and in the end he was pardoned. The Court lost a great deal of reputation by this trial, for besides that Rosewell made a strong defence, he proved that he had always been a loyal man even in Cromwell's days, that he prayed constantly for the king in his family, and that in his sermons he often insisted upon the obligations to loyalty."

The manner of his escape was quite unusual. For once a Dissenter who had been condemned to death and who was bitterly hated by Jefferies did not suffer the full penalty of the law. Sir John Talbot, who had been present at the trial, went to the King, and speaking quite plainly, told him, "that he had seen the life of a gentleman and a scholar dependent on such evidence as he would not hang his dog on." He also said, "Sir, if your Majesty suffers this man to die, we are none of us safe in our houses." Just at this moment Jefferies, delighted with what he had done, burst into the room, and with much joyful pleasure told the King what a good deed he had accomplished, and what great service he had rendered to his Master. The surprise of Jefferies may be imagined when Charles II. told him that Rosewell should not die, but that he must by some means make a way of escape. This was most unpalatable to Jefferies, who was simply thirsting for the blood of Rosewell, but a new trial was ordered, and Counsel was assigned the condemned man in order to plead the insufficiency of the indictment in arrest of judgment. There was an adjournment until the following term, and in the meantime the King granted Rosewell a pardon and he was discharged.

The prosecution of Rosewell was particularly unjust in that whilst a strong Puritan, he always had a very kindly feeling towards the Stuart family. While he was a schoolboy at Bath during the Civil War, the King's army seized the town, and the school was broken up. It was about this time that while he was taking a walk from home, he saw Charles I. in a field, sitting at dinner under a tree with a few persons around him. This occurrence always disposed him to be loyal to the Royal Family, but it in no way influenced Jefferies in his decision.

His death took place on February 14th, 1692, in the 62nd year of his age, so that he outlived his trial about seven years.

TWO EPITAPHS.

Here lyeth the Body of John Dent,
Son of John and Ann Dent, who
dyed April the 5th, 1710, aged One Year
and a Half and Six Months.

After a short, but sharp affliction here,
I take my Leave of you, my Parents dear.
Low here I lye, in this soft bed of Dust,
Waiting the Resurrection of the Just.
I, Phœnix like, have my first rising known,
And on the Wings of Love am upward flown:
My Heavenly Part's ascended up on high,
Whilst on Earth my Earthly Part doth ......
'Till it shall rise again in Glory blest,
With all the saints, in their eternal Rest.
My Parents dear, my Time was short, you see:
So live and dye, that you may rest with me.

Lucia Smith dyed Octob. the 6, 1682, within a day of 12 years; who lived much beloved, and dyed greatly lamented by all her Acquaintance; as not having known her Equal for Natural Endowments, At her Age.

D

JOHN, THOMAS AND BENONI ROWE.

THIS tomb is only a few paces from that of Thomas Rosewell. The original inscriptions were as follows :—

Here lies the body of JOHN ROWE, some time preacher in the Abbey of Westminster, who died October 12th, in the 52nd year of his age. Anno, 1677.

Under this stone is the body of Mr. THOMAS ROWE, the eldest son of Mr. John Rowe ; late minister of the Gospel in London. He departed this life the 18th day of August, in the year of our Lord 1705, in the 49th year of his age.

Here also lies the body of Mr. BENONI ROWE, minister of the Gospel in London, who departed this life the 30th day of March, in the year of our Lord 1706, in the 49th year of his age.

(The present stone was erected by Walter W. Law, Esq., of Briar Cliffe Manor, New York, on the 11th February, 1910.)

JOHN ROWE.

Mr. John Rowe was born in the year 1626 at Crediton in Devonshire, and after spending some time at Cambridge he removed to Oxford in 1648. He was appointed to a Fellowship in Corpus Christi College, and became a lecturer at Witney in Oxfordshire, but afterwards was engaged in the work of the ministry at Tiverton. In 1654 Mr. Rowe was appointed to succeed William Strong as minister of the Independent Church, which met in Westminster Abbey during the Commonwealth. His congregation was quite a remarkable one, as numbers of the leading Puritans were constant attendants upon his ministry.

On the 14th March, 1659, he was appointed by Act of Parliament one of the Approvers of Ministers, but at the Restoration in 1660 he was ejected from his pastorate at Westminster Abbey. After the Act of Uniformity he preached privately as often as he could, with his old people gathered round him. He was noted for his great gravity and piety, whilst "his sermons were judicious and well studied, fit for the audiences of men of the best quality in those days." It is interesting to notice, too, the words with which he closed his last sermon : " We should not desire to continue longer in this world than to glorify God, to finish our work, and to be ready to say, 'Farewell, Time ; welcome, blessed Eternity ; even so, come, Lord Jesus.'" One of his other expressions when preaching this sermon was, "that he knew no other bottom whereon to lay the stress of his Salvation, than the incarnation and atonement of the Son of God."

Thomas Rowe.

Mr. Thomas Rowe was chiefly noted for the number of distinguished pupils which attended his Academy, amongst them being Daniel Neal, the author of "The History of the Puritans," Doctor Isaac Watts and Mr. Samuel Say, all of whom are buried in Bunhill. Thomas Rowe was the son of John Rowe, and was born about the year 1657. He had quite a remarkable mind, and having a great desire for knowledge he soon became one of the best instructed men of his times. Soon after his father's death he accepted the oversight of the congregation which was then removed to Girdler's Hall, Basinghall Street. His predecessor as a teacher was none other than Theophilus Gale, whose body is resting so close to his own. Dr. Watts was not only a pupil, but also a member of his church.

The Revolution of 1688 naturally made a great difference to Mr. Rowe, and considerable prosperity attended his latter days, but his end was very sudden. He was riding through the City when he was seized with a fit, and falling from his horse near the Monument immediately expired. This took place on the 18th August, 1705, when he was only in his 49th year.

Benoni Rowe.

Benoni Rowe was also son to John Rowe, and was the younger brother of Thomas Rowe. The date of his birth was about 1658, and the early days of his ministry began

when Dissenters were under a dark cloud.   Through the
reigns of Charles II. and James II. he was sorely persecuted, and his services were often disturbed.   After the
Prince of Orange ascended the throne Benoni Rowe
moved to Epsom, and stayed there about a year, when
he accepted an invitation to become the pastor of the
Independent Church in Fetter Lane.   Amongst other
memorable services in which he took part was that of
the ordination of Isaac Watts, at which his brother
Thomas preached a sermon from the text, "I will give
you pastors according to Mine heart, which shall feed
you with knowledge and understanding" (Jer iii. 15).

He died just about seven months after Thomas, and
was buried in the same vault, where their father's body
had been placed some years previously.

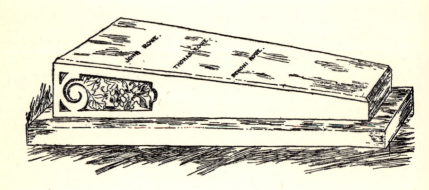

THEOPHILUS GALE.

This grave is a little nearer the path than Rowe's tomb, and on the low headstone there is to be seen the inscription:—

THEOPHILUS GALE. Born 1628. Died 1678.

Mr. Theophilus Gale was the son of Dr. Thomas Gale, Prebendary of Exeter. He was born in 1628, and in 1650 he was unanimously chosen Fellow of his College, in preference to many others who were his seniors. He frequently preached at the University, and also enjoyed a considerable reputation as a tutor—Bishop Hopkins, who always paid him very great respect, being one of his pupils.

During the Commonwealth, in 1657, he was called to the Cathedral at Winchester, where he remained as a preacher till the Restoration, when he was ejected. As he also lost his Fellowship, he went to France in September, 1662, as the tutor to the two sons of Lord Wharton, and stayed for two years at Caen. He left his pupils there and returned to England, reaching the Metropolis just as it was being devastated by the Great Fire.

He was much alarmed and distressed when told that the house was burned in which he had left his MSS., amongst these being his famous work, "The Court of the

Gentiles." These MSS. represented the labour of twenty years, but after he had given up all hope, he received the welcome news that certain of his goods had been preserved. He was told that amongst the things saved was a desk, which a friend who had placed no value upon it had intended leaving behind, but having just enough room, he placed it upon the cart to make up the load. In this desk were his much loved papers, and Gale was thus enabled to complete his work.

Upon Mr. John Rowe's death he was chosen as joint pastor with Mr. Lee, and it is recorded that he was " a man of great reading, and an exact philologist, and philosophist, and a learned and industrious person." He died of consumption in 1678, when only 49 years of age, leaving all his estate in the charge of Nonconformist ministers for the purpose of educating poor Dissenters.

ALMOST in a line with Gale's stone, but close to the railings and facing the path, is the small headstone which is now the oldest one in the grounds.

INSCRIPTION.

PRUDENCE JAMES, Jun., died March 24th, 1668, aged 23 years.

When cleaned this is quite legible, but being so near to the earth is often covered with dust or mud. To see the face of the stone one must be standing upon the path itself.

RICHARD WAVEL, B.A.

A FEW rows eastward, in about the centre of this section of the ground, is the small, fast-decaying headstone of Richard Wavel, B.A. The words are practically obliterated, but the stone will not be very difficult to identify.

INSCRIPTION:

This adjourns to the family vault of the late REV. RICHARD WAVEL.

Here is the resting-place of one of the victims of the Act of Uniformity. He was born in the Isle of Wight on April 3rd, 1633, and after he had taken his degree of B.A. he studied Divinity under the tuition of the Rev. W. Reyner, at Egham, in Surrey. He afterwards married Mr. Reyner's step-daughter, and constantly preached in the church at Egham.

When the Act of Uniformity came into force he was compelled by his conscience to sever his connection with the Established Church, although many tempting offers of good livings were made to him. For a time he preached privately at Egham, in his own house, but was compelled to cease, as stern measures were taken against him. He afterwards became minister at Pinner's Hall, and on doing so "told his people that he would venture his person if they would venture their purses; which they did, and they were put to no small expense by it." It is recorded that "his preaching was plain, and tended very much to exalt Christ, and the grace of God in him; and yet it was his dying advice to his church that they would choose one to succeed him of whom they should have some ground to hope that he would preach Christ crucified more than he had done. He excelled in prayer, more especially upon particular occasions, to which he would apply Scripture expressions with great propriety. It was a most frequent petition in his prayer, which he would express with a warmth and relish that was very remarkable, 'Father, glorify Thy name; Father, glorify Thy Son.' During the time of his last illness, for a fortnight before his death, he enjoyed a continued serenity of mind, expressing to those about him his desire to depart, and rejoicing that his work was finished. To a minister who visited him, telling him that he had suffered much for his Master, Christ, his answer was, 'He owes me nothing.' As he sat in his chair, he lifted up his hands and blessed his children; and as he was going to bed died in his chair, December 19th, 1705, in the 72nd year of his age."

TWO EPITAPHS.

Here lyeth interred the Body of the
Reverend and Learned Divine, Mr.
Anthony Fidoe, who 'till the Year
1660, was a Fellow of Trinity College
in Cambridge; but soon after (his
Conscience not permitting him to comply
with the Act commonly known by the
Name of The Bartholomew Act) he
resigned not only his Fellowship but a
considerable Living he was then in
Possession of, in the County of Cambridge;
and since that time, has continued a
Minister of the Gospel in several
Parts of England; but for the last
Thirty Years of his Life, in the City
of London. He dyed a Batchelor,
on the 17th Day of January, 1715.
Aged 75 Years.

Here lyes the Body of Mr. John Dickonson,
who dyed Dec. 11, A.D. MDCLXXXIX.,
aged LV., an Israelite indeed, exem-
plarily pious, humble, useful, labouring
for Acceptance with God, not the
Praise of Man.
X. Prov. VII.   The Memory of the Just is
Blessed.

THOMAS GOODWIN.

THE tomb of Thomas Goodwin, as shown in the photograph, lies slightly to the south-east of Wavel's. During a terrific thunderstorm a flash of lightning split the top, and all that can now be deciphered is, " Thomas Goodwin, D.D."

INSCRIPTION.

Here lies the body of the Rev. THOMAS GOODWIN, D.D., born at Rolesby, in the county of Norfolk. He had a large and familiar acquaintance with ancient, and above all, with ecclesiastical history. He was exceeded by none in the knowledge of the Holy Scriptures. He was at once blessed with a rich invention, and a solid and exact judgment. He carefully compared together the different parts of holy writ, and with a marvellous felicity discovered the latent sense of the Divine Spirit who indited them. None ever entered deeper into the mysteries of the gospel, or more clearly unfolded them for the benefit of others. The matter, form, discipline, and all that relates to the constitution of a true Church of Christ, he traced out with an uncommon sagacity, if he was not rather the first Divine who thoroughly investigated them. He was eminently qualified, by the light of sacred truth, to pacify troubled consciences, to dispel the clouds of mistake, and to remove needless scruples from perplexed and bewildered minds. In knowledge, wisdom, and eloquence, he was a truly Christian pastor. In his private discourses, as well as in his public ministry, he edified numbers of souls, whom he had first won to Christ; till having finished his appointed course both of service and sufferings, in the cause of his Divine Master, he gently fell asleep in Jesus. His writings already published, and what are now preparing for publication (the noblest monuments of this great muse's praise), will diffuse his name in a more fragrant odour than that of the richest perfume, to flourish in those far distant ages, when this marble, inscribed with his just honour, shall have dropt into dust. He died, February 23, 1679, in the 80th year of his age.

Dr. Thomas Goodwin, one of the most eminent of the

Puritan Divines, was born on October 5th, 1600. His parents, wishing him to be devoted to the ministry, had him educated in a careful and thorough manner, and being blessed with good natural abilities he so improved by diligent study as to become noted even at the early age of thirteen. He had strong impressions of religion upon his mind from the time he was six years old, but when at Christ College, Cambridge, to which he was sent in 1613, he was much engrossed in ambitious designs, and his whole desire was to obtain high offices and the good word of man. When nineteen years of age he removed to Katherine Hall, where his tutor was the famous Puritan, Dr. Sibbes. "On Monday, the 2nd of October, 1620, in the afternoon," while going from Katherine Hall to enjoy himself with his former friends of Christ College, he heard a bell toll for a funeral, and one of his companions saying there was to be a sermon, pressed him to hear it. The preacher was Dr. Bambridge, who was accounted a witty man, and though his remarks, based on Luke xix. 41, 42, were quite ordinary on this occasion, they made an impression upon the mind of Goodwin. Instead of going on with his companions he returned to his college, having a most powerful sense of sin and a dread of its consequences. It pleased God in a little time gently to speak peace to his soul, and he now saw very clearly how vague and empty had been his previous profession. He had a very real yet peculiar evidence of a true conversion, for he was led to search out the sins which he had loved most, and was by grace enabled to gain the victory over them.

In 1628 he was appointed lecturer at Trinity Church, Cambridge, in spite of the opposition of the Bishop, but in 1634, his conscience being disturbed with the terms of Conformity, he resigned his preferment and left the University.

When referring to this memorable event in after years Goodwin said, "I freely renounced for Christ, when God converted me, all those designs of pride, and vain-glory, and advancement of myself, upon which my heart was so strongly set that no persuasions of men, nor any worldly considerations, could have diverted me from the pursuit of them. No, it was the power of God alone that prevailed with me to do it. It was He alone that made me willing to live in the meanest and most afflicted condition, so that I might serve Him in all godly sincerity. I cheerfully parted with all for Christ, and He hath made me abundant compensation, not only in the comforts and joys of His love, which are beyond comparison above all other things, but even in this world. What love and esteem I have had among good men, He gave me. He alone made my ministry in the gospel acceptable, and blessed it with success, to the conversion and spiritual good and comfort of many souls."

Goodwin was now a marked man, and Archbishop Laud persecuting him, he left England and went to Holland in 1639. Here he enjoyed liberty of conscience, and became pastor of the English Church at Arnheim. He, however, returned to England during the Long Parliament, and became minister of an Independent Congregation meeting in Thames Street. Being chosen a member of the Assembly of Divines, which met at Westminster in 1643, he took a leading part in the deliberations, and won high esteem by his ability, modesty and meekness. He afterwards published his notes of these transactions, and was himself one of the Dissenting ministers.

His first marriage took place in 1638, his second in 1649, and he was very happy in both. The great Protector, who held him in high favour, appointed him in 1654 to the Presidency of Magdalen College, Oxford. He formed a church in this university town, and his members numbered amongst others, Thankful Owen, Theophilus Gale and Stephen Charnock. Soon after the Restoration he retired from the college and removed once more to London, many of his fellow members and friends following him. Another Independent Church was formed in Fetter Lane, and he preached here until his death.

During the Great Fire of 1666 he lost a large portion of his library, and he felt this blow to be a very severe one. He, however, expressed his thankfulness that his works of divinity were for the most part saved, and that those lost were in the main books of human knowledge.

He continued to preach in spite of the Conventicle
and Five Mile Acts, and was for the most part unmolested.
Except when preaching he lived a very retired life,
dividing his time between prayer, reading and meditation.
He had his favourite authors, such as Augustine and Cal-
vin, but his son says, " The Scriptures were what he most
studied. . . . The love and free grace of God, the
excellencies and glories of our Lord Jesus Christ, were
the truths in which his mind soared with the greatest
delight."

The last scene of all was also described by his son as
follows :—

" In February, 1679, a fever seized him, which in a few days
put an end to his life. In all the violence of it, he discoursed
with that strength of faith and assurance of Christ's love, with
that holy admiration of free grace, with that joy in believing,
and such thanksgivings and praises, as he extremely moved
and affected all that heard him. That excellent man, Mr.
Collins, praying earnestly for him, offered up this petition,
' That God would return into his bosom all those comforts
which he had by his ministry of free grace poured into
so many distressed souls.' My dear father felt this prayer
answered in the abundant comforts and joys with which
he was filled. He rejoiced in the thoughts that he was
dying, and going to have a full and uninterrupted communion with God. ' I am going,' said he, ' to the Three
Persons, with whom I have had communion : They have taken
me ; I did not take Them. I shall be changed in the twinkling
of an eye ; all my lusts and corruptions I shall be rid of, which
I could not be here ; those croaking toads will fall off in a
moment.' And mentioning those great examples of faith,
Heb. xi., ' All these,' said he, ' died in faith. I could not have
imagined that I should ever have had such a measure of faith
in this hour ; no, I could never have imagined it. My bow
abides in strength. Is Christ divided ? No, I have the whole
of His righteousness ; I am found in Him, not in mine own
righteousness, which is of the law, but in the righteousness
which is of God, which is by faith of Jesus Christ, who loved
me and gave Himself for me. Christ cannot love me better
than He doth : I think I cannot love Christ better than I do ;
I am swallowed up in God.'

" Directing his speech to his two sons, he exhorted them to
value the privilege of the covenant. ' It hath taken hold on

me,' said he; 'my mother was a holy woman; she spake
nothing diminishing of it. It is a privilege cannot be valued
enough, nor purchased with a great sum of money,' alluding to
the words of the chief captain to Paul, Acts xxii. 28. Then he
exhorted them to be careful that they did nothing to provoke
God to reject them. 'Now,' said he, 'I shall be ever with the
Lord.' With this assurance of faith and fulness of joy, his
soul left the world, and went to see and enjoy the reality of
that blessed state of glory which in a discourse on that subject
he had so well demonstrated. He died February, 1679, and in
the eightieth year of his age."

Extract from Goodwin's "Child of Light Walking
in Darkness," kindly selected by Mr. W. BROOKE, pastor
of West Street Chapel, Croydon :—

"The fourth direction is, to make diligent search into, and
to call to remembrance what formerly hath been between God
and you. The remembrance of former things doth often up-
hold, when present sense fails. This David practised in the
like case, Psalm lxxvii. 5, 6, when his soul had refused comfort,
as I told you, ver. 2 ; yet in the end he began not only to be
willing to listen to what might make for him, but set himself
a-work to recall to mind, to 'consider the days of old, to make
diligent search,' namely, into the records and register of God's
dealings, ver. 11, to see if there were never a record extant
which might help him, now the devil pleaded against his title.
Even as if your houses and lands were called into question,
you would search over old writings and deeds ; so do you in
this. 'I considered,' says he, 'the songs in the night,'—that
is, that joyful communion he had enjoyed with God, when
God and he sang songs together,—and 'I communed with
mine own heart, and made diligent search;' I tossed and
tumbled over my heart, to see if no grace formerly had been
there, and if no grace at present were there. He searched into
what might comfort him, as well as into the causes might provoke God thus to deal with him ; for I take it both may be
meant.
"And so Job did, when he was thus stricken and forsaken
of God ; he views over every part of his life ; he seeks what
dry land he could find to get footing upon in the midst of seas
of temptations ; recounts what a holy life he had lived, with
what fear and strictness he had served God, chap. xxix. and
chap. xxx., and chap. xxxi. throughout, and tells them plainly,
chap. xxvii. 5, 6, that let them plead and argue what they

could against him, and go about to prove him a hypocrite, ' till
I die,' says he, ' I will not remove mine integrity from me, nor
let go my righteousness ; ' I will never give up mine interest
in God's mercies, nor the evidences I have to shew for them.
And, says he, chap. xix. 27, 28, ' Though my reins be at present
consumed, yet the root of the matter is in me,'—that is,
though God deals thus hardly with me, as you see, yea, though
the exercise of grace is much obscured, the sunshine of God's
favour withdrawn, His face hidden from me, and the joyful
fruits of righteousness, and comfortable fresh green speeches,
and leaves you have known to grow upon this now withered
stock fallen off ; yet there is the root of the matter still in me
—a root of faith that decays not, a constant frame of grace
that still remains, which hateth sin, loveth God ; and you shall
all never beat me from it.   And canst thou call nothing to remembrance betwixt God and thee, which argues infallibly His
love ?   What ! nothing ?   Look again.   Did God never speak
peace unto thy heart, and shed His love abroad in it ?   Hast
thou at no time found in thine heart pure strains of true love
and good-will to Him, some pure drops of godly sorrow for
offending Him, and found some dispositions of pure self-denial,
wherein thou didst simply aim at His glory more than thine
own good ?   Hast thou never an old tried evidence which
hath been acknowledged and confirmed again and again in
open court ?   What ! not one ?   And if thou canst now call to
mind but one, if in truth, it may support thee.   For if one promise do belong to thee, then all do, for every one conveys
whole Christ, in whom all the promises are made, and who is
the matter of them.   And if thou canst say, as the church of
Ephesus, Rev. ii. 6, ' This thing I have, that I hate sin,' and
every sin, as God hates it, and because He hates it : as Christ
owned them for this one grace, and though they had many
sins and many failings, yet, says He, ' This thou hast,' &c.   If
Christ will acknowledge thee to be His for one ear-mark, or if
He sees but one ' spot of His child ' upon thee, Deut. xxxii. 5,
thou mayest well plead it, even any one, to Him.   Yea, though
it be but in a lesser degree, in truth and sincerity.   For God
brings not a pair of scales to weigh your graces, and if they be
too light refuseth them ; but He brings a touchstone to try
them ; and if they be true gold, though never so little of it, it
will pass current with Him ; though it be but smoke, not flame,
though it be but as a wick in the socket, Matt. xii. 20 (as it is
there in the original), likelier to die and go out than to continue,
which we use to throw away ; yet He will not quench it, but
accept it.

"These things you are to recall and consider in time of distress: to remember former graces and spiritual dispositions in you; and God's gracious dealings with you. God remembers them to have mercy on you; and why should you not remember them to comfort you? Therefore, Heb. vi. 9, 10, 'We hope,' says he, 'better things of you; for God is not unrighteous to forget your labour of love;' namely, to reward you. And therefore He calls upon them in like manner, Heb. x. 32, 'to call to remembrance the former days' to comfort them; how they held out when their hearts were tried to the bottom; when shipwreck was made of their goods, good names, and all for Christ,—yet they made not shipwreck of a good conscience. And if thou dost thus call to remembrance things of old, and yet canst find no comfort at first from them,—as often ye may not, as was David's case, Psalm lxxvii., for after his 'remembrance of his songs in the night,' still his soul was left in doubt, and he goes on to say, 'Will God ever be merciful?'—yet have recourse to them again, and then again, for though they comfort not at one time, yet they may at another; that it may be seen that God comforts by them, and not they alone of themselves. Hast thou found a promise (which is a 'breast of consolation,' Isa. lxvi. 11) milkless? Yet again suck; comfort may come in the end. If after thou hast empanelled a jury and grand inquest to search, and their first verdict condemns thee, or they bring in an *ignoramus;* yet do as wise judges often do, send them about it again, they may find it the next time. Jonah looked once, it seems, and found no comfort, chap. ii. 4, for he said, 'I will look again towards Thine holy temple.' A man's heart is like those two-faced pictures; if you look one way towards one side of them, you shall see nothing but some horrid shape of a devil, or the like; but go to the other side and look again, and you shall see the picture of an angel or of some beautiful woman, &c. So some have looked over their hearts by signs at one time, and have to their thinking found nothing but hypocrisy, unbelief, hardness, self-seeking; but not long after, examining their hearts again by the same signs, they have espied the image of God drawn fairly upon the table of their hearts."

THANKFUL OWEN.

(Same Tomb as Goodwin.)

TRANSLATION OF LATIN INSCRIPTION.

THANKFUL OWEN, S.T.B. Here mingles his sacred dust with that of Goodwin ; to whom in life he was most dear. He scarce survived an hour the finishing of a Preface which he had been writing to that great work of Goodwin's on the Epistle to the Ephesians, the publication of which had fallen to his care. Dying with the same calmness with which he had lived, without a groan, save of the heart to Christ, on the 1st April, 1681, in the 63rd year of his age.

Thankful Owen was born, according to one account, at Taplow in Buckinghamshire, but another authority states that he was born in London. While quite a youth he had a remarkable preservation from drowning, for as he was swimming near Oxford he sank twice under the water.

He received his education chiefly at Exeter College, Oxford, where his tutor was a Puritan. He became a man of much learning, and was greatly admired for the easy fluency of his language and compositions, and for the quite exceptional purity of his Latin style. He joined the Independent Church, afterwards becoming one of their preachers, and he was also chosen Proctor of the University in 1650, whilst in the same year he became President of St. John's College.

At the Restoration he was ejected by the Commissioners, and like Goodwin, removed to London. Here he lived very quietly, preaching as often as he could and steadfastly maintaining his nonconformity. On the death of Goodwin he was chosen to succeed him, but was only pastor for a fortnight, as he died quite suddenly at his house in Hatton Gardens. His last labour was, as stated in the Inscription, to write a Preface for Goodwin's work on the Ephesians, and he had almost finished a work of

(1) RICHARD WAVEL, B.A   (2) THOMAS GOODWIN, D.D.
(See page 39.)   (See page 41.)

(1) WILLIAM JENKYN, M.A.   (2) JOHN STAFFORD, D.D.
(See page 49.)   (See page 55.)
(3) THE MORLEY FAMILY TOMB. In it, amongst others, are buried Mr. and Mrs. JOHN MORLEY, the father and mother of the late Samuel Morley, M.P.

(See page 64.)

CHANDLER'S FAMILY VAULT. (See page 62.)

his own, entitled " Imago Imagins," which was designed
to show that Rome Papal was simply an imitation of
Rome Pagan.   Dr. John Owen said of Thankful Owen
that he had not left his fellow behind him for learning,
religion, and good humour.

WILLIAM JENKYN, M.A.

THE massive stone tomb of William Jenkyn will readily
catch the visitor's eye, as it lies only a little to the south-
east of Thomas Goodwin's.   The original inscription on
this tomb was in Latin, but was replaced by an English
one, now undecipherable, which was as follows :—

> " Sacred to the remains of WILLIAM JENKYN, Minister
> of the Gospel, who during the heavy storms of the Church
> was imprisoned in Newgate.   Died a martyr there in the
> 72nd year of his age and the 52nd of his Ministry, 1684."

This " martyr of Jesus " was born at Sudbury, Suffolk,
in the year 1612, and was blessed with godly parents.
That his father was a good man is clear, for he had
already sacrificed all prospects of wealth and honour
rather than yield obedience to laws, rites, and doctrines
which he deemed unscriptural.   Indeed, so exceedingly
enraged was his own father at his turning from
the path which led to the highest positions in the
Church of England, that he disinherited him.   This
cruel action of William Jenkyn's grand-father, however,
had no effect, for his father became the minister at Sudbury,
where God was pleased to smile upon his labours.   The
mother of Jenkyn was a grand-daughter of noble John
Rogers, who was burned to death in the reign of that poor
mis-guided but cruel daughter of Rome known as "Bloody

E

Mary." When William was still quite young his father died, and his mother somewhat reluctantly agreed to trust him to the care of his paternal grandfather, who was willing to educate him and to train him as a gentleman. After the lad had been with his grandfather for a few years, fearing that the godless habits of those with whom he lived would have an ill effect upon him, his mother, like a wise woman, took William under her own care, and with her second husband trained him up after a godly manner. In 1626 arrangements were made for him to go into residence at Cambridge, the college chosen being that of St. John's, and his tutor was Anthony Burgess, who found him an apt pupil. Indeed, he made such progress in his studies that his fame spread abroad, but best of all his mind was exercised concerning his spiritual standing. His walk, conversation and conduct alike proclaimed him to be a godly character, and he was mercifully preserved from falling into those outward sins of dissipation and vice which ruin so many young men. Having taken his M.A. degree he accepted a lectureship at St. Nicholas, Acons, London, but soon after moved to Hythe in Essex, where he preached to a small congregation.

A number of his friends, being desirous of sitting under his ministry, persuaded him in 1641 to return to the Metropolis, where he became vicar of Christ Church, Newgate, and afterwards he was also appointed lecturer of St. Ann's, Blackfriars. He laboured with much earnestness and success, but his political views brought him into trouble at the overthrow of the Monarchy. So thankful were the people at being freed from the hateful yoke of the Stuarts, that Parliament appointed special thanksgiving services, but Jenkyn, whilst a stalwart Puritan, refused to take part in these. As a consequence he was banished from London, suspended from his ministerial office and his benefices were sequestered. He removed to Billericay, in Essex, for some six months; then returned to London, only to be sent to the Tower for taking some little part in a foolish plot. On the advice of friends he afterward petitioned Parliament for his release, although it was a difficult matter for those interested in him to obtain his signature to the document. It is pleasing to relate that it was resolved to pardon Jenkyn " both for life and estate," and he was thus free not only to return to his home, but also to his ministry. Showing a very magnanimous spirit he refused to eject the Mr. Feak who had been appointed to Christ Church, but an early morning lectureship was arranged, and a large subscription was raised for this purpose. He also recommenced his lectures at Blackfriars, and on the death of Dr. Gouge he was chosen rector. When afterwards Mr. Feak was dismissed by the Government, Jenkyn was reappointed by the Governors of Bartholomew's Hospital, and thus once again he became vicar of Christ Church. Each Lord's Day he preached morning and evening to large auditories, for in addition to his parishioners, people flocked from all parts to listen to this prince of preachers. He possessed very considerable abilities, and was called by Baxter, " that elegant and sententious preacher." When the deceived and foolish people made another Stuart, Charles the Second, King of England, Jenkyn's troubles began again.

On Tuesday, January 2nd, 1661, he was compelled to appear before a special council, where he " was reproved for not praying for the King." When afterwards the Uniformity and Oxford Acts in 1662 and 1665 were passed, Jenkyn could not take the oaths that were required ; and once again he sacrificed his living, retiring to Langley in Hertfordshire, where he preached to a few friends in private. When the King issued a Declaration of Indulgence in 1671, he returned to London, and a chapel was erected for him in Jewin Street, where once again great numbers of people sat under his ministry. The Indulgence was not confirmed by Parliament, and was withdrawn ; but although not immediately, Jenkyn's sorest trial was fast approaching. As was only to be expected, Jenkyn declined to conform, and from that time he was " in dangers oft," for although the King decreed, this man and hundreds of others refused to have their voices silenced, and continued to preach under the most adverse circumstances. Meetings were held in secrecy as often as possible until September 2nd, 1684, when he was apprehended by soldiers, who broke in upon the numerous company which had met for prayer. With the exception of Jenkyn, all the ministers, amongst whom were Reynolds and Flavel, escaped, the latter stating that it was a piece of foolish vanity on a lady's part, combined with an act of politeness by the famous preacher, that cost him his liberty. In the rush for safety Jenkyn stood aside to allow this lady to pass before him, and her long train only too effectually prevented his hastening down the stairs and reaching a place of safety. The officers were delighted at their capture, and treated the aged and venerable servant of God in as cruel and rude a manner as possible, whilst the two magistrates, who were mere tools of the Court, were exceedingly violent and unjust. According to the law, by the payment of £40, the offender could obtain his release, but these creatures set all order at defiance and committed the preacher, now 71 years of age, to Newgate Prison, where most severe restrictions where imposed. What mattered it that this much loved and highly respected man had suffered greatly for the Royalist cause? What cared his persecutors that the foul air and stench of Newgate would surely poison him? What anxiety did the statement of Jenkyn's physician that "his life was in danger from close confinement" cause the evil king and his counsellors? What effect had all the pleadings of his friends and petitions of his followers? Answers to these questions are found in the regulations by which Jenkyn was bound. He was not allowed to pray with anyone—not even his daughter. He was never permitted to leave the prison, although full security was offered, and neither was he granted the ordinary rights of a prisoner. It is not to be wondered that his physical health soon began to fail, although as his natural strength decayed his spiritual powers seemed to increase. On one occasion he exclaimed to some of his friends, " What a vast difference is there between this and my first imprisonment! Then I was full of doubts and fears, of grief and anguish; and well I might, for going out of God's way and my own calling to meddle with things that did not belong to me. But now being found in the way of my duty, in my

Master's business, though I suffer even to bonds, yet I
am comforted beyond measure. The Lord sheds His
love abroad in my heart; I feel it; I have the assurance
of it." Some of his loving hearers giving way to tears, he
exclaimed, " Why weep ye for me? Christ lives; He is
my Friend; a Friend born for adversity; a Friend that
never dies. Weep not for me, but weep for yourselves
and for your children." On January 19th, 1685, after
some four months' confinement, Jenkyn exchanged a
prison cell for a heavenly mansion. In the former he
suffered privation, persecution, hunger, thirst, and a
thousand indignities, but in heaven all these things were
done. The prison doors were kept securely fastened, but
it is recorded of the Celestial City, " The gates of it
shall not be shut at all by day; for there shall be no
night there."

For fifty years he had been a minister of the Gospel
upon the earth, faithfully rebuking sin and setting forth
Christ as the one hope of a sinner and the only way to the
Father, but now he " sees Him as He is," and is joining
in the song of the redeemed from among men.

It was not long ere the news of the death reached the
court, and one courtier was bold enough to say to the
King, " May it please your majesty, Jenkyn has got his
liberty." With surprise the monarch replied, " Aye, who
gave it to him?" "A greater than your Majesty, the
King of kings," was the explanation, and even so callous
and perfidious a man was for once silent.

To Bunhill Fields the mortal remains of Jenkyn were
taken, " his corpse being attended by at least one hundred
and fifty coaches," and were there laid to rest. He was
undoubtedly a martyr, for in Newgate, as he stated, " a
man might be as effectually murdered as at Tyburn;" and
his daughter boldly gave mourning rings with the inscription, " Mr. William Jenkyn murdered in Newgate." As a
politician Jenkyn is not easily understood, for he seemed
to change his views quickly and often, but this compared
with eternal matters is of small moment.

His great work is an exposition upon the Epistle of
Jude, which was preached in Christ Church. A revised
and corrected edition was published in 1839, the editor

being Mr. James Sherman, who was then the minister of the Surrey Chapel.

The extract given is from Jenkyn's sermon on the afternoon of August 17th, 1662, before he was ejected. The text was Exodus iii. 2—5.

" Lastly, to name no more, labour to preserve the holiness of God's true institutions, those things which are of divine consecration. What is human consecration without divine institution? The sabbath day is of divine institution, labour to keep it holy; this is a holy day indeed, and this labour to keep your families from profaning of ; but for other holy days, and holy things, they are much alike for holiness ; the Lord's day is a holy day indeed, and for shame, do not let your children gad abroad on this day. Truly I do verily believe, that though here be a great company of people in the congregation, yet they are but a handful in comparison of what are drinking in ale-houses, and walking in the fields, that one can hardly get home to their house for the crowd of the people that are going thither. For shame let not this be told in Gath, nor published in Askelon. What! shall we stand up for the holiness of places, and yet oppose the holiness of the Lord's day, which God hath enjoined and instituted ? Oh ! that the magistrates of London.—Oh ! that England's king— Oh ! that England's Parliament would do something for the reformation of this, to oppose wickedness and profaneness, which will otherwise bring upon us the judgments of Sodom and Gomorrah, and make us guilty and worthy of a thousand punishments. And labour by prayer in your families to overcome that flood of profaneness, which you cannot by your strength prevent. And then for the Lord's message and Word, that is a holy thing, and therefore love His messengers : the messengers of God delivering His message with fear and reverence, you are to hear them with the same fear, reverence, and resolution to be holy, as if Christ were present. And for the Word of God, it is not enough for you to have a choice sentence written upon the walls of your churches, but let God's law be written in your hearts and consciences, and practised in your lives, that all the world may see that you live as men dedicated to the true God, in all the duties of His ways and obedience. Many of these things might have been enlarged. What I have given you with the right hand, I pray you Christians, do not take with the left ; for if you do, you will make yourselves guilty of a double sin. First, because you do not obey the truth you hear. And secondly, for putting a wrong construction upon it. But I have better hopes of you, my beloved hearers, and hope that the Lord will be better unto your souls than His ministers, than His Word, or any thing else can be. God bless you and His ordinances, and discover His mind and will at this time to you."

DR. STAFFORD.

INSCRIPTION.

The Rev. JOHN STAFFORD, D.D., 42 years Pastor of the Congregational Church meeting in New Broad Street. In refuting error he was skilful, in defending truth he was bold; in his work as a Christian minister, and in his duty as a pastor, he was zealous and faithful. He departed this life, February 22nd, 1800, in the 72nd year of his age.

THIS stone tomb is to the south-east of Jenkyn's, and quite near to the path.

Dr. Stafford was born in the town of Leicester in the month of August, 1728. Quite early in life he met with some experiences which made a deep impression on his mind. Having received an experimental acquaintance with the deep things of the Gospel he left his secular employment, that of a wool comber, and devoted himself to the ministry. His first tutor was Dr. Doddridge at the Northampton Academy, but he completed his studies in London under Dr. Conder. During the latter period he united with the church in New Broad Street, over which Dr. Guyse was the pastor, but when his studies were completed, he went first to Royston and then St. Neots as pastor. When, owing to the advanced years and failing strength of Dr. Guyse, the church was compelled to obtain a co-pastor, their choice fell upon Dr. Stafford.

He accepted the invitation, and was ordained on May 11th, 1758. A very solemn charge was delivered at the ordination to the new pastor by Mr. Thomas Hall, and an account of the services was afterwards published. During his remarks Mr. Hall said, " Let me earnestly beseech, and solemnly charge you, my brother, in the presence of the Lord Jesus, and in the midst of this church of the living God, that you constantly watch and pray, that you may never in any instance, at any season, or upon any occasion, desert or balk the truth ; no, not through the flattering smiles of the dearest worldly friends, or the threatening frowns of the most avowed and bitter enemies. Shun not to declare any one truth of divine revelation. O, with what insolence and boldness, do some contradict the Scripture-doctrines of the Eternal Deity of the Son of God ; of the infinite merit of His atonement, and the imputation of His righteousness ; together with the personality and deity of the infinitely blessed and Holy Spirit. They deny the absolute necessity of His discriminating, efficacious, and omnipotent grace, by which precious souls are renewed, and the heart of sinners turned to God. How many are there who dispute the sovereignty of God's mercy ; the immutability of His love ; and openly deny the doctrine of the saints' certain and final perseverance in grace to glory ; with other grand articles of the Christian religion, in which the glory of God, Father, Son and Spirit ; the comfort of believers, and the power of true godliness are most nearly concerned ! O watch and pray, that you may with all boldness, as well as meekness, and patience, speak the truth as it is in Jesus."

After the death of Dr. Guyse in 1761, Stafford became the pastor, and occupied this position for a period of nearly 42 years. He preached his final sermon on October 6th, 1799, and attended the chapel for the last time on November 10th, in order to administer the Lord's Supper. This service is said to have been a most impressive one, and many tears were shed as the aged pastor resigned himself and his people into the Lord's hands to receive whatever He was pleased to send them. He also earnestly prayed that if they were permitted to meet no more upon earth they might all through the Redeemer's blood and righteousness meet around His throne in heaven. A short time before his death he remarked, "I have been favoured for so many years with an habitual readiness for death that I never expected to meet with much difficulty in it. I find the same faith, the same hope, the same trust, the same precious promises to support me ; so that I have not one trouble on my mind either respecting this world or that to come." To the last he was quite sensible and resigned, and was overheard to say, " So shall I be ever, ever, ever with the Lord."

WILLIAM GUYSE and JOHN GUYSE, D.D.

THIS stone tomb nearly touches the City Road railings, and is the third from the middle path.

INSCRIPTION.

Here lye interred the remains of the Rev. Mr. WILLIAM GUYSE, who departed this life, Dec. 8th, 1759, aged 54 years. Also the remains of the Rev. JOHN GUYSE, D.D., who departed this life the 22nd day of Nov., 1761, in the 81st year of his age. Whose life, character, and excellent writings, will long perpetuate his memory.

John Guyse was the father of William and was born at Hertford in the year 1680, and whilst quite a young man he was chosen to be assistant to an old ejected minister, Mr. W. Haworth. On Black Bartholomew's day, Mr. Haworth preached his last sermon as vicar of St. Peter's Church, in the town of St. Albans, and in due course became a dissenting minister in Hertford. After his death John Guyse was chosen pastor, but in 1727 left the county town and moved to London, where he became pastor of a people meeting at Girdler's Hall, and afterwards in a new chapel in New Broad Street. He enjoyed a considerable reputation as preacher and scholar, and took a rather notable part in some of the great controversies of his day. His physical strength was maintained in a marked degree, although he lost his eyesight some time before his death. The words that fell from his lips as the end drew near are clear evidence that his sun set in peace. "Thanks be to God I have no doubt as to my eternal state. I know whom I have believed ; here my faith rests. The peculiar doctrines of the Gospel, which I have long preached, are now the support of my soul; I live upon these every day, and thence I derive never-failing comfort. How good is my God to me. How often has He made to me that promise, 'As thy day so shall thy strength be.'" When a company of friends had gathered in the room he requested some to read and pray, and the portion chosen was 2 Cor. v. As the words were read he made amongst others the following remarks :—at ver. 1, "O when shall it be dissolved indeed ! When shall this mortal put on immortality?" at ver. 2, "This is my earnest desire and what I am waiting for " ; and at ver. 5, "This earnest I have; this I enjoy, and therefore I am confident. I am not afraid of death ; I am afraid lest I should err on the other hand, being too desirous of it."

His last day upon earth was a Sabbath, and during the morning he exclaimed, "When shall I get through this valley?" The final words that reached a human ear, were, "O my God, Thou who hast always been with me will not leave me." William for a time assisted his father, and was a man of ability. His physical health was so poor, however, that he was not able to undertake the regular services of a pastor, and for some time before his death he was quite incapacitated from preaching.

DAVID DENHAM.

It is much to be lamented that the flat tombstone which marked the resting-place of this gifted hymnwriter has entirely disappeared. The position of the grave is, however, not in doubt, as there is full evidence to prove that it is in the front row near the railings, next to the last tomb that is standing at the south-east corner. Surely the many congregations who use "Denham's Selection" might erect a stone with a suitable inscription! The grave originally belonged to a Mr. James Wood, but was bought by Mr. Josiah Elias Denham on December 15th, 1848, which was the date of the funeral.

INSCRIPTION.

Sacred to the memory of the Rev. DAVID DENHAM, minister of the Gospel, who departed this life, December 8th, 1848, age 58 years.

David Denham was born on April 12th, 1791, and early in life he experienced much hardship and great privations, for at the age of eight he was employed as an errand boy. Afterwards he was placed apprentice to a glass-cutter, and when he was about eighteen years of age became a teacher in the Sunday School at a famous old round chapel in Blackfriars Road.

After he was baptised he became a preacher at Gainsford Street, Southwark, and afterwards at Horsell Common Chapel, in Surrey. This place is about a mile out of Woking, and the building, which has been thoroughly renovated, still stands

> "As a palace built for God,
> To show His milder face."

He afterwards moved to Reading, then to Bath, and again to Plymouth. In the naval port he preached at a chapel in Willow Street, and this building becoming too small for the congregation, a larger chapel was built, in which he preached about seven years. During his stay at Plymouth there was much excitement owing to the secession from the Established Church of several ministers. Many of these joined the Baptists, but instead of being a help they caused much distress and discord. They fought most strenuously against the doctrines of free and sovereign grace; also denying the Deity and the distinct personality of the second and third Persons in the Trinity—the Son and Holy Ghost. Their evil doctrines for a time spread very rapidly, and although Mr. Denham opposed them with great ability and vigour, he was unable to make any headway, and eventually was compelled to leave Plymouth.

He then went to Birmingham and afterwards to Margate, but in the year 1834 he came to the world's metropolis as pastor of the Baptist Church at Unicorn Yard, Southwark. Here he remained for several years, and then went to Oxford, Cheltenham and other places. Accepting an invitation, he visited Yeovil in November, 1848, but on the fourth day that he was there, namely, November 26th, as he went to the chapel he complained of pain and heaviness in his head and eyes. He bravely stood up in the pulpit to read, but his voice seemed quite muffled, and after leaning on his Bible he sat down. The friends then requested him to leave the pulpit, and make no attempt to preach, but he said in reply, "Well, I will try." Although he opened his Bible and spoke a little with a faltering voice, he gave out no text. Some expressions were distinctly heard, amongst them being, "How blessed to be brought to see the perfections of Jehovah harmonising in the salvation of a sinner, and the Father embracing him through the blood and righteousness of Jesus." After speaking for a very few minutes, and pronouncing the benediction, he was conveyed to his home by the friends. He suffered great physical agony for twelve days, but through it all "his soul struggled to exalt, hold forth, and speak well of his Lord and Master." Once he woke up and exclaimed, "My soul thirsts for God, yea, for the living God. Christ is precious to me; exceedingly precious! His mercies are great!" The end came between nine and ten o'clock on the morning of December

8th, 1848, and his remains were removed from Yeovil to London. They were taken into Unicorn Chapel on Friday, the 15th, where there was a large congregation of friends who had assembled to show their respect and love for the departed minister, and their sympathy with his sorrowing family. After addresses by Mr. W. H. Bonner and other ministers, there was a long procession to Bunhill Fields, where his body was placed in a brick vault.

Mr. Denham published in 1837 an excellent collection of hymns, which is still largely used. Since his death there have been a Supplement and an Appendix added, but in the portion which he compiled there are some 70 hymns written by himself. In the preface of the Hymnbook he states: " The great object of praise is Jehovah—the Father, the Son, and the Holy Ghost,— the Self-Existent (Exod. iii. 14), Independent (Isa. xlvi. 9), Eternal (Deut. xxxiii. 27), Immutable (Job xxiii. 13) and All-Mighty God (Gen. xvii. 1), who alone is worthy to be adored for His mighty acts and excellent greatness in Creation and Providence ; but above all, for the manifestation of Himself in His Beloved Son : and the harmony of all His attributes, in the great work of Salvation—eternal election, particular redemption, effectual call, free justification, complete sanctification, final perseverance, and the everlasting glorification of all whom He foreknew and ordained to eternal life (Rom. viii. 29, 30), and of whom the Apostle says, ' I beheld, and lo, a great multitude, which no man could number, of all nations, and kindreds, and people, and tongues, stood before the Throne and before the Lamb, clothed with white robes, and palms in their hands ; and cried with a loud voice, saying, Salvation to our God which sitteth on the throne, and unto the Lamb ' (Rev. vii. 9, 10)."

———

" I am with you, saith the Lord of hosts."—HAG. ii. 4.

Jehovah dwells in Zion still,
    Our ever-present Lord !
His ancient covenant to fulfil,
    And magnify His Word.

He's with us in His pardoning blood,
　And Holy Spirit given;
He's with us, as our gracious God,
　In Christ, the Way to heaven.

He's with us in temptation's hour,
　Fresh succour to impart;
He's with us in His love and power,
　To heal each broken heart.

He's with us in His faithfulness,
　In every fire and flood;
He's with us to correct and bless,
　And working all for good.

He will be with us to sustain
　When heart and flesh shall fail,
And we with Him shall live and reign
　In heaven, within the vail.

DAVID DENHAM.

SAMUEL CHANDLER.

THIS stone tomb is on the south side of the path, near the iron railings of the Artillery buildings, and is the second from them. In the west panel is, " Chandler's Family Vault."

Chandler, who was a famous Presbyterian minister, died on May 8th, 1766, in the 73rd year of his age, but there was no inscription placed upon his tomb. His father officiated many years as a dissenting minister at Hungerford, whence he removed to Bath. Samuel Chandler was placed as a pupil with a Presbyterian minister, John Moore, and he was afterwards removed to the academy of Samuel Jones, at Tewkesbury. While a student he had as a daily companion Joseph Butler, the future author of the famous "Analogy," and also Thomas Secker, who became Archbishop of Canterbury. The friendship between these three was never broken, although their paths were so divergent. Chandler left Tewkesbury in his 21st year, and became a minister of a Presbyterian congregation at Peckham in 1716. He was quite inexperienced in many matters, and as a result he invested his wife's dowry, which was a considerable sum, in some wild speculations, which brought such terrible ruin on the collapse of the " South Sea Bubble." In order to lessen the blow he opened a bookselling business in the Poultry, and here he was brought into close touch with William Bowyer, the celebrated printer.

A lecture was founded at the Old Jewry about this time, and the appointed preachers were Chandler and Dr. Lardner. When this was abandoned Chandler completed a series of his own, and these were eventually published. His abilities produced many offers of Anglican preferment, but they were always declined, for he was a most conscientious Nonconformist. In 1735 there was much excitement over the spread of Popery, and this was closely connected with the future rebellion in favour of the Young Pretender. Some Dissenters engaged a number of leading ministers to point out the character of Popery, and to warn the people against it. Chandler's lectures aroused particular interest; he did not spare either Rome or the Establishment, for he pointed out that a blind subjection " to priestcraft is the soul and essence of Popery." There was great need for these lectures, and also for the debates which were arranged between Protestant ministers and Papist priests. Dr. Chandler had a heart hatred of the Papacy, and he translated " Limborch's History of the Inquisition," the publication of this being followed by a very excited controversy. He also actively used his pen in 1736, when taking part with those who attempted to obtain a repeal of the Corporation and Test Acts. In 1745 there was much turmoil, and ten editions of his Memorial against the Pretender were freely distributed. The leaders of the Papists and of the Jacobites feared his tongue, his pen, and his influence, for they were quite unable to overcome these. When Chandler died the cause of Nonconformity and of religious liberty sustained a severe loss.

LIEUT.-GEN. CHARLES FLEETWOOD.

THIS tomb, which is in a good state of preservation, is three rows to the west of Chandler's. In the north panel is, "Lieut.-General Fleetwood, 1692;" and in the south, "Dame Mary Hartopp." The tomb was found about six feet under the ground, and was raised when the City authorities came into possession of Bunhill.

Charles Fleetwood was the third son of Sir Miles Fleetwood of Aldwinkle, Northamptonshire, and of Anne, daughter of Nicholas Luke, of Woodend, Bedfordshire. His father died in 1641, and the eldest son, Sir William, who succeeded to his father's estates and office, took the side of the King in the great struggle and died in 1674. George, the second son, sought his fortune in the service of Sweden, and Charles, who was much younger than his brothers, was left by his father an annuity of £60, chargeable on the estate of Sir William Fleetwood. On the outbreak of the Civil War, he and other young gentlemen of the Inns of Court entered the Life Guards of the Earl of Essex. Though only a simple trooper, Fleetwood was in September, 1642, employed by Essex in the confidential task of bearing a letter to the Earl of Dorset containing overtures of peace to the King. The tactlessness of Charles and his advisers was strikingly manifested, as Fleetwood was dismissed without an answer. Had the Royalists acted differently the whole history of England would probably have taken another course. Fleetwood was wounded at the battle of Newbury, by which time he had risen to the rank of Captain, and in 1653 he was in command of a regiment in the Earl of Manchester's Army. "Look at Colonel Fleetwood's regiment," writes a Presbyterian; "what a cluster of preaching officers and troopers there!" The progress of Fleetwood was rapid, for in May, 1646, he entered the House of Commons as Member for Marlborough, and he was appointed on 14th August, 1649, Governor of the Isle of Wight in conjunction with Colonel Sydenham.

When in the summer of 1650 Cromwell marched into

(1) ANDREW GIFFORD, D.D.
(See page 69.)

(2) WILLIAM ROSS.
(See page 72.)

(3) JOHN CHIN.   (See page 73.)

ANDREW GIFFORD, D.D.   (See page 69.)

JOHN OWEN, D.D.

JOHN BUNYAN.

Bunyan's fame reached Charles II., and the King, ridiculing John Owen on one occasion for hearing an illiterate tinker prate, received from the learned and eloquent Puritan the reply: "May it please your Majesty, could I possess that tinker's ability for preaching, I would most gladly relinquish all my learning." (See page 23.)

Scotland, Fleetwood accompanied him and helped to gain the Battle of Dunbar. During his absence Fleetwood was elected a member of the Third Council of State, and being recalled from Scotland, was charged with the command of the forces retained in England. On the subsequent invasion of England by Prince Charles, he co-operated with Cromwell, meeting him on 24th August at Warwick. It was Fleetwood who commenced the slaughter of September 3rd, 1651, by forcing his way across the Teme, and driving the Royalists into Worcester. In this historic battle he particularly distinguished himself, and Charles suffered a total defeat, barely escaping after many adventures to the Continent. His services were acknowledged by the thanks of the House of Commons, and his re-election to the Council of State. A few weeks after the Battle of Worcester, Fleetwood lost his wife, Frances, daughter of Thomas Smith of Winston, Norfolk, who was buried in St. Anne's, Blackfriars,* November 24th, 1651. In the following year, 1652, his importance was further increased by his marriage with Cromwell's eldest daughter, Bridget (whose first husband, the famous Henry Ireton, had died in November of the previous year), and by his appointment as Commander-in-Chief in Ireland. Fleetwood held this high position from September, 1652, to September, 1655, and on August 27th, 1654, or earlier, he was also given the higher rank of Lord Deputy, and continued to hold this title until superseded by Henry Cromwell in November, 1657. It was to Fleetwood that Cromwell wrote one of his most characteristic letters :—

To the Lord Fleetwood, Lord Deputy of Ireland.

Whitehall, 22nd June, 1655.

Dear Charles,—I write not often : at once I desire thee to know I most dearly love thee ; and indeed my heart is plain to thee, as thy heart can well desire ; let nothing shake thee in this. The wretched jealousies that are amongst us, and the spirit of calumny, turn all into gall and wormwood. My heart is for the people of God ; that the Lord knows, and will in due

* This church was afterwards the scene of Romaine's labours. It has indeed through its long history been favoured to have some of the most eminent men as preachers in its pulpit. Several buried in Bunhill have been closely connected with it.

F

time manifest; yet thence are my wounds;—which though it grieves me, yet through the grace of God doth not discourage me totally. Many good men are repining at everything; though indeed very many good are well satisfied, and satisfying daily. The will of the Lord will bring forth good in due time. It's reported that you are to be sent for, and Harry to be Deputy; which truly never entered into my heart. The Lord knows, my desire was for him and his brother to have lived private lives in the country: and Harry knows this very well, and how difficultly I was persuaded to give him his commission for his present place. This I say as from a simple and sincere heart. The noise of my being crowned, &c., are similar malicious disfigurements. . . .

Dear Charles, my dear love to thee; and to my dear Biddy, who is a joy to my heart, for what I hear of the Lord in her. Bid her be cheerful and rejoice in the Lord once again: if she knows the Covenant (of Grace), she cannot but do so. For that transaction is without her; sure and steadfast, between the Father and the Mediator in His blood. Therefore, lean upon the Son, or looking to Him, thirsting after Him, and embracing Him, we are His Seed;—and the Covenant is sure to all the Seed. The Compact is for the Seed; God is bound in faithfulness to Christ, and in Him, to us. The Covenant is without us; a transaction between God and Christ. Look up to it. God engageth in it to pardon us; to write His law in our hearts; to plant His fear so that we shall never depart from Him. We, under all our sins and infirmities, can daily offer a perfect Christ; and thus we have peace and safety, and apprehension of love, from a Father in the Covenant—who cannot deny Himself. And truly in this is all my salvation; and this helps me to bear my great burdens.

If you have a mind to come over with your dear wife, take the best opportunity for the good of the public and your own convenience. The Lord bless you all. Pray for me, that the Lord will direct, and keep me His servant. I bless the Lord that I am not my own; but my condition to flesh and blood is very hard. Pray for me; I do for you all. Commend me to all friends. I rest, Your loving Father,

OLIVER P.

In December, 1654, Fleetwood had been appointed one of Cromwell's Counsel, and on his return to England, September, 1655, he at once resumed a leading place in the Protector's Court. He was appointed also one of the Major-Generals, having under his charge the counties of

Norfolk, Suffolk, Essex, Oxford, Cambridge, Huntingdon, and Buckingham, but seems usually to have exercised his functions through a deputy.

He opposed the proposal to make Cromwell king, but accepted quite willingly the rest of the articles of the Petition and Advice. In foreign as well as domestic policy, Fleetwood, moved by his strong religious sympathies, was in complete accord with Cromwell. He firmly believed that the latter was "particularly raised up" to be a shelter to poor persecuted Protestants in foreign parts, and he held the cause of the "Protestant interest against the common enemy," to be the supreme concern of England. So for public, as well as for personal reasons, Fleetwood watched with anxiety Cromwell's last illness, and lamented his death. "There is none," he wrote, "but are deeply concerned in this that have a true love of this blessed cause. His (Cromwell's) heart was full of love to the interest of the Lord's people, and made everything else bow down to it."

Fleetwood's position as head of the army and his thorough agreement with Cromwell's views lend some plausibility to the story that Cromwell once designed him to be his successor. It is stated that the Protector some time before his death nominated him in writing, but that the document was lost or destroyed. If a Protector were to be chosen other than one of Cromwell's sons, no one had stronger claims than Fleetwood.

He took some part in the elevation of Richard Cromwell, presenting the address in which the army declared their resolution to support him, and writing to Henry Cromwell to express his joy at his brother's peaceable accession. It, however, soon became apparent that the new Protector would not be adequately or fairly supported by Fleetwood his brother-in-law, Desborough his uncle, Lambert, and other leading officers of the Army. These joined in demanding that the appointment of officers should be taken out of the Protector's hands on the ground of his being a lawyer, and this was really the beginning of Richard's downfall. Henry Cromwell, who was in Dublin, wrote to his brother on October 20th, 1658, in terms which clearly showed that he was fully acquainted with the disaffection of his relatives and the others. " I thought," he said, "those whom my father had raised from nothing, would not so soon have forgot him, and endeavoured to destroy his family before he is in his grave. . . . I am almost afraid to come over to your Highness, lest I should be kept there, and so your Highness lose this army. I also think it dangerous to write freely to you. . . . God help you and bless your Councils."

To Fleetwood himself Henry Cromwell wrote the same day, beseeching him to reflect carefully upon his actions before it was too late. " Let me beg of you to remember how his late Highness loved you, how he honoured you with the highest trust by leaving the sword in your hand which must defend or destroy us. . . . Let us remember his last legacy, and for his sake, render his successor considerate, and not make him vile, a thing of naught and a by-word." But this and other appeals were in vain, and finally Richard, feeling the position was hopeless, vacated his exalted position, and became for twenty long weary years a fugitive and exile, and after his return home an ordinary and harmless unit of the nation.

At the retirement of Richard, Fleetwood and the Council of officers assumed command, and finally the way was made quite clear for the return of the Stuart Prince, who became King Charles II. Fleetwood's escape from death and punishment at the Restoration was due to the fact that he had taken no part in the King's trial, and was not regarded as politically dangerous. When the Act of Oblivion and Indemnity came before the Lords, the Earl of Lichfield exerted himself, and thanks to his influence and that of other friends, Fleetwood was ultimately included in the list of eighteen persons whose sole punishment was perpetual exclusion from all offices of trust. The rest of his life was passed in comparative obscurity. Shortly after the Restoration, Bridget Fleetwood died, and was buried in St. Anne's, Blackfriars, July 1st, 1662, whilst eighteen months later, January 14th, 1663-4, Fleetwood married Dame Mary Hartopp, daughter of Sir John Coke, of Melbourne, Derbyshire, and widow of Sir Edward Hartopp, Bart. From the date of his third marriage he resided at Stoke Newington, in a house belonging to his wife, which was afterwards known as Fleetwood House, and was not demolished until 1872. During this period he was a member of the congregation of Dr. John Owen, who wrote his last letter to him.* Fleetwood's third wife died on December 17th, 1684, her name being inscribed on the south panel as Dame Mary Hartopp, whilst Fleetwood himself died on October 4th, 1692.

ANDREW GIFFORD, D.D.

ONE row west from the tomb of Fleetwood, but nearer the path, is the half-size headstone of Andrew Gifford. The exact position of the graves of Ross and Chin are clearly shown in the illustration. Gifford's stone is in a very poor condition and scarcely any word can be deciphered.

H. S. E., A. GIFFORD, D.D., P.F., vix. ann. 83, 1784.

Gifford was born in August, 1700, and as he died in June, 1784, he was in the 84th year of his age, about sixty of which had been spent in the ministry. Of this golden jubilee fifty-five years were spent at Baptist churches in Little Wild Street, Lincoln's Inn, and Eagle Street, Holborn. He was about five years at his two first churches, but nearly fifty at his last, and he was also for twenty-seven years sub-librarian of the British Museum. His father, Emanuel Gifford, had endured much suffering because of his Dissenting principles, whilst his

* See page 90.

grandfather was put in prison four times because of his stedfastness to the Scriptures. On one occasion Emanuel was set to watch for the coming of the persecutors, and he sat down to rest. There was a very intense frost, and when he tried to move he found that he was frozen to the ground. He was obliged to cut off portions of his new frieze coat and leave these fastened to the ground. He died when Andrew was twenty-four years of age, and by this time the latter had himself become a preacher.

June 6th, 1784, was the last occasion when Gifford presided at the Lord's Supper. He was very weak, and the first sentence he uttered was, "With my soul have I desired to eat this passover with you before I suffer." Although he broke the bread, he was unable to pour out the wine, but had sufficient strength to speak with considerable power upon the words, "Thou hast, in love to my soul, cast all my sins behind Thy back." The following evening he preached in his loved chapel from Heb. xiii. 7 : "Let brotherly love continue." He said farewell with a cheerful voice to some of his members and left them, but returned and took a further look at the Meeting House, and at his old friends, repeating with great emphasis, "Farewell." Three days before he died he said, "I am in great pain, but, bless God, this is not hell! O, blessed be God for Jesus Christ!" When the end was nigh, he was asked whether any friend should be sent for, but he replied, "I want no friend but Christ. I want to see no friend but Christ." He also murmured, "O what should I do now if it were not for Jesus Christ? What should I do now, but for an interest in Jesus?"

He died on Saturday morning, June 19th, 1784, and his remains were buried in Bunhill at six o'clock on Friday morning, July 2nd. This was according to his own request, for he had often expressed the wish that he might be buried at an early hour, in order to testify his faith in the resurrection of Jesus, who arose early on the first day of the week; and he thereby declared also his own hope of the resurrection morning at the Last Day.

It was on this occasion that John Ryland delivered, in the presence of two hundred ministers and a vast concourse of persons, one of the most remarkable grave-side addresses. The closing paragraphs were, " Farewell, thou dear old man! We leave thee in the possession of Death until the Resurrection Day, but we will bear witness against thee, O King of terrors, at the mouth of this dungeon—thou shalt not always have possession of this dead body; it shall be demanded of thee by the Great Conqueror, and at that moment thou shalt resign thy prisoner. O ye ministers of Christ, ye people of God, ye surrounding spectators, prepare, prepare to meet this old servant of Christ at that day, that hour when this whole place shall be nothing but life, and death shall be swallowed up in victory! "

TWO EPITAPHS.

Here lyes interred the body of
Mr. Edward Bagshawe, Minister of the Gospel,
who received from God Faith to embrace it,
Courage to defend it, and Patience to suffer for it;
When by the most despised, and by many persecuted,
Esteeming the advantages of Birth, and Education,
and Learning (all eminent in him) as Things of Worth,
To be accounted Loss for the Knowledge of Christ;
From the Reproaches of professed Adversaries,
He took Sanctuary by the Will of God in Eternal Rest,
the 28th of December, 1671.

Here also lyes the Body of Mrs. Margaret, late Wife of Mr. Edw. Bagshawe, who departed this Life the 20th of February, 1692.

Here the Wicked cease from Troubling,
And here the Weary be at Rest;
Here the Prisoners rest together,
They hear not the Voice of the Oppressor.

Here lyeth the Body of Elizabeth Twistle,
the eldest Daughter of the Right Honourable the
Lord Viscount James Fynes, Say and Seale, Wife to
John Twistleton, Esq.; at Dartford in
Kent. She Dy'd on the 28th Day of
March, Anno Dom., 1673.

WILLIAM ROSS.

INSCRIPTION.

Here rests until the morning of the Resurrection, all
that was mortal of the Rev. WILLIAM ROSS, late minister
of Salem Chapel, Shadwell, who died Dec. 23rd, 1808,
aged 31.

> When time has worn these characters away,
> And this frail stone may totter o'er his clay ;
> The truths he preached shall stand the general shock,
> And rise superior as a mighty rock.
> Yea, he shall live and reign thro' endless days,
> While heaven's high arch resounds with Jesu's praise.

It is now true that "Time has worn these characters
away," for the inscription is practically undecipherable.
The truths however that William Ross preached—the
infallibility of the Scriptures, the Atonement of Christ,
the invincible work and operations of the Holy Ghost,
with many others, have well stood "the general shock."

JOHN CHIN.

INSCRIPTION.

The Rev. JOHN CHIN, died August 28th, 1839, aged 66 years. He was thirty-two years pastor of the Baptist Church in Lion St., Walworth. He was a faithful, zealous and successful Minister of the Gospel of Jesus Christ. His unwearied labours were owned of God and blessed. Numerous seals were given to his Ministry, and many were added to the Church. His memory was long cherished, and held sacred by his flock ; and his kind, humble, pious and consistent conduct long lived in the remembrances of grateful and benefited people, the mourning widow, and a numerous and affectionate family.

JOHN CHIN was born at Hinton, near Blandford, in May, 1773, and was the youngest member of a large family. His parents resided upon a small farm, and John always spoke in the highest terms of his father and mother ; especially of the latter, because she took the greatest pains in teaching her children the Scriptures.

When about eight years of age John was brought under conviction of sin, but for a time this wore away, and after he had left his home and was an apprentice boy at Bristol he deviated very considerably from the paths of morality and rectitude. In Bristol at this time there was an Independent minister, Mr. Hey, who preached some-times in the open air, and through hearing him John became a fairly regular attendant at the chapel in Horsley Down. He once again experienced deep distress of mind, but under the contemplation of the words, " What manner of man is this, that even the winds and the sea obey Him ? " he proved that He who had calmed the angry billows in the days of His flesh could give peace to a tempest-tossed sinner. He now united him-self to the church, and Mr. Hey observing his zeal and ability encouraged him to visit cottages and do a little preaching when there was an opportunity.

At the close of his apprenticeship he obtained a situation in London, and became closely associated with

several young men who were members of the Baptist
Church meeting in Church Street, Blackfriars.

In Walworth about this time there were a few persons
who assembled in the East Street for public worship,
and amongst those who were invited to preach was
Mr. Joseph Swain, who ultimately became the minister.
Mr. Chin went as often as possible to hear Mr. Swain
preach, although being engaged himself in the public
ministry his opportunities were not many.

After the death of Mr. Swain there was a division
amongst the congregation, and a separate church was
formed, which ultimately obtained ground in Lion Street,
Walworth, on which a chapel was erected. A considerable congregation was gathered together, and an invitation
was given to Mr. Chin to be the pastor ; he hesitated for
some two or three years, but ultimately accepted the
call, and was ordained on December 29th, 1807. Mr.
Ivimey and Mr. Upton took part in the services, and
thus united minister and church, who continued to love
each other for the long period of thirty-two years. The
congregations increased very rapidly, and the chapel was
enlarged several times until it would accommodate at
least 900 persons. In his latter days Mr. Chin endured
great affliction, but he was wonderfully sustained. The
following are some of the words which fell from his lips
during his last illness :—

"I am obliged to come to first principles, and daily
look to Christ as a poor perishing sinner."

"My prevailing desire is to glorify God in this
affliction ; continual affliction is a scene of continual
temptation."

"The prospect of a change seems most pleasing as
introducing to a state free from sin."

"I have never been tried by doubts as to the reality of
religion itself, but my mind has often been in doubt
about my interest in its blessings ; but this does not
affect my interest."

"Sweet peace . . . I little thought of dying so.
. . . Father, I long to see the place of Thine abode."

"I have such sweet peace, such tranquillity, and it is
all tranquillity in an eternal world."

"I will sing of the mercy of God, that He should have called me by grace."

"Good men have over-rated me; I am the chief of sinners; but it is all of grace."

> " 'I the chief of sinners am,
> But Jesus died for me.' "

On the last morning his sufferings were excruciating, and being asked how he felt, he replied, "I feel like a dying man—I am dying; dying is hard work, but all the days of my appointed time will I wait till my change come; yes, I will patiently wait. But

> " 'Welcome, sweet hour of full discharge,
> That sets our longing souls at large;
> Unbinds our chains, breaks up our cell,
> And gives us with our God to dwell.' "

He requested his wife to come to him, took her hand, and pressing it, said, "My dear, I have prayed much for you, that God may support and comfort you when I am no more seen. The time is come—we must part; I feel it much. But 'thy Maker is thy husband: the Lord of hosts is His name.'" A short time before his departure one of his sons said to him, "My dear father, you will soon see those in glory who will be stars in your crown—those to whom you have been so useful; they are surely waiting to welcome you to glory." With a smiling face he replied, "I shall; but all I want is that I may be found in Him, accepted in the Beloved." Looking stedfastly upwards he exclaimed, "My God, My Saviour! Dear Lamb, precious blood! eternity will be too short to praise Thee for Thy mercies." He then requested his youngest daughter to read the 19th chapter of John, and when she came to the 30th verse, he placed her finger on the words, "It is finished!" and said, "I leave you these words, my dear child, as my dying text, the same as Christ left to His sorrowing disciples, to show you the work of redemption is complete—ever value it, my child, and live upon it." He now engaged in prayer almost incessantly, the last words that were audible being, "Come, Saviour, come, and take me to Thy bosom!"

His remains were buried on Wednesday, September 4th. A service having been previously held in the chapel, an address was given at the grave by Mr. Samuel Green.

THOMAS HOPKINS.

THE stone of Hopkins is near the middle of the ground, but about four rows west from Chin. The inscription is entirely obliterated.

INSCRIPTION.

Here lie the remains of the Rev. THOMAS HOPKINS, late pastor of the Church of Jesus Christ met in Eagle St., Holborn, who died on the 16th day of November, 1787, in the 30th year of his age.

> He was a Christian most sincere,
> A preacher powerful and clear;
> In sweet obedience moved along,
> Christ was his theme and Christ his song.

His successor, Mr. Ivimey, has left an account of Hopkins, which is complete and interesting. He was born at Devizes in the year 1758, and both his parents died before he had reached his tenth year. An uncle took compassion on the orphan and apprenticed him in due course to a cooper at Frome. As a lad, Hopkins took great delight in reading foolish and profane books, and he sold all those which his father had left in order to procure these. He was, however, firmly resolved not to part with his father's Bible, although at this time he read very little out of it. There was an old man named Hall living at Frome, who was blind, but he had made a very considerable fortune by begging close to the wall of Bethlem Hospital in Moorfields. The old mendicant had retired to Frome to live comfortably and peaceably, and being anxious to have the Scriptures read to him he arranged with Hopkins to come each Sunday, when he would reward him with 2d. for his trouble. This led to a practice of Bible reading, and serious reflections were awakened in the mind of the lad. He continued reading to Hall until his death, though he did not obtain a watch and other things which had been promised him.

The meeting place at Frome was supplied by ministers in fellowship with Lady Huntingdon, and Hopkins now missed no opportunities of hearing the gospel preached, and his character and seriousness very favourably im-

pressed the people. He made the acquaintance of
Mr. Boddily when he was twenty-two years old, and was
asked by him to go and read a sermon to a small village
congregation. He did so, and the people were very much
taken with the manner and sweetness of his prayer, so
they desired him to come again, not to read, but to preach
a sermon. He accepted the invitation and the villagers
were delighted.

From this time he was very frequently employed at
this and other places, until he was invited to Devizes to be
an assistant to Mr. Sloper, the Independent minister. He
left the Wiltshire town through embracing the doctrines
of the Baptists, and this brought him for the time being
into destitution, for he resigned his assistant pastorate.
Soon afterwards, however, he received an invitation from
the Baptist Church at Bradford, Wiltshire, to supply, and
his preaching met with much acceptance. He was often
solicited to become the pastor of the church, but he felt
unable to comply with the request. About this time the
church at Eagle Street, Holborn, was often in a difficulty
owing to the failing health of Dr. Andrew Gifford, and
they were compelled to obtain outside assistance.
Amongst other ministers Hopkins was asked to go some-
times, and being there during the whole of the month of
April, 1784, was afterwards requested to come again for
three months. He was eventually called to the pastoral
office on July 13th, 1785, Mr. Abraham Booth giving
the charge, which has so often been published under the
title "Pastoral Cautions."

Mr Hopkins' first text as the minister was from
Romans x. 30 : "Now I beseech you, brethren, for the
Lord Jesus Christ's sake, and for the love of the Spirit,
that ye strive together with me, in your prayers to God
for me." In just over two years one hundred persons
were added to the church, a number of these being seals
to his own ministry.

His death was very sudden, for he had preached
three times with his usual ability and solemnity on
Sunday, November 11th, 1787. It was raining in the
evening, and as he had to walk about a mile from the
chapel to his house and he had no coat, he tried to borrow

one, but could not succeed. He was therefore very wet when he reached home, and the next day when he met and dined with Mr. Medley the famous hymn writer, he complained of excessive fatigue. On the Tuesday he visited one of his members who was ill, and returning to his home, he never left it again. Alarming symptoms soon appeared, and when he was first told of his danger he felt great distress of mind at the thought of leaving his young family unprovided for. His wife was afflicted, and the outlook was dark. He called his little boy, then about four years of age, to his bedside, and said, " Poor dear fellow! I had intended to have given him a good education; but it is all over now; though I doubt not but God will provide." His little girl, who was only twelve months old, was brought to him, but being unable to bear the sight of her, he cried, " Take her away; take her away." In a peaceful and calm manner he charged his wife to trust in God who had said, " Leave thy fatherless children, I will preserve them ; and let thy widows trust in Me."

He was buried quite close to his immediate predecessor, Dr. Gifford, and it is pleasing to record that a sufficient sum of money was raised for the support of his wife and children by the church and the Christian public. His old Independent friends at Devizes sent a noble contribution of £50 to the fund, thereby showing a truly Christian spirit.

SAMUEL HAYWARD.

THE positions of the headstones of Hayward and Nicholson, with the tomb of John Owen, will be easily identified by the illustration.

INSCRIPTION.

Only lent to the bosom of the tomb, till Christ shall come to claim His ransomed at the last. The Rev. SAMUEL HAYWARD, minister at Silver St., died July 23rd, 1757, aged 39 years.

> In spirit fervent, and in conduct pure,
> In Christ triumphant, and of heaven secure,
> Hayward undaunted met his nature's foe,
> And smiled exulting as he felt the blow.

ISAAC NICHOLSON.

INSCRIPTION (now almost entirely obliterated).

Here rests from his labours, the Rev. ISAAC NICHOLSON, formerly tutor of the Countess of Huntingdon's College, at Cheshunt, Herts, and afterwards minister of Mulberry Garden Chapel, Bell Street, St. George's-in-the-East, London, who exchanged mortality for everlasting life, June 29th, 1807, in his 47th year. "Christ is all and in all." Col. iii. 2.

THE birthplace of Isaac Nicholson was Netherwasdale, in Cumberland, and the date was January 5th, 1761. He received his education at the Grammar School in St. Bees' Head, and he early displayed a marked aptitude for learning. Day after day he protracted his studies until the early morning, but although he made rapid headway, he, like Dr. John Owen, afterwards much regretted that he had thus seriously undermined his constitution. He entered the ministry of the Established Church, and was ordained deacon at Chester in the month of September, 1783.

Being elected curate of the parish of Woodale-Head in his native county, he embarked upon his duties with great zeal but little knowledge. It was a dark neighbourhood, and the only people with whom he could really mix were the members of a Baptist family. He much objected to their doctrine, but liked their conduct; and although, for the most part, the "language of Canaan" which they spoke was a foreign tongue to him, he was much impressed by their insistence that salvation was of grace alone, and also by the stress they laid upon the importance of vital and personal religion.

A great change, however, took place, for one day whilst in the midst of a warm discussion, a lady member of the company lifted up her hands and her heart unto the Lord, "imploring that the Holy Spirit would enlighten his mind and bring him forth as a preacher of those very doctrines he was now opposing." This prayer was heard and answered, for what had been dark hitherto now became light, and Nicholson began very earnestly to seek the Lord by prayer, and also fervently and seriously to study the sacred Scriptures. What had taken place was soon made known, for after a severe struggle he renounced dancing, card playing, and many other things in which he had taken such pleasure. He was much impressed and helped by noting an old saying of the Puritans, viz., "That praying will make a man leave off sinning; or sinning will make him leave off praying." This caused him to exclaim, "Well, then; I will pray against my sins as long as I have breath to do it." Deliverance from many evils came to him, and he was afterwards greatly helped by reading Hervey's "Theron and Aspasio," and also John Owen on "Justification." These works were much blessed to him, and he was established in the doctrines of his most holy faith, especially concerning the ground of a sinner's acceptance with God.

The curacy at Woodale-Head only lasted a short time,

for in 1784 he was appointed curate to Coddington, where he laboured for eight years. Owing to his manner of life and preaching, he met with much persecution from the people generally and especially from one wealthy gentleman, but there were a few humble souls who heard him gladly. One day he was greatly distressed and retired to his room for prayer, and opening the Bible whilst upon his knees his eyes caught these words : " Watch thou in all things, endure afflictions, do the work of an evangelist, make full proof of thy ministry " (2 Tim. iv. 5). This portion imparted fresh strength, courage and hope, and when he left the room he was determined to preach the gospel at all costs.

His mind now became greatly exercised with respect to his position as a minister of the Establishment, for he had many scruples with respect to the baptismal and burial services, and also indiscriminate communion. There were likewise points of discipline which caused him much anxiety; and after a season of waiting, of watching and of prayer, he felt bound to resign his curacy and to renounce those things which he now believed to be errors. It was a very important step to take, and caused him much distress, but as he frequently said, " It was one of the severest trials of my life, but, if all the world had forsaken me, I dared not to have staid there."

He bade farewell with many tears to his beloved flock, but although he knew it not, God was preparing for him a place for which he was eminently qualified. The trustees of Cheshunt College gave him an invitation to become a tutor, and he accepted the position after earnest prayer and careful consideration. He believed it was the voice of God speaking to him in providence, and he entered upon his appointment as president and tutor on July 14th, 1792. The college had just been removed from Trevecca, the furniture, library and communion-plate having been bequeathed by the Countess of Huntingdon for the use of the college. The opening service was quite remarkable, and of the four ministers taking part three are buried in Bunhill. These are William Francis Platt, Anthony Crole, Lemuel Kirkham, whilst the name of the other was John Eyre.

G

The first hymn was,

" Jesus, where'er Thy people meet,
 There they behold Thy mercy-seat ;
 Where'er they seek Thee Thou art found,
 And every place is hallowed ground."

It does not appear that Mr. Nicholson took any very prominent part, as the four ministers conducted the services, delivering the charges, addresses and sermons, whilst some students read suitable lessons. Concerning the appointment of Mr. Nicholson, it is recorded that he was " a man eminently qualified for the office, who proved an honour to the institution, a blessing to the students put under his care, and to the neighbourhood where he resided."

In addition to his duties as tutor Mr. Nicholson became pastor of a church at Chase-side, Enfield, and here blessing attended his ministry. Personal and family suffering and sorrow were soon his portion, for in addition to the loss of his wife from consumption, his father and sister-in-law were removed by death. The fact that his wife caught the cold which brought on the dread complaint while nursing him during a very severe illness, added so much grief and distress that he was compelled to go North for a change and rest and thus obtain a measure of relief. He married again in due course, but ere long relapsed into a very sad and dark state both of mind and body.

There was no other course for him than to resign both his tutorship and pastorate, and with his wife he went once more to his native place, and then to the borders of Scotland. Being favoured with an increase of strength he preached ocasionally ; one sermon from the text, "This Man receiveth sinners," being particularly blessed to a woman who had suffered much anguish through being in a backsliding state.

After returning to London, on the invitation of the church meeting in the Mulberry Gardens, Pell Street, he became its pastor, and continued until his death three and a half years later. Remarkable blessings rested upon him and his labours, for one hundred and forty members were added to the church, and he enjoyed much liberty in preaching.

The last time he addressed his own people was at the morning service on June 21st, 1807, when the text was Rev. i. 4, 5. Many of his hearers were deeply moved, one exclaiming, "He seemed to be fast ripening for glory." He was at Stratford for the evening service, preaching from Hosea vi. 3, and this seems to be the time when his last affliction seized hold upon him.

For a short season it did not appear that his sickness was unto death; and, indeed, he hoped that he would once again be able to preach the everlasting gospel. On the Sabbath evening, which was the day previous to his death, he exclaimed to his two deacons: "I am very happy; I have enjoyed some great views of Christ; and, if I should come out again, I shall have no reason to speak of Him in lower strains than I have ever done!"

He was not aware of his real condition until Monday morning, but the near prospect of death caused him no terror. His conversation was most animated, and amongst other things he said, "I am in death, but death is not in me. 'O Death, where is thy sting? O Grave, where is thy victory?'" Speaking of Christ, he exclaimed, "I will testify of the love of Christ and of His glories before you all; and I hope to do it before ten thousand times ten thousand more." His friend, Mr. Bennet, inquiring whether the Lord Jesus was precious, the fast-dying man replied, "O yes, He is All in all! He is all my hope and all my salvation! God forbid that I should have any other hope!"

A little wine was given him, and this caused his mind to dwell upon the ordinance over which he had presided so many times. "Let us," he said, "in the wine commemorate the sufferings and death of our dear Lord;" and when it was remarked that he would shortly drink it new in the Father's kingdom, he added, "Yes, and there will be no going out there for ever—that's the mercy."

No clouds were now allowed to cause distress, and his few remaining hours were singularly triumphant. "Joyous, joyous! Jesus is with me," was a sentence that fell from his lips in reply to a question as to the state of his mind. A friend then repeated the words, "In His presence is fulness of joy;" and Mr. Nicholson finished the quotation with a face beaming with pleasure and most victorious energy, exclaiming, "And at His right hand there are pleasures for evermore—for evermore! Eternity! Eternity!" No other words fell from those eloquent lips, and thus on June 29th, 1807, in the 47th year of his age, Isaac Nicholson went to his eternal rest. His years were not many compared with others whose bodies have been laid in Bunhill, yet after his call by grace he wasted no time, but devoted his talents with sustained and tremendous energy in preaching the "truth as it is in Jesus." It was well said "that in him were combined the two great ministerial qualifications—he was the Son of Thunder to sinners, and the Son of Consolation to mourners in Zion."

JOHN OWEN, D.D.

TRANSLATION of inscription by Dr. Gibbons :—

JOHN OWEN, D.D., born in the county of Oxford, the son of an eminent minister, himself more eminent, and worthy to be enrolled among the first divines of the age; furnished with human literature in all its kinds, and in its highest degrees, he called forth all his knowledge in an orderly train to serve the interests of religion, and minister in the sanctuary of his God. In divinity, practice, polemic, and casuistical, he excelled others, and was in all equal to himself. The Arminian, Socinian, and Popish errors, those hydras, whose contaminated breath and deadly poison infested the Church, he, with more than Herculean labour, repulsed, vanquished, and destroyed. The whole economy of redeeming grace, revealed and applied by the Holy Spirit, he deeply investigated, and communicated to others, having first felt its divine energy, according to its draught in the Holy Scriptures, transfused into his own bosom. Superior to all terrene pursuits, he constantly cherished, and largely experienced, that blissful communion with Deity he so admirably describes in his writings. While on the road to heaven,

systems. Outside the Scriptures there is no armoury like the writings of John Owen from which to obtain weapons to combat them. In the 1850 edition of his works, which was edited by a Scottish minister, William H. Goold, there are twenty-four volumes, and few, if any, vitally important points of controversy are untouched.

His first work was "A Display of Arminianism," and this unrivalled treatise was written in order to combat the doctrines of Arminius which had worked such havoc and caused such disturbances on the Continent and especially in Holland. The contest between the celebrated theologians, Gomar and Arminius, had produced in the Dutch church two sharply divided parties, and whilst the former obtained the chief of his support from the clergy and members of the Church, the latter relied for the most part upon political aid. Gomar was very earnest in desiring a national Synod, so that the questions of Free-grace as expounded by himself, and Free-will as upheld by Arminius, could be openly and clearly debated. Being desirous of avoiding public discussion Arminius used his influence with the State authorities to prevent this, and as he succeeded in his endeavours very violent proceedings followed. During the confusion Arminius died, and the "Arminians," or Remonstrants, elected Episcopius as their leader, and made themselves ready for an appeal to arms instead of to the "Sword of the Spirit." There were military preparations on every hand and the prospect was most dark, when Maurice, the head of the House of Orange, by extraordinary and daring means seized the political power, and thus became head of the State. At the request of Gomar and much to the alarm of the Arminians, Maurice convened a general Synod which met at Dort, on the 13th of November, 1618. After much searching debate the doctrines which had been so zealously propagated by Arminius were condemned, and the Synod drew up five special Articles which were published as their judgment upon the points in dispute.

These are of great importance, and are consistent with several Articles of the Church of England, and have been since incorporated in many other Confessions and Declarations of Faith.

The first of the five Articles maintained election by grace, in opposition to election on the ground of any fore-seen excellence. In the second the doctrine of particular redemption is clearly asserted, for God is declared to have decreed that Christ should efficaciously redeem all those, and those only, who from eternity were chosen to salva-tion. By the third and fourth articles definite statements are made with respect to the moral impotence of man and the work of the Holy Spirit in regeneration, whilst the glorious and comforting doctrine of the perseverance of the Saints is affirmed in the fifth and last. There were four English theologians at the Synod, viz., Drs. Carleton, Davenant, Ward, and Joseph Hall, who afterwards became the famous Bishop of Norwich, whilst Dr. Balcanquhal went from Scotland. These all gave their sanction to the proceedings and conclusions of the Synod, and there is no doubt but that the Articles of the State Church in England were considered to express the same fundamental truths.

The advent of Laud, however, wrought a great change, and he being fearful of discussion like Arminius, caused a royal decree to be issued prohibiting references to, or preaching upon, the disputed points. Error has always desired to avoid investigation, for it loves silence more than speaking, and darkness more than light. Laud having much influence over the King, all the preferments in the gift of the Crown were placed at the disposal of those who openly professed or who leaned to Arminian views. Owen makes reference to this state of affairs in his note, " To the Christian Reader," which is prefixed to "A Display of Arminianism," in the following words : " The fates of our Church having of late devolved the government thereof into the hands of men tainted with this poison, Arminianism became backed with the powerful arguments of praise and preferment, and quickly prevailed to beat poor naked truth into a corner."

The position of affairs obliged Owen to show publicly by his preaching and writings that he had no sympathy with the Arminians, and that he foresaw great and increasing danger. He said, " It is high time, then, for all the lovers of the old way to oppose this innovation before our breach grow great like the sea, and there be none to heal it."

To Owen the lawless spirit then abounding in the Established Church, as manifested in the disregard of the Thirty-nine Articles, portended grave disaster, and he looked upon the Ritualists of his day as men who should have been dealt with in a firm and just but merciful manner. Well might he exclaim, "Had a poor Puritan offended against half so many Canons as they (the Ritualists) opposed Articles, he had forfeited his livelihood, if not endangered his life." This, Owen's first publication, was issued in 1642, and immediately brought him into prominence. It was dedicated "To the Right Honourable the Lords and Gentlemen of the Committee for Religion," which was composed of ten earls, ten bishops, and ten barons; and it was this particular body who appointed Owen to the living of Fordham, in Essex.

Owen was married when Vicar of Fordham, in Essex, and although eleven children were born, not one survived him. To follow him to the battle-field, to Dublin with Cromwell, and to go with him on his preaching expeditions, would entail covering the ground of one of the most thrilling periods of English history. His sermons delivered before Parliament, to the army, and on many special occasions, are masterpieces, and the pity is that they are so neglected in these degenerate days. But to read of his expulsion from the office of Vice-Chancellor at Oxford, and the many afflictions which befell him after the Restoration, takes us to a period when truth was reviled, Popery honoured, purity derided, and godly men persecuted—indeed, to the time of the abominable Act of Uniformity. It was not Owen's lot to suffer such indignities as Baxter, Bunyan, and numbers of other ministers; and, indeed, he used his influence to secure a measure of relief for the "tinker of Bedford" during his years of imprisonment, and was instrumental finally in obtaining his release.

It is strange that so little is known of Owen's domestic life, but his first wife died in 1676, and he married again some eighteen months after. His second wife was a lady of means, and thus the closing days of the great

Puritan divine were spent in comparative comfort. His
physical frame was racked with asthma and other distressing ailments, but his mind was clear and vigorous.
The letter written on the day before his death to the
famous General Fleetwood is most touching, and must
be inserted in full :—

"Dear Sir,—Although I am not able to write one word myself, yet I am very desirous to speak one word more to you in
this world, and do it by the hand of my wife. The continu-
ance of your entire kindness, knowing what it is accompanied
withal, is not only greatly valued by me, but will be a refreshment to me, as it is, even in my dying hour. I am going to
Him whom my soul has loved, or rather who has loved me
with an everlasting love, which is the whole ground of all my
consolation. The passage is very irksome and wearisome,
through strong pains of various sorts, which are all issued in
an intermitting fever. All things were provided to carry me to
London to-day, according to the advice of my physicians ; but
we are all disappointed by my utter disability to undertake the
journey. I am leaving the ship of the church in a storm ; but
whilst the great Pilot is in it, the loss of a poor under-rower
will be inconsiderable. Live, and pray and hope, and wait
patiently, and do not despond ; the promise stands invincible,
that He will never leave us, nor forsake us. I am greatly afflicted
at the distempers of your dear lady ; the good Lord stand by
her, and support and deliver her. My affectionate respects to
her, and the rest of your relations, who are so dear to me in
the Lord. Remember your dying friend with all fervency. I
rest upon it that you do so, and am yours entirely.
                                          "J. OWEN."

The last scene is well described by Andrew Thomson,
B.A., as follows :—

"The first sheet of his 'Meditations on the Glory of Christ'
had passed through the press under the superintendence of the
Rev. William Payne, a dissenting minister at Saffron Waldon,
in Essex; and on that person calling on him to inform him of
the circumstance on the morning of the day he died, he exclaimed, with uplifted hands, and eyes looking upward, 'I am
glad to hear it, but, O brother Payne! the long wished for day
is come at last, in which I shall see that glory in another
manner than I have ever done, or was capable of doing, in this
world.' Still it was no easy thing for that robust frame to be
broken to pieces, and to let the struggling spirit go free. His

physicians, Dr. Cox and Sir Edmund King, remarked on the unusual strength of that earthly house which was about to be dissolved ; while his more constant attendants on that consecrated hour were awe-struck by the mastery which his mighty and heaven-supported spirit maintained over his physical agonies. In respect of sickness, very long, languishing, and often sharp and violent, like the blows of inevitable death, yet was he both calm and submissive under all. At length the struggle ceased ; and with eyes and hands uplifted, as if his last act was devotion, the spirit of Owen passed in silence into the world of glory. It happened on the 24th of August, 1683, the anniversary of St. Bartholomew's Day—a day memorable in the annals of the Church of Christ, as that in which the two thousand Nonconformist confessors had exposed themselves to poverty and persecution at the call of conscience, and in which heaven's gates had been opened wide to receive the martyred Protestants of France. Eleven days afterwards, a long and mournful procession, composed of more than sixty noblemen, in carriages drawn by six horses each, and of many others in mourning coaches and on horse-back, silently followed the mortal remains of Owen along the streets of London, and deposited them in Bunhill Fields—the Puritan Necropolis."

Is Owen read to-day ? Numbers of people have blessed God for him, but it is to be feared that for the most part his writings are now consigned to the library shelves, and are rarely looked at or studied. Why is this ? Doubtless it may be truly replied that his style rather repels by its very fulness and massiveness ; but is not the true reason because the spiritual apprehension of present day people is so small and Owen is altogether too deep and profound ? He himself readily acknowledged that he made no attempt to use a polished literary style, being more intent on stating truth in unadorned language than in using flowery metaphors of speech. But if and when a true revival comes, once again will the writings of this man of God be valued and esteemed.

Mr. J. K. Popham, Pastor of "Galeed," Brighton, and Editor of the "Gospel Standard," has very kindly chosen an extract from the works of John Owen, prefacing it with a short note of his own :—

"It is impossible in an extract of four hundred words to

fairly represent the author of twenty-four volumes. But as Owen was particularly led by his Divine Master to dilate on the Person of Christ, to set Him forth as the substance, fulness, and glory of all divine truths, the following may be taken as a good example of his general drift.

"EXTRACT FROM OWEN ON THE PERSON OF CHRIST.

"'(1) *Efficacy* or power is the second property of divine truth. And the end of this efficacy is to make us like unto God : Eph. iv. 20—24. The mortification of sin, the renovation of our natures, the sanctification of our minds, hearts, and affections, the consolation of our souls, with their edification in all the parts of the life of God and the like, are the things that God hath designed to effect by His truth (John xvii. 17) ; whence it is able to " build us up, and give us an inheritance among all them that are sanctified " (Acts xx. 32). But it is from their relation unto the Person of Christ that they have anything of this power and efficacy. For they have it no otherwise, but as they are conveyances of His grace unto the souls of men. So 1 John i. 1, 2.

"' Wherefore, as professors of the truth, if separated from Christ as unto real union, are withering branches—so truths professed, if doctrinally separated from Him, or their respect unto Him, have no living power or efficacy in the souls of men. When Christ is formed in the heart by them, when He dwelleth plentifully in the soul through their operation, then, and not else, do they put forth their proper power and efficacy. Otherwise, they are as waters separated from the fountain— they quickly dry up or become a noisome puddle; or as a beam interrupted from its continuity unto the sun—it is immediately deprived of light.

"' (2) All divine spiritual truths are declarative, either of the grace and love of God unto us, or [of] our duty, obedience, and gratitude unto Him. But, as unto these things, Christ is All and in all ; we can have no due apprehensions of the love and grace of God, no understanding of the Divine truths of the Word—wherein they are revealed, and whereby they are exhibited unto them that believe—but in the exercise of faith on Christ Himself. For in, by, and from Him alone, it is that they are proposed unto us, that we are made partakers of them. It is from His fulness that all grace is received. No truth concerning them can, by any imagination, be separated from Him. He is the life and soul of all such truths—without which, they, as they are written in the Word, are but a dead letter.'—*Vol. i., P. 81.*"

SAMUEL POMFRET.

THE position of this grave is two rows to the south, i.e., at the back of John Owen's. The tomb has sunk considerably in the ground, and there is no trace of any inscription upon the moss-covered top.

As a preacher Samuel Pomfret was well known in his day, large congregations highly valuing his scriptural and experimental ministry. He was born at Coventry in the year 1651, and was nineteen years old when the death of his much-loved mother was the means used in his regeneration. He studied for a time at Cambridge, but finished his education in Islington, London, under a private tutor. He began preaching in Lincoln's Inn Fields, where he was much appreciated, but after a time accepted a pastorate at Sandwich in Kent. Here he remained for seven years, but was compelled to move by the persecuting priests and government of Charles II. He then began to preach as often as possible in and around London, generally delivering three or four sermons each Lord's Day. As he usually visited a different congregation each time, the arduous nature of his labours may be surmised, and it must be remembered also that he was in constant danger and peril. When the Stuart power and tyranny were broken, Pomfret began to preach in a building in Winchester Street in the City of London, but such tremendous crowds gathered at a service, that the floor gave way. As there was a merciful Providence watching over the congregation no one was hurt, and the friends soon erected a special building in Gravel Lane, Hounsditch. This was capable of holding fifteen hundred persons and was filled to overflowing. Indeed, there were often as many as eight hundred members attending the ordinance of the Lord's Supper, and the solemn scenes at these services were among the most remarkable in the history of any church or preacher. As a student of the Scriptures, Samuel Pomfret was unwearied, whilst his power in prayer was surpassed by none and equalled by very few. He often spent almost the whole of Saturday night beseeching the Lord to be with him at the services, and at the close of the day he was engaged for hours in supplicating pardon for anything not pleasing to God, and asking a blessing upon all that was acceptable to Him.

One marked feature of his character was his absolute indifference to money and creature comforts. He was quite prodigal in his gifts to the poor, not infrequently taking the food from his own table and the clothes from his person to help those in distress. His declining years were spent in much pain, for he suffered very severely from asthma and other distressing ailments. When unable to walk he was carried in a chair to his pulpit, and at such seasons so intense was his earnestness and so fervent his speech that it seems impossible for his physical weakness and pain to have been so great. His expressions during his last days upon earth clearly show that he had a most lively hope that he would go to heaven. Some were as follows:—" Come, see, see a dying man under exquisite pain, yet not afraid to die." " Let Him do His pleasure. Absent from the body, present with the Lord. Outward pain but inward peace." " Here we are imperfect, but at my dissolution I shall be presented faultless to my dear Redeemer ; faultless and spotless without a wrinkle." He was much in prayer the night before he died, and on being asked how things were with him, replied, " Nature disputes every inch of ground." To a sorrowing friend he exclaimed, " O ! you should rather rejoice." As death came upon him and he felt its presence, he said, " Better and better," and just before his departure uttered the words, " Almost well ! " He then entered into the joy of the Lord.

For nearly fifty years he had been a most faithful and unwearied minister of the Gospel, opposing error, rebuking sin and maintaining the truth. He died on January 11th, 1721, in the seventy-first year of his age, and was buried in the presence of a mighty concourse of people. Some years after his death the church and congregation erected and moved to a building in Great Alie Street, Whitechapel, but owing to the inroads of Arianism and Socinianism the people were soon scattered and the building closed. It was later, however, opened again by Mr. John

Bailey, who called it "Zoar Chapel," and was only pulled down in 1909, the last sermon being preached by Mr. J. K. Popham, of Brighton, from Isa. xvi. 5, on June 21st. The last minister of the Baptist Church and congregation which were formed here was Mr. Eli Ashdown, who died in 1904.

THOMAS BRAND.

ABOUT three rows west of Pomfret's, but in direct line with Hayward's, is the grave of Thomas Brand. The flat stone which marks his resting-place is split into several pieces, and scarcely a letter can be deciphered.

ORIGINAL INSCRIPTION.

In memory of the Rev. Mr. THOMAS BRAND, who upon principle of piety and charity, devoted his life and estate to the interests of religion and the good of the Gospel, died December 1st, 1691.

Thomas Brand was born at Leaden Rooding, Essex, in the year 1635. His father, who held a position in the Church of England, sent Thomas to Oxford, intending that he should follow the law as a profession, but the course of his life was changed, and he entered the ministry of the Established Church. He is said to have become "one of the brightest mirrors of piety and charity, and one of the most fervent useful preachers the age hath afforded." He was one of the victims of the Act of Uniformity, but he lived to see Protestantism firmly established in England after the banishment of the popish James II. and the crowning of William III. One of Brand's great desires was to educate the young, and he was continually striving to instruct them in the Scriptures. His attached friend, Dr. Annesley, in preaching the funeral sermon, said of him:—

"Besides his own weekly catechizing at home, and in all the schools which he erected, he hired some persons in distant places to catechize children, and others who were willing to learn ; and once a month and oftener he rode from place to place to catechize them himself. And to encourage those who did well he gave some reward either in books or money. He would often say that he never experienced more of the goodness of God in any duty than this."

ROBERT BRAGGE, SEN.

THIS headstone is in the next row west, but in a direct line with Brand's.

ORIGINAL INSCRIPTION.

Here lyeth in hope, the precious dust of the Rev. ROBERT BRAGGE, Minister of the Gospel, who died April 14, 1704, aged 77 years.

HERE LYETH IN HOPE THE PRECIOUS DUST OF THE Rev. ROBERT BRAGGE MINISTER OF THE GOSPEL WHO DIED APRIL 14. 1704 AGED 77 YEARS.

This Robert Bragge, who was born in the year 1627, is the father of Robert Bragge, who is buried in the same tomb as Bunyan. His early life was an exciting one, as his own father was a Captain in the Parliamentary Army. On the surrender of Oxford by the Royalists to the Roundheads, Robert Bragge went there to live, and was in due course chosen Fellow. He afterwards moved to London, and was appointed Rector of Allhallows the Great, in Thames Street, but like so many other godly men he suffered greatly after the Restoration and through the Act of Uniformity. After this period he became minister of a congregation which met in Pewterers' Hall, Lime Street, London, and preached here to the end of his life. It is only with the greatest difficulty that any portion of the inscription can now be made out.

(1) Isaac Nicholson. (See page 79.)   OWEN'S TOMB.   (2) Samuel Hayward. (See page 79.)

JOHN OWEN, D.D.

(1) SAMUEL POMFRET. (See page 92.)   (2) South Panel of JOHN OWEN'S TOMB.
(3) THOMAS BRAND. (See page 95.)   (4) ROBERT BRAGGE, SEN. (See page 96.)

THE TOMBS OF THE CROMWELLS. (See page 99.)

WILLIAM BUTTON.

FROM the grave of Bragge to that of Button's the visitor must pass along the path, leaving the tomb of Bunyan on the right hand. The headstone with the almost obliterated inscription adjoins the path on the left hand.

WILLIAM BUTTON.
DIED AUGUST. 2. 1821.
AGED 67. YEARS

INSCRIPTION.

Mr. W. BUTTON, Pastor of the Baptist Church in Dean Street, Tooley Street, upwards of 40 years, died August 2nd, 1821, aged 67 years.

William Button's father was a deacon of Dr. John Gill's, and when his mother died in 1766 the Doctor preached a funeral sermon from Psalm xl. 11. In the same tomb as William Button are buried his father, his mother, his widow, his youngest son, and his only daughter. The celebrated John Ryland, Senr., was selected to be William Button's tutor, and the lad made his way to Northampton to attend the famous Academy. Through a funeral sermon preached on the occasion of a school-fellow's death, he and another pupil had their minds brought to a state of serious concern. In 1767 John Ryland, Junr., and he were baptized together in the river,

H

and sat down to the Lord's Supper the same day. Button was only thirteen years and six months, and Ryland was fourteen years and nine months, and the former commenced preaching when he was only nineteen. In the meantime he had returned to London, and was a member of the Baptist Church in Unicorn Yard, Southwark. His own minister, Mr. Clarke, Samuel Stennett, Benjamin Wallin, and John MacGowan all bade him God-speed, and he first supplied the church at Hitchin, who had lost their Pastor, Mr. Samuel James, by death. After Gill's death there was a division on the choosing of Dr. John Rippon as pastor, and Button was requested by those who had separated to preach to them for the period of twelve months. The new chapel was in Dean Street, and this was opened in November, 1774, Mr. Button being ordained pastor on July 7th, 1775. More than forty years after this occasion he wrote a letter to his church, from which the following is taken :—

" The church in Dean Street has long lain near my heart. I have been many years pastor over it. I have endeavoured to feed the flock of God committed to my charge with knowledge and understanding, looking to Jesus, the great and good Shepherd, for supplies. When I take a retrospective view of my life and labours among you, I perceive ten thousand defects ; I sink into the dust of abasement, and there bewail my numerous faults. I am filled with admiration and gratitude to God, who has borne with my manners in the wilderness, and with my imperfections in the church. Brethren, I have had my joys and my sorrows, my elevations and depressions. The church at Dean Street has been my sanctuary, the place of my delight. Hither I was sent by the Lord in the year 1774. Here the Lord has given me children, who have been nourished and brought up, and taken to glory. Here I have enjoyed the most pleasant communion with my Christian friends ; and here, which is still more delightful, I have truly had fellowship with the Father, and with His Son, Jesus Christ. I have had soul-elevating seasons in the pulpit, at the Lord's Table, and at our weekly prayer meetings. Here also I have heard many persons declare their experiences, and relate what God has done for their souls under my poor ministry, which has warmed my heart. In short, I have repeatedly seen the power and glory of God evidently displayed in this little sanctuary, to the joy of my soul."

CROMWELLS' TOMB (1).

THE tombs of the Cromwells will now be seen at the left hand of the path. In the north panel is the name,

HENRY CROMWELL.

Henry Cromwell was the second son of the Lord-Lieutenant, Henry Cromwell, and was thus the grandson of Oliver, being born in Dublin Castle, then his father's residence (as Chief Governor of Ireland), on March 3rd, 1658. After his eldest brother's death, he succeeded him in the estate at Spinney Abbey, which he enjoyed for several years, until by the enthusiasm and zeal of his good wife (Hannah Hewling) in supporting the persecuted Dissenters, he was obliged to dispose of that estate ; after which he experienced many misfortunes. These evidently caused him to leave England, for he afterwards to a friend urged as a qualification for the horse service, that "he had rode a long time in the Academy abroad." In his distress he applied to the Countess Fauconberg, his aunt, for her ladyship's protection and support, but she at first exhibited so little tenderness for and desire to help her family, that Henry often under great melancholy wished himself of another name, thinking as he says, "his burden would be lighter to him " ; he subjoins, " Though our family is low, and some are willing it should be kept so ; yet I know that we are a far ancienter family than many others; Sir Oliver Cromwell, my grandfather's uncle and godfather, his estate that was, is now let for above £30,000 a year ! " He might also have said that Sir Oliver had £30,000 per annum in Huntingdonshire only, besides very great estates in other counties. However, he said that he patiently submitted to what God was pleased to order—but he purposed, when in circumstances, to appear as others ; it would then be his great endeavour to maintain the reputation of his family.

Finally, through the good offices of the Duke of Ormond, Henry was appointed "A Major of foot in Fielding's Regiment." He went with the troops to

Portugal, and while there contracted a fever, of which
he died on September 11th, 1711. So that although his
name is cut in the north panel of the tomb, he was
actually buried at Lisbon.

HANNAH CROMWELL.

Hannah Cromwell, the wife of Henry Cromwell, is
better known as Hannah Hewling, and was the grand-
daughter of William Kiffin. Hannah had two brothers,
Benjamin and William, and when their father died the
three children were cared and provided for by Kiffin.
He gave them a good education and training, sending
William to a seminary in Holland. He was there when
the weak and ill-fated Duke of Monmouth was making
arrangements for his invasion of England, and was one
of the Duke's company that landed with him at Lyme
Regis. Of Benjamin, too, we find that " conversing with
those that were under great dissatisfaction, seeing Popery
encouraged and religion and liberty like to be invaded,
did furnish himself with arms, and went to the said
Duke." Both brothers took part in the fatal battle of
Sedgemoor, and it was generally acknowledged afterwards
that had Benjamin been all the time upon the disastrous
field, matters might have gone differently. He, however,
dashed off to bring up some artillery from Minehead, and
the damage done in his absence could not be repaired.
They both escaped to the coast and put to sea in a
barque, but the winds being contrary, they were driven to
land again. Being captured, they were lodged for a time
in Exeter Jail and then taken to London, and were
placed in Newgate, remaining there about three weeks.
Here they were loaded with irons, and it was only by
great determination and the overcoming of many obstacles
that any members of the family were allowed to see the
doomed brothers. After three weeks in the London
dungeon they were taken to Dorchester, and here one of
those scenes took place which will ever remain a disgrace
to the justice of England. Their aged grandfather put
forth every effort to save them, but met with no manner
of success. " It being given out," says Mr. Kiffin, " that
the King would make only a few who had been taken

examples, and would leave the rest to his officers, to compound for their lives, I attempted with my daughter, their mother, to treat with a great man, agreeing to give him three thousand pounds if he would obtain their deliverance. But the face of things was soon altered, so that nothing but severity could be expected. Indeed, we missed the right door, for the Lord Chief Justice (Jeffreys), finding that agreements were made with others, and so little attention paid to himself, was the more provoked to use all manner of cruelty to the poor prisoners, so that few escaped, and amongst the rest those two young men were executed."

Their sister, Hannah, though delicately nurtured, endured many hardships and insults in attempting to save their lives. When everything else had failed she determined at all cost to present a petition to King James. She was introduced by Lord Churchill, who afterwards became the famous Duke of Marlborough, and he assured the sorrowing sister that she had his most hearty wishes for success, "But, Madam," said he, " I dare not flatter you with any such hopes, for that marble," pointing to the chimneypiece, " is as capable of feeling compassion as the King's heart." Hannah, in the "Life of Kiffin," has made a record of the sad yet glorious deaths of her brothers, and although the quotation will be somewhat long it is worth giving in full :—

" At Salisbury, the 30th of August, I had the first opportunity of conversing with them. I found them in a very excellent composure of mind, declaring their experience of the grace and goodness of God to them in all their sufferings, in supporting and strengthening and providing for them, turning the hearts of all in whose hands they had been, both at Exeter and on shipboard, to show pity and to favour them, although since they came to Newgate they were hardly used, and now in their journey loaded with heavy irons and more inhumanly dealt with. They with great cheerfulness professed that they were better, and in a more happy condition than ever in their lives, from the sense they had of the pardoning love of God in Jesus Christ to their souls, wholly referring themselves to their wise and gracious God to choose for them life or death, expressing themselves thus :—' Anything what pleaseth God ; what He sees best, so be it. We know He is able to deliver ;

but if not, blessed be His name, death is not terrible now, but desirable.'

"The sixth of September, Mr. Benjamin Hewling was ordered to Taunton, to be tried there. Taking my leave of him, he said, ' Oh ! blessed be God for afflictions. I would not have been without them for all this world.' I remained still at Dorchester, to wait the issue of Mr. William Hewling, to whom, after trial, I had free access, and whose discourse was much filled with admirings of the grace of God which had been manifested towards him in calling him out of his natural state. He said, God by His Holy Spirit did suddenly seize upon his heart when he thought not of it, in his retired abode in Holland, as it were secretly whispering in his heart, ' Seek ye My face,' enabling him to answer His gracious call and to reflect upon his own soul, showing him the evil of sin and the necessity of Christ, from that time carrying him on to a sensible adherence to Christ for justification and eternal life. Hence he found a spring of joy and sweetness beyond the comforts of the whole earth.

" When I came to him the next morning, when he had received news that he must die the next day, and in order to it was to be carried to Lyme that day, I found him in a more excellent, raised, and spiritual frame than before. He was satisfied, he said, that God had chosen best for him. ' He knows what the temptations of life might have been. I might have lived and forgotten God ; but now I am going where I shall sin no more. Oh, it is a blessed thing to be freed from sin and to be with Christ ! Oh ! how great were the sufferings of Christ for me, beyond all I can undergo ! How great is the glory to which I am going. It will soon swallow up all our sufferings here !'

" As they passed through the town of Dorchester to Lyme, multitudes of people beheld them with great lamentations, admiring his deportment at his parting with his sister. Passing on the road, his discourse was exceedingly spiritual, taking occasion from everything to speak of the glory they were going to. Looking at the country as he passed, he said, ' This is a glorious creation, but what then is the paradise of God to which we are going ? It is but a few hours, and we shall be there, and be for ever with the Lord.'

" At Lyme, just before they went to die, reading John xiv. 8, he said to one of his fellow-sufferers, ' Here is a sweet promise for you—" I will not leave you comfortless ; I will come unto you." Christ will be with us to the last !' One taking leave of him, he said, ' Farewell, till we meet in heaven. Presently we shall be with Christ. Oh, I would not change conditions with any one in this world. I would not stay behind for ten thousand worlds.'

" Afterwards he prayed for three-quarters of an hour with the greatest fervency, exceedingly blessing God for Jesus Christ, adoring the riches of His grace in Him, in all the glorious fruits of it towards him, praying for the peace of the Church of God, and of these nations in particular; all with such eminent assistance of the Spirit of God as convinced, astonished, and melted into pity the hearts of all present, even the most malicious adversaries, forcing tears and expressions from them; some saying, they knew not what would become of *them* after death, but it was evident *he* was going to great happiness.

" When just departing out of the world, with a joyful countenance, he said, ' Oh, now my joy and comfort is that I have a Christ to go to; ' and so sweetly resigned his spirit to Christ.

" An officer who had shown so malicious a spirit as to call the prisoners ' devils,' when he was guarding them down, was now so convinced, that he afterwards told a person of quality that he was never so affected as by his cheerful carriage and fervent prayer, such as he believed was never heard, especially from one so young ; and said, ' I believe, had the Lord Chief Justice been here, he would not have let him die.'

" The Sheriff having given his body to be buried, although it was brought from the place of execution without any notice given, yet very many of the town, to the number of two hundred, came to accompany him ; and several young women of the best of the town laid him in his grave in Lyme churchyard, September 13th, 1685.

" When I came to Taunton to Mr. Benjamin Hewling, he expressed himself to this effect :—' We have no cause to fear death, if the presence of God be with us ; there is no evil in it, the sting being taken away. It is nothing but our ignorance of the glory the saints pass into by death which makes it appear dark to ourselves or our relations ; if in Christ, what is this world that we should desire an abode in it ? It is all vain and unsatisfying, full of sin and misery.' He also intimated his own cheerful expectations soon to follow (he had just heard of his brother's death), discovering then and all along great seriousness and sense of spiritual and eternal things, complaining of nothing in his present circumstances but want of a place of retirement to converse more uninterruptedly with God and his own soul; saying that his lonely time in Newgate was the sweetest in his whole life.

"When there was a general report that no more should die, he said, 'I do not know what God hath done contrary to our expectations ; if He doth prolong my life, I am sure it is all His own, and by His grace I will wholly devote it to Him.' But on the 29th of September, between ten and eleven at night, we found the deceitfulness of this report, they being then told that they must die the next morning, which was very unexpected as to the suddenness of it. But herein God glorified His power, grace, and faithfulness, in giving suitable support and comfort by His blessed presence, which appeared upon my coming to him at that time and finding him greatly composed. He said, 'Though men design to surprise, God doth and will perform His Word, to be a very present help in trouble.'

"The next morning, when I saw him again, his cheerfulness and comfort were much increased, waiting for the Sheriff with the greatest sweetness and serenity of mind. . . . With a smiling countenance, he discoursed of the glory of heaven. . . . His hope and comfort still increasing with the assurance of an interest in that glorious inheritance to the possession of which he was now going, he said, 'Death was more desirable than life, and he would rather die than live any longer here.' . . . Then, reading the Scriptures and musing with himself, he intimated the great comfort which God conveyed to his soul in it; saying, 'Oh, what an invaluable treasure is this blessed Word of God ! In all conditions here is a store of strong consolation.' One desiring his Bible, he said ; 'No, this shall be my companion to the last moment of my life.'

"Thus, praying together, reading, meditating, and conversing of heavenly things, they waited for the sheriff, who, when he came, void of all pity and civility, hurried them away, scarcely suffering them to take leave of their friends. Notwithstanding this, and the doleful mourning of all about them, the joyfulness of his countenance was increased. Thus he left the prison, and thus he appeared in the sledge, where they sat about half-an-hour before the officers could force the horses to draw; at which they were greatly enraged, there being no visible obstruction from weight or way. At last the Mayor and Sheriff haled them forward, themselves, Balaam-like, driving the horses.

"When they came to the place of execution, which was surrounded with spectators, many that waited their coming said, that when they saw him and them come with such cheerfulness and joy, and evidence of the presence of God with them, it made death appear with another aspect. They first embraced each other with the greatest affection ; then, two of the elder persons praying audibly, they joined with great seriousness. Then he (Benjamin) required leave of the Sheriff to pray particularly ; but he would not grant it, and only asked him whether he would pray for the King. He answered, ' I pray for all men.' He then requested that they might sing a hymn. Tho Sheriff told him it must be with the rope round their necks ; which they cheerfully accepted, and sung with such heavenly joy and sweetness that many who were present said it both broke and rejoiced their hearts. Thus in the experience of the delightfulness of praising God on earth, he willingly closed his eyes on a vain world, to pass to that eternal enjoyment.

"All present of all sorts were exceedingly affected and amazed. Some officers who had before insultingly said, ' Surely these persons have no thoughts of death, but will find themselves surprised by it,' now acknowledged that they saw he and they had something extraordinary within, which carried them through with so much joy. Others said that they were so convinced of their happiness that they would be glad to change conditions with them. The soldiers in general, and all others, lamented exceedingly, saying, ' It was so sad a thing to see them so cut off, that they scarcely knew how to bear it.' Some of the most malicious in the place, from whom nothing but railing was expected, said, as they were carried to their grave in Taunton church, ' These persons have left sufficient evidence that they are now glorified spirits in heaven.' A great officer also in the King's army has often been heard to say, ' If you would learn to die, go to the young men of Taunton.' "

Hannah was married to Henry Cromwell on May 25th, 1686, and shielded her persecuted family and the Cromwells in every possible way. During the reign of James II. she was engaged night and day in her good work, spending her own and her husband's substance most liberally. She rejoiced exceedingly when the popish king was driven out of the country and William III. was seated upon the throne. She ended her days, according to the inscription on the next tomb, on March 27th, 1732, aged 79.

CROMWELLS' TOMB (2).

INSCRIPTIONS.

TOP OF TOMB.

This monument was erected by Mr. Richard Cromwell
to the memory of Mrs. ELEANOR GATTON, widow, his
mother-in-law, who died 27th day of September, 1727, in
the 60th year of her age.

ELEANOR CROMWELL, his third daughter, died 24 day
February, 1727, aged two months.

M. MARY CROMWELL, spinster, his sister, who died 9
day July, 1731, in the 41st year of her age.

Mrs. HANNAH CROMWELL, his mother, who died 27
day March, 1732, in the 79th year of her age.

HENRY CROMWELL, Esq., his father, who was a Major
in the Army, died at Lisbon 11th day of September, 1711,
aged 53, and was buried there.

Here rests the body of Mrs. ELEANOR GRACEDEIU,
spinster, daughter of Sir Bartholomew Gracedeiu, Knt.,
who died 26th February, A.D., 1737, in the 53rd year of
her age.

NORTH PANEL.

Here lies the body of Mrs. MARY CROMWELL, the
beloved wife of William Cromwell, Esq., and daughter of
William Sherwill, late of London, Merchant, died 4th
March, 1752, aged 62 years.

SOUTH PANEL.

Here lies the body of WILLIAM CROMWELL, Esq.,
(husband of Mrs. Mary Cromwell mentioned on the other
side of this monument). He died 9 July, 1772, aged 79
years.

EAST PANEL.

Mrs. ELIZABETH CROMWELL died Nov. 12, 1772, in the
68th year of her age.

WEST PANEL.

Mrs. LETITIA CROMWELL died Nov. 15th, 1789, in the
56th year of her age.

It must be pointed out that none of Oliver's children
are buried in Bunhill. Hannah Hewling was his

grandson's wife, and the other Cromwells are either great-grandchildren or their descendants. In addition to these two vaults there was another on the north side of the grounds, but this cannot be found. The brothers, Thomas and Henry Cromwell, who were sons of Henry and Hannah, were buried in it. Of William Cromwell only is it necessary to give some little account, for this celebrated family had lost all position, and the members of it were, for the most part, tradesmen or lawyers.

WILLIAM CROMWELL.

William Cromwell was the fourth son of Hannah and Henry Cromwell, and was born in Cripplegate parish, London, April 24th, 1693. He resided in the City, where he spent the greater part of his life, having been designed for the law. In 1750 he married Mary, the daughter of William Sherwill, of London, and after marriage they resided about two years at Bocking, in Essex, where Mrs. Cromwell died, March 4th, 1752, aged 62, leaving him a moderate fortune. Upon her death he returned to London, and died in Kirby Street, Hatton Garden, July, 1772, in the 80th year of his age. He was buried in Bunhill Fields with his wife. His funeral sermon, which was preached at the Haberdashers' Hall, by Dr. Thomas Gibbons, has been published, with a short genealogy of the Cromwell family. Dr. Gibbons thus speaks in his sermon of Mr. William Cromwell.

" He was a member of this church, I suppose near, if not quite fifty years, or more, and was a deacon of it for thirty ; and I never heard of a single blemish upon his character during the whole period of either his deaconship or communion with us ; and methinks, it is no small thing for the lamp of a Christian profession to be maintained through such an unknown space without its ever having been so much as once damped, or obscured. He appeared to be a Christian indeed, not only by abstaining from what was gross and scandalous, profane and ungodly, but by a spirituality of temper ; and an attention to inward religion, and the pulse of his soul towards God ; and indeed his sentiments and conduct manifested a happy union of experimental and practical godliness. He met, and no wonder in so long a pilgrimage, with very heavy afflictions, but never did I hear him murmur or repine, though I am persuaded he was not without quick and keen sensations. He appeared to be of a humble spirit, and I well remember his saying to me not long before his decease that he would lie at the foot of God. In the frequent visits I made him in his decay of nature, I did not perceive him in high and overflowing joys, nor on the other hand did he seem left to consternation and terror. How have I found him—with some good book of the divines of the last age in his hand, or on his table? And where are there writings that ever excelled them for deep penetration, spirituality, and Christian experience and favour? He might have had gentle provision made for him in life, beyond what Providence had otherwise given him, if he could have qualified as a member of the Church of England; but he chose rather to preserve his conscience inviolable, and to remain a Nonconformist, than advance himself in the world, and depart from what appeared to him a line of duty."

WILLIAM WILLIAMS.

On left side of path, in the row which starts between the Nos. 40 and 41 on the wall is the headstone of William

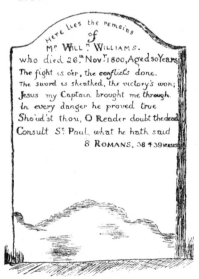

Williams. The tomb of Hume is in the next row west, but nearer the Artillery wall.

Also inscribed on the stone is the following verse of Joseph Hart's:—

"Earthly cavern, to thy keeping
   We commit our brother's dust;
Keep it softly, softly sleeping,
   Till our Lord demand thy trust.
Sweetly sleep, dear saint, in Jesus;
   Thou with us shalt wake from death;
Hold he cannot, though he seize us;
   We his power defy by faith."

ABRAHAM HUME.

INSCRIPTIONS (now undecipherable).

Here lyes interred the body of the Reverend Mr. ABRAHAM HUME, minister of the Gospel, who departed this life the 29th of January, 1706. Aged about 92 years.

And near this place lyes the body of Mrs. LUCY HUME, his first wife who dy'd No. 19th, 1681. And also the Rev. Mr. WILLIAM GILLCHRIST, his son-in-law who dy'd Oct. 26th, 1684. And his grandson, WM. GILLCHRIST, who dy'd March 18th, 1683.

This tomb of stone originally stood on a brick foundation some height above the ground, but it has now sunk so low that only the flat top stone can be seen. It was much damaged on one occasion by a large mob of people who flocked to Bunhill on the report that a Dr. Emms would have an immediate resurrection. It appears that during the early part of the eighteenth century a strange set sprang up in France called Camisars, which believed in prophetical impulse, and that a new dispensation would be proclaimed in every nation under heaven within three years. A number of these people came into England in 1706 and preached that this country was to be the first in which great things would be accomplished. Incredible as it might seem many converts were made, some being persons of wealth and learning. One was Sir Richard Bulkeley, " a gentleman of learning, who was very short and crooked, but fully expected under this dispensation to be made straight in a miraculous way, though he happened to die before the miracle was even wrought upon him, to his no small mortification and disappointment." The antics practised by these deluded fanatics were very ridiculous, but the great sign of the truth of their teachings was to be the resurrection of Dr. Emms, who had been buried in Bunhill. This was to take place on May 25th, 1708, and much excitement was caused by the approach of the date. It was announced " that the prophet spirit had declared, he would attest the publication of our Lord's approach as a bridegroom, and return as a King, by raising Dr. Emms from the dead on that day, above five months after his interment."

One of the leading Camisars declared, "Which if it be performed by the power of Him who is the resurrection and the life, none that believe Moses and the prophets, will doubt that the fulfilling of the glorious things written of Him by them, is at the door, according to the tenour of this prophetic voice of late sounding." When the day came multitudes of people assembled in Bunhill, and much damage was done to this and other tombs. In spite of their disappointment the faith of the Camisars was unshaken, but their power was shattered and very few adherents were afterwards made.

Abraham Hume was a Scot and he lived in troublous times. After he had completed his education at St. Andrew's he became Chaplain to the Countess of Hume, and travelled with her to London, where he made close observations of people, the court, and the state of the government generally. When he returned to Scotland he became connected with the Duke of Lauderdale and journeyed with him to the Continent, staying there some two years. After another visit to London at the time of the Assembly of Divines he was ordained minister of a Presbyterian Church at Benton near Newcastle. All went well with him until his zeal for the royalist cause led him into trouble and he was banished from England. Sir Arthur Haselrigg was chiefly instrumental in bringing this about, but in after years he more than made amends for his conduct in persecuting Hume. Until Oliver Cromwell was firmly established in his Protectorate, Hume remained in Scotland, and Sir Arthur Haselrigg instead of pursuing him, now united with others in persuading him to accept a Church at Wittingham. But no kindness or love that were ever shown to Hume could make him own Cromwell as the rightful governor of the country. Yet in spite of this he was turned out of his living by Charles II. because he could not and would not conform to the Church government and worship enacted by the Act of Uniformity. His sufferings were extreme, but in spite of many tempting offers he stedfastly stood by his principles, although this attitude cost him nearly all his influential friends. He finally settled in London as minister of a congregation meeting in Drury Lane, which position he occupied until his death.

JOHN RIPPON, D.D.

THE tomb of Rippon is in the last row at the west end, i.e., near to Bunhill Row.

INSCRIPTIONS.

SOUTH PANEL.

The Rev. JOHN RIPPON, D.D., for 63 years pastor of a Baptist Church in Carter Lane, Southwark: as a man and as a minister, he was endeared to all who intimately knew him. His talents pre-eminently qualified him for the useful and acceptable discharge of his Public Duties. Affable in manner, affectionate in disposition, animated in the pulpit, in doctrine incorrupt, unwavering in principle : his preaching was attractive, and his labours were abundant and successful. Among his varied services in the cause of religion, by none was he better known, or will be longer remembered in the Churches at home and abroad, than by the judicious and comprehensive Selection of Hymns bearing his name, which has aided the devotions and inspired the praises of myriads of his fellow Christians.

NORTH PANEL.

Dr. RIPPON, pastor of the Baptist Church, Carter Lane, Tooley Street, Southwark, sixty-three years, died 17th December, 1836, in the 86th year of his age.

IT is very appropriate that John Rippon's body should rest in Bunhill Fields, as when alive he spent many hours in copying the inscriptions then discernible upon the tombs, which the hand of time has now erased. There is an old diary extant in which a certain lady used to record her movements, and as she frequently visited Bunhill her remarks are specially interesting. One entry is as follows :—

" We had this day dinner with our worthy minister, Mr. Winter, who was pleased to say he should wish to meet our good friend, Mat. Wilks, for conferring and prayer upon matters which greatly concern the peace of our church just at present. After they had talked the affairs over and over, and sought the best direction, we were asked to go over to the Tabernacle to tea, and our pastor, Mr. Winter, never having seen Dr. Owen's grave, we went into the ground by the Old

Royal (now City) Road—not our usual way. There we found
a worthy man known to Mr. Wilks, Mr. Rippon by name, who
was laid down upon his side between two graves, and writing
out the epitaphs word for word. He had an ink-horn in his
button-hole, and a pen and book. He tells us that he has
taken most of the old inscriptions, and that he will, if God be
pleased to spare his days, do all, notwithstanding it is a
grievous labour, and the writing is hard to make out by
reason of the oldness of the cutting in some, and defacings of
other stones. It is a labour of love to him, and when he is
gathered to his fathers, I hope some one will go on with the
work."

When Mr. Rippon had completed his task, it was
found impossible to publish the result of his labours, but
these are still preserved, and may be seen by anyone
who has the wish. In the Official Guide there are these
words :—

"Rippon is not without his monument. It is to be found
within the great courtyard of the College of Heralds, in
Doctors' Commons. There, right and left, are the apartments
of Garter, Clarencieux, and Norroy, the Kings-at-Arms, and
Rouge Croix, Portcullis, Bluemantle, and others of the
fraternity of Heralds and pursuivants : and there is the Court
of Honour and the rare and ancient library gathered with the
greatest pains, and kept with the utmost care. Here, fit place
for such a treasure, and in the midst of all the genealogical
trees of the great, the gallant, and the noble of the land, is preserved the treasured record of the names and pious worth of
those whose pedigree is of the highest, and whose honour is of
the brightest that earth can show. Good Dr. Rippon little
thought of such a depository for his work, but so it is, and so
it will remain, as long as books may last, safeguarded by all the
gaunt lions and griffins, the grim supporters of Old England's
historic heraldry."

The birth-place of Rippon was Tiverton in Devonshire,
and the date was April 29th, 1751. His father was the
Baptist minister in that town, and it was here that
Rippon himself was baptized. When Dr. Gill died in
October, 1771, according to custom the church in Carter
Lane engaged with several ministers to supply the pulpit,
amongst these being Mr. Rippon. He afterwards received
an invitation to become the pastor, and in his letter
dated April 7th, 1773, in answer he said : "Various

The flat stone is the TOMB OF ABRAM HUME. (See page 109.)

JOHN RIPPON, D.D. (See page 111.)

JOHN GILL, D.D. (See page 123.)

THE TOMB OF JOHN GILL, D.D.
× SAMUEL BURFORD. (See page 131.)

have been the workings of my mind upon this weighty subject since I left you. Often and daily have I laid it before the Divine throne, impartially sought counsel of the All-wise and Infallible Counsellor, and now I judge it proper that I should beg leave of you, my dear and honoured brethren and sisters in the Lord, to spend some time longer amongst you before I return an absolute and decisive answer to the call you have given me; which I am the rather inclined to, as I apprehend this would be agreeable to some of my much esteemed friends, and I hope disagreeable to none."

After preaching amongst the people a little longer he became the pastor, and was ordained on November 11th, 1773. As a portion of the congregation was not satisfied with his ministry, they left Carter Lane and formed a new church. In contradistinction to many other ministers who have been placed in a similar position, Rippon showed a magnanimous spirit, for he actually collected money amongst his own church and congregation toward the expenses of the new chapel. In the Minute Book of the Baptist church, now meeting in the famous building known as the Metropolitan Tabernacle, there is a statement from which the following is an extract:—

"The pastoral charge of this church was accepted by Dr. Rippon, August 1st, 1773. He was ordained November 11th, in the same year. He held the office of pastor for 63 years; and if it be borne in mind that his predecessor, the learned Dr. John Gill, occupied the same office for 51 years, it would appear that during the period of 114 years, this church has had but two pastors! When Dr. Rippon first accepted the charge, the church was worshipping in Carter Lane, Tooley Street, Southwark, but in consequence of the building of the new London Bridge, they erected another edifice in New Bridge Street, which was opened May 6th, 1833. Dr. Rippon for a series of years occupied the pulpit with great success. He was instrumental, in the hand of the Spirit, in 'turning many from darkness to light'; numbers of whom have entered upon their rest before him, and ere this, have doubtless hailed his emancipated spirit to the same glory. Nor should we omit the instruction and comfort he was enabled to impart to the church. As a valuable and popular preacher our dear pastor occupied a prominent place in the denomination, for a lengthy

I

series of years: and, if in addition to the usefulness of his
public ministrations the urbanity and warm-heartiness of his
private manner be considered, we may be at a loss to know
whether he was more to be revered as a minister of Jesus
Christ or to be esteemed as a friend. From his long standing
in the ministry, he enjoyed an influence in his own denomination of the most flattering nature; not to advert to the
general respect he acquired in other sections of the Church of
Christ."

The statement goes on to mention his Selection of
Hymns, which a century ago was used in numbers of
chapels in England and in America. This, however, is
now practically unobtainable.

Dr. Rippon died on December 17th, 1836, the funeral
taking place on Christmas Eve, and his body was placed
in a tomb not far from that of his illustrious predecessor,
Dr. John Gill. The service was previously held in the
chapel in New Park Street, when Dr. Cox gave a
funeral address.

At the grave Mr. Charles Room delivered an oration,
and Dr. Collier preached the funeral sermon the next
day at New Park Street Chapel, from Hebrews ix. 27, 28.

In addition to collecting hymns for publication, Dr.
Rippon also penned some of his own. A somewhat
striking one was evidently written during one of his
visits to Bunhill Fields.

" My thoughts that often mount the skies,
    Go, search the world beneath,
Where nature all in ruin lies,
    And owns her sovereign—Death.

The tyrant, how he triumphs here!
    His trophies spread around!
And heaps of dust and bones appear
    Through all the hollow ground.

These skulls, what ghastly figures now,
    How loathsome to the eyes!
These are the heads we lately knew,
    So beauteous and so wise.

But where the souls, those deathless things,
    That left their dying clay?
My thoughts, now stretch out all your wings,
    And trace eternity.

O that unfathomable sea !
    Those deeps without a shore !
Where living waters gently play,
    Or fiery billows roar !

There we shall swim in heavenly bliss,
    Or sink in flaming waves ;
While the pale carcase breathless lies
    Amongst the silent graves.

' Prepare us, Lord, for Thy right hand ! '
    Then come the joyful day ;
Come death, and some celestial band,
    To bear our souls away."

DAVID NASMITH.

FROM Rippon's tomb pass towards the middle path, and this headstone is the eighth from the railings of the path.

INSCRIPTION.

Sacred to the memory of DAVID NASMITH, founder of City Missions, born in Glasgow ; died at Guildford, November 17th, 1839, in his 41st year.

The parents of David Nasmith were members of the College Church in Glasgow, and on March 21st, 1799, the babe was born, whose comparatively short life was such a busy and useful one.

Young David was sent to the City Grammar School, but did not receive much instruction, although he remained here four years. He was only sixteen years old when he became a member of the church in Nile Street, Glasgow, and he immediately took considerable part in the establishment of adult schools, besides being secretary to some prison societies. In the year 1826 he formed a Glasgow City Mission, and two years later went to Dublin and succeeded in establishing a City Mission there. He next went to America, where his labours were great, for he travelled over 3,000 miles, visiting forty cities and towns of America and two of Canada. He was instrumental in forming sixteen City Missions and other societies, returning to Scotland in December, 1831. He afterwards visited Paris, and established a work there. As might be expected, he met with much opposition, particularly from clergymen, but nothing could daunt his courage or abate his vigour. The London City Mission was formed on May 16th, 1835, in a room of his own house in Canning Terrace,

Hoxton. When the work was well-established in the Metropolis, he visited Wales and many English towns; not courting the smile or fearing the frown of any man.

He journeyed from London to Guildford in November, 1839, hoping to form a Mission, but when he reached the place on Saturday afternoon the 16th, he was in much pain. The doctors were called in, but nothing could afford him the slightest relief, and his agonies were most excruciating. One remark he passed was, " There is nothing but the simple Truth that will be of any avail to us in extremity. I am a sinner; Christ is my Saviour. I can let all else go ; the finished work of Christ is all my hope." One friend began to repeat to him the verse,

" If on my face, for Thy dear name,
　　Shame and reproach shall be ; "

when Mr. Nasmith took up the words and with great emphasis and feeling went on,

" All hail reproach, and welcome shame,
　　If Thou remember me."

He died the next afternoon, November 17th, without dain or a struggle, in a strange bed, with strange faces around him, yet with a sure and certain hope in the mercy of God. The funeral was largely attended, as beside the six mourning coaches containing about thirty friends, all the London City Missionaries were present.

JOSEPH IVIMEY.

FROM Nasmith's grave it is needful to return to Rippon's tomb, and then pass on to the grass. There will be no difficulty in discovering the tall headstone of Joseph Ivimey.

INSCRIPTION.

Here lie interred the mortal remains of the Rev. JOSEPH IVIMEY, in his lifetime the respected Pastor of the Baptist Church, which met in Eagle Street, Red Lion Square, for upwards of 29 years. He departed this life on the 8th day of February, 1834, aged 60 years. " Grace reigns."

THIS famous Baptist historian is buried in the same grave as many other members of his family. As he wrote so faithfully yet kindly of numbers of other ministers, he deserves some special attention himself. It is very appropriate that he should be buried in Bunhill Fields, for he himself knew what it was to visit the tombs and to record the lives of many interred there.

Ivimey was born at Ringwood on May 22nd, 1773, and was the eldest of a family of eight children. His education was elementary, and he was early in life taught the trade of a tailor, as it was necessary that the youth should contribute at least something towards the maintenance of the family. The religious instruction he received was of a sad nature, as he was under Arian influence. Owing to home troubles, he was placed with an uncle while still young, and it was while with him that he heard the Gospel preached for the first time. His early spiritual experience was very gloomy, but through the singing of the following verse :—

" In the world of endless ruin,
      It shall never once be said,
' There's a soul that perished suing
      For the Saviour's promised aid,' "

he was much comforted, although his mind was still in
confusion. A measure of hope was however granted him,
and his views upon doctrine were much influenced through
reading Elisha Coles' work on " Divine Sovereignty."
He now wished to hear the Gospel faithfully proclaimed,
and so often walked with two friends from Ringwood to
Wimborne, a distance of some nine miles. In April,
1793, he removed to London, and as well as other
ministers, he heard Mr. Martin at Keppel Street and Mr.
Swain at Walworth and Devonshire Square. His stay
in the Metropolis, however, was very short, and he returned to Ringwood, saying to himself as he mounted
the coach, " I will never see this London again." From
Ringwood he moved to Portsea, where he commenced
village preaching. After his " public call " he visited
Lymington, Romsey, Southampton, and other towns.
For a short time he was assistant to Mr. Lovegrove at
Wallingford, but receiving an invitation from the Baptist Church at Eagle Street, London, to preach for three
Lord's Days, he acceded to the request. This led to an
invitation to return to the Metropolis and preach to the
church with a view to becoming their pastor. As he was
well received by the church and people, he was ordained
on January 16th, 1805.

It was about 1808 that Mr. Ivimey became an author,
and although his " Life of Bunyan " has been severely
criticised by Southey and others, yet it is generally
acknowledged that most of the criticisms passed upon it
are quite unjust. His largest work is " The History of
the English Baptists," which is highly prized for the
information it contains, and is in most respects entirely
to be relied upon.

As a Protestant, Mr. Ivimey uttered faithful warnings
against Popery, for he watched its steady and stealthy
advance, and as a Dissenter he was always contending
for civil and religious liberties. He was also connected
with several societies, so that his labours were quite
herculean.

In 1826 he published his "Pilgrims of the 19th Century; a Continuation of the 'Pilgrim's Progress,' under the Plan Projected by Mr. Bunyan; Comprising a History of the Visit to the Town of Toleration; with an Account of its Charter, and a Description of the Principles and Customs of its Inhabitants under the Similitude of a Dream." In this he attempted to follow up what he considered to have been John Bunyan's train of thinking. In the preface he says, " I have endeavoured especially to avoid every statement which would be justly offensive to members of the Established Church. The Protestant Dissenters are not now oppressed and persecuted by the ruling church, and it therefore becomes them, when defending their dissent, not to use provoking expressions even in regard to those errors in that system which prevent their conformity. That the Protestant Dissenters should be placed upon the same level in regard to civil disabilities with the Roman Catholic Dissenters, I consider to be unjust and oppressive; and think it becomes us to take every suitable occasion to represent those hardships for the purpose of procuring the repeal of the Corporation and Test Acts." In this work he describes a visit to the "Pilgrims' Burial Ground," his companion being Matthew, whom he described as "The eldest of the great-grandsons of those excellent pilgrims, Christian and Christiana." Of the "large cemetery consisting of several acres of land," he quotes Matthew as saying, "This has been the place of our fathers' sepulchres for nearly two centuries past; long before our town was fortified. This was the place where the wicked should no longer trouble them, and where the weary found themselves at rest. I take it that more of those bodies, which when living were temples of the Holy Ghost, and purchased by the blood of the Son of God, are congregated here than in any other field beneath the sun." He then goes on to speak of the inscriptions on the monuments, most of which now, alas! are quite undecipherable. Pointing to one tomb,* he remarked, " You perceive that handsome monument; it perpetuates the memory of one who was an eminent inhabitant and public teacher in our town,

* That of Isaac Watts.

who died in a good old age, honoured and beloved by all
parties; he is usually known by us as ' The sweet singer
of British Israelites!'   It might be said, of a number of
his poetical pieces, as of Solomon, ' His songs were a
thousand and five.'   Many of the productions of his pen
have been sung by my neighbours, not only in the house
of their pilgrimage, but as they have been passing through
' The valley of the shadow of death.'   It would seem as
if his lips had been touched with seraphic fire from the
altar of God, and almost as if the same Spirit spake by
him as taught David his evangelical and heavenly strains.
He soared towards the skies as on eagles' pinions, teaching us to gaze on and admire the radiance of the Sun of
Righteousness; then descends to earth, and like the doves
of the valley, utters his pious mournings with the sons
and daughters of woe."   Reference in the book is also
made to the tombs of Chandler and Stennett, although
Ivimey makes a curious mistake, for he states that the
three Stennetts are buried here.   Apparently feeling that
his own end could not be very far off, Ivimey writes most
beautifully of death.   Pointing to a grave-stone he sighed
and said, " There they buried Abraham and Sarah his
wife, there they buried Isaac and Rebecca his wife; and
there I buried Leah.   In that grave it is my wish that I
and my dear Mercy may find our last home.   .   .   .   It
is not probable the period will arrive in my time when the
Lord of the Hill will make His second advent, not as at
the first, but with all the glories of His exalting Majesty.
To be prevented from falling asleep, and to be changed in
the twinkling of an eye into the likeness of the mortal
body of my Lord and Saviour, is what doubtless many
will experience, but which I do not expect.   It is most
probable my slumbers will be disturbed, and that I shall
be awakened to a new state of existence by the voice of
an archangel and with the voice of the trump of God.
Oh, what a shout of victory! victory! victory! will arise
from thousands and tens of thousands who will then
ascend from these graves.   Oh! may then I hear the
joyous acclamation of myriads exclaiming with seraphic
delight, ' Now is come to pass the saying that is written,
Death is swallowed up in victory.' "

During the latter years of Mr. Ivimey's life he was much afflicted with asthma, and other ailments. His last sermon was preached on December 8th, 1833, from the words, "I know whom I have believed, and am persuaded that He is able to keep that which I have committed unto Him against that day." He took to his bed on the 22nd of the month, feeling sure that he would never again leave it. His mind was quite calm, the fear of death being entirely removed. He said, "I have nothing to do. I am quite safe and perfectly happy. Satan has shot his sharpest dart at me in former times, but he is now restrained." When the words, "And the blood of Jesus Christ cleanseth us from all sin," were read, he cried, "Ah! that is it. There's the foundation, there's my hope." During the same evening there was read to him the account of the pilgrims, Christian and Hopeful, passing the river. This he enjoyed very much, and exclaimed, "I feel the bottom like Hopeful, and it is good." In answer to a remark that it was encouraging

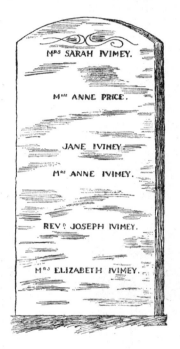

to see him supported in such a trying hour by the truths of the Gospel, he replied, "I am glad that my dying experience does not contradict the doctrines which I have preached." To a friend he said, "I enjoy perfect peace, only differing in degree from the peace of heaven. I am called to wait ; and, through mercy, I have no distress.

> " ' Not a wave of trouble rolls
> Across my peaceful breast.' "

Three hours before he died he was heard to say, " My struggles will soon be at an end. Dr. Ryland said, ' Oh ! for the last groan,' and I say, ' Oh ! for my last groan.' The wicked will never have a last groan!'" An hour later he said, " I have waited for Thy salvation, O Lord;" and also quoted several passages of Scripture, concluding with, "Behold, God is my Salvation. I will trust and not be afraid." His last request, made about eleven o'clock, was to be raised up, and looking at his wife his dying words were, "It's all over." In his will he had stated his wishes with respect to his funeral, in the following words : " I desire to be buried in my family grave, in Bunhill Fields, and that on the head stone, after my name and date, there be added, and that only, ' Grace reigns.' "

WILLIAM ANDERSON, Bapt.

MOVE south-east from Ivimey, about three rows, and this headstone will be found adjoining the path.

INSCRIPTION.

Sacred to the memory of the Rev. Mr. WILLIAM ANDERSON, Pastor of a church of Christ, meeting in Grafton Street; who being led into an experimental acquaintance with the great things of God, was animated to declare the same with much zeal and spiritual affection, to the great comfort and joy of many who now mourn the loss of so valuable a servant of Christ. He fell asleep, September 8th, 1767, in the 67th year of his age.

DR. JOHN GILL.

MOVING from Anderson's grave towards the middle path, the large tomb of John Gill will be seen. The original inscription, which was in Latin, was drawn up by Samuel Stennett, and engraved on the top of the massive stone. This is now practically obliterated, but there is no mistaking the tomb, as at the west end may still be seen the small original headstone.

INSCRIPTION.

In this Sepulchre are deposited the remains of JOHN GILL, Professor of Sacred Theology, a man of unblemished reputation, a sincere disciple of Jesus, an excellent preacher of the Gospel, a courageous defender of the Christian faith ; who, adorned with piety, learning, and skill, was unwearied in works of prodigious labour for more than fifty years. To obey the commands of his Great Master, to advance the best interest of the Church, to promote the salvation of men, impelled with unabated ardour, he put forth all his strength. He placidly fell asleep in Christ the 14th day of October, in the year of our Lord, 1771, in the 74th year of his age."

John Gill was born at Kettering on November 23rd, 1697 (old style), of parents in a comfortable position in life.

In Kettering there was a dissenting congregation made up of Presbyterians, Independents and Baptists, the teaching Elder being a Mr. William Wallis, who administered baptism by immersion to all adult persons who desired it. As might be expected, this mode of government caused some discomfort, and finally there was a separation and a Particular Baptist Church was formed. Of this church Mr. Edward Gill was in due time chosen to the office of Deacon, and continued in it until the end of his days.

John Gill was early sent to the Grammar School in Kettering, and soon showed remarkable talents and an extraordinary aptitude for receiving instruction. Latin and Greek became simple languages to him, and instead of playing games with other boys, his spare time was taken up with the classics. He was soon made to feel the disabilities under which he laboured as a dissenter, for his master insisted that all children should go to church every school day for the reading of prayers. This led to the removal of a number of boys from the school, Gill being amongst them. But with all the obstructions thrown in his way, he continued to make progress. He took great delight in Logic, Rhetoric, Natural and Moral Philosophy, Hebrew and Divinity. When about twelve years of age he heard Mr. Wallis preach a sermon from Genesis iii. 9, " And the Lord God called unto Adam and said unto him, Where art thou ? " The question, " Sinner, where art thou ? " was continually upon his mind, and he was brought to serious concern. His feelings were deepened by the death of Mr. Wallis, and he now began to see more clearly the depravity of his nature, the exceeding sinfulness of sin, his need of the Saviour, and of a better righteousness than his own, even the righteousness of Christ to be received by faith.

It was his happiness shortly after to be favoured with a comfortable persuasion of his interest in the life, death, blood and righteousness of Christ, and the doctrines of the Gospel became exceedingly dear to him. On Thursday, 1st of November, 1716, Gill made a public profession of his faith before the Church, and on the same day was baptized by immersion in a river.

It is clear that he had convinced the members of the Church of his godliness and abilities, for the next Lord's Day when there was a meeting for prayer he read and expounded the 53rd chapter of Isaiah. Those who heard were so favourably impressed that he was asked to preach the next Sabbath evening. His text then was 1 Cor. ii. 2, " For I am determined not to know anything among you, save Jesus Christ and Him crucified." At the commencement of this his ministry he exhibited those qualities of seriousness, solemnity, affection and love which afterwards so characterised his long and most useful labours. Having a desire to continue his studies to the best advantage, he removed to Higham Ferrers, and although he was disappointed in this matter, yet he became most useful as a village preacher. He also met Elizabeth Negus, whom he married in 1718, and in finding Elizabeth his wife, he found "a good thing." As she died on October 10th, 1764, in the 68th year of her age, they were favoured to enjoy more than forty-six years of married life.

During his stay at Higham Ferrers he frequently visited his home and friends in Kettering to preach to the Church and congregation, and after his marriage he returned there to live. His ministry was much blessed, but in the beginning of the year 1719 he received an invitation from the Church at Horsley Down, Southwark, to go to the great Metropolis in order to preach. In the following March he was ordained pastor, and so became the successor of Benjamin Keach and Benjamin Stinton. The congregation soon increased, and although he was much occupied by his public labours, Gill's pen was moving very fast in the quiet of his study.

He was twenty-six years of age when he began his "Exposition of the Book of Solomon's Song," the sermons occupying 122 Lord's Day mornings. He also dealt with the question of baptism, with the prophecies of the Old Testament respecting the Messiah and with many other subjects. At this time error with respect to the Godhead was rife, and it was decided by a number of gentlemen to ask nine ministers to deliver discourses on this and other important doctrines. These preachers included at least three who are buried in Bunhill, viz., Robert Bragge, Thomas Bradbury and John Gill.

Year after year the writings of Gill were published, but to attempt to speak of all these would be to review a long and important period of controversy, which dealt with practically every doctrine of the Christian faith. The words of Mr. Toplady must be given, although these are well-known and often quoted. In referring to one of Gill's publications Toplady says in his diary : " Between morning and afternoon service read through Dr. Gill's excellent and nervous tract on Predestination against Wesley. How sweet is that blessed doctrine to the soul when it is received through the channel of inward experience! I remember a few years ago Mr. Wesley said to me concerning Dr. Gill: ' He is a positive man, and fights for his own opinions through thick and thin.' Let the doctor fight as he will. I am sure he fights to good purpose, and I believe it may be said of my learned friend as it was said of the Duke of Marlborough, that he never fought a battle which he did not win."

It should be noticed that in addition to his pastorate, Gill was the Wednesday evening Lecturer in Great Eastcheap for more than twenty-six years.

On October 9th of the following year, 1757, a new chapel was opened in Carter Lane near London Bridge, and Gill preached two sermons from Exodus xx. 24. These were afterwards published and the following striking paragraph is abstracted :—

" As we have now opened a new place of worship, we enter upon it, recording the name of the Lord by preaching the doctrines of the grace of God, and of free and full salvation alone by Jesus Christ, and by the administration of gospel ordinances as they have been delivered to us. To do this, from time to time, is our present design, and what, by Divine assistance, we shall endeavour to pursue in the course of our worship and administrations here. What doctrines may be taught in this place after I am gone is not for me to know; but as for my own part, I am at a point; I am determined, and have been long ago, what to make the subject of my ministry. It is now upwards of forty years since I entered into the arduous work, and the first sermon I ever preached was from those words of the Apostle, ' For I am determined not to know anything among you save Jesus Christ, and Him crucified; ' and through the grace of God I have been enabled in some good measure to abide by the same resolutions hitherto, as many of you are my witnesses; and I hope, through Divine assistance, I ever shall, as long as I am in this tabernacle and engaged in such a work. I am not afraid of the reproaches of men; I have been inured to these from my youth upwards : none of these things move me."

Towards the end of his life Gill used his pen in writing and his time in preaching much upon the eternal Sonship of Christ. His pamphlet upon this great subject is well worthy of a perusal, and the following paragraph clearly shows the view that Gill held concerning this doctrine :—

"I cannot see any reason to object to the use of the phrase, 'that of the eternal generation,' as applied to the Sonship of Christ, since one Divine Person is said to beget (Psa. ii. 7), and therefore must be a Father, and another Person is said to be begotten (John i. 14, 18, and elsewhere), and therefore must be a Son; and if a begotten Son, as He is often said to be, then He must be a Son by generation; for he is an illiterate man indeed who does not know that to beget and generate are the same; and therefore generation, if used of the Father, in the Divine nature, then of the Son in the Divine nature; and there being nothing in the Divine nature but what is eternal, then this generation must be eternal generation, a phrase which is no more a contradiction than a Trinity in Unity, or a Trinity of Persons in one God."

The Doctor was particularly careful to make himself clear upon the difference between the Personality and the Persons of a Triune Jehovah.

The labours of Dr. Gill were herculean, and when asked by Mr. Ryland how he was able to perform these, he answered that it was not done by very early rising nor by sitting up late, for the latter, he was confident, must be injurious to any student, and could not be helpful. The fact was, he rose as soon as it was light in the winter, and usually before six in the summer, although towards the end of his days he took a little more rest. He was not accustomed to visit his people very much, but he always endeavoured to meet ministerial brethren at some coffee house, or under the roof of his friend, Mr. Thomas Watson. He had quite a sense of humour, and often expressed himself with rugged wit.

There was a female member of his church who considered that part of her duties was to attend to the personal appearance of her famous minister. She went to his house one day, and told him that his white preaching bands were too long, and asked that he would allow her to put this matter right. To her joy the Doctor consented, and she stated that, believing he would be willing, she had brought her scissors with her, and soon these did what she felt was so necessary. When the task was accomplished, Gill said, "Now there is something about you that is a little too long. Will you allow me to cut that off, as I have allowed you to cut my preaching

bands?" "Yes, certainly," she replied, being willing to
please her minister. "Then give me the scissors, and
put out your tongue," replied Gill.

In his congregation there was a godly woman who one
day visited him in great trouble about the singing, for it
appears that in some three years the clerk had introduced two new tunes. This pleased the young people,
but this good woman could hardly bear it. The Doctor
listened patiently to her complaint, and then asked her
whether she understood singing. Her reply was, "No,
and neither did her aged father before her." She also
said that "though they had had about a hundred years
between them to learn the Old Hundred tune, they could
not sing it nor any other tune." Instead of openly telling her that people who could not sing were the last who
should interfere in this matter, the worthy Pastor meekly
asked, "Sister, what tunes would you like us to sing?"
"Why, Sir," she replied, "I should very much like
David's tunes." "Well," said he, "if you will get
David's tunes for us, we will then try to sing them."

There were many men called by grace under Gill's
preaching, who afterwards entered the ministry, amongst
others being John Brine, William Anderson, and James
Fall. Of these three Gill thought with much pleasure
and gratitude, and when Anderson and Fall died he
preached and published special funeral sermons. He
was also always ready to give advice to those who were
desirous of forming churches, and his own Articles were
adopted by several companies of people. During the last
two years of his life he rarely preached more than once
each Lord's day, and this caused a falling off in the
attendance.

It was appropriate that he should be seized for death
whilst in his loved study; but he was wonderfully supported, and his faith and hope were clear and strong. To
his nephew, Mr. John Gill, of St. Albans, he wrote, "I
depend wholly and alone upon the free, sovereign, eternal,
unchangeable love of God, the firm and everlasting covenant of grace, and my interest in the Persons of the
Trinity for my whole salvation, and not upon any
righteousness of my own nor on anything in me, nor
done by me under the influence of the Holy Spirit."

To one of his friends he said, " I have nothing to make me uneasy ; " and then repeated the well-known lines of Dr. Watts :—

> " He rais'd me from the deeps of sin,
>   The gates of gaping hell ;
>   And fixed my standing more secure
>   Than 'twas before I fell."

The last words he was heard to utter were, " O my Father ! my Father ! " and all who were with him were much impressed by the wonderful faith, joy, and peace of mind which never left him.

He had been pastor of his church for more than fifty-one years, and his loss was greatly felt. The friends were desirous of meeting all the expenses of, and making the necessary arrangements for the funeral, but the family being in comfortable circumstances, and wishing to show their own loving affection, declined this proposal. He was buried in Bunhill, and a vast train of mourning coaches accompanied the remains to their last resting-place, the service being conducted by Mr. Benjamin Wallin. His great friend and admirer, Mr. Toplady, very earnestly desired to officiate at the grave, but his wishes could not be met, as Gill was a conscientious Dissenter, and wished to show it in every respect. This, however, did not alter the affection and love of Toplady, and his testimony to the qualities, industry, faithfulness, and character of Gill was most generous and striking.

Mr. George Alexander, the pastor of the Strict and Particular Baptist Church at Birkenhead, has kindly selected an extract from the writings of John Gill. As the author of " The Myrtle Tree,"* as a stalwart Protestant, as a writer to Magazines over the initials, " G. A.," and as a preacher, Mr. Alexander is known and loved far beyond the confines of his own church and town.

" GILL ON I COR. v. 23 : ' Afterwards they that are Christ's at His coming.'

" ' Afterwards they that are Christ's ' ; not immediately after,

* C. J. Farncombe & Sons, Ltd., 1s.

K

for now (1747) seventeen hundred years are elapsed since the resurrection of Christ, and yet the saints are not raised; and how many more years are to run out before that is not to be known. But as there was an interval between the first fruits and the ingathering of the harvest, so there is a considerable space of time between the resurrection of Christ as the first fruits, and the resurrection of His people which will be the harvest. The persons who shall rise first, and next after Christ, are they that are His ; who were chosen in Him before the foundation of the world, and were given to Him by His Father as His spouse, His children, His sheep, His portion and His jewels ; who were purchased and redeemed by His blood, are called by His grace and regenerated by His Spirit ; who give up themselves to Him and are possessed by Him. The interest that Christ has in them, here expressed, carried in it a strong argument of their resurrection ; which may be concluded from their election in Christ, which can never be made void ; from the gift of their whole persons to Christ by His Father, with His declaration of His will that He should lose nothing of them, but raise it up at the last day ; from His redemption of their bodies as well as their souls ; from the union of both unto Him ; and from the sanctification of both, and His Spirit dwelling in their mortal bodies as well as in their souls.

"The time when they will be raised by Christ is *at His Coming* ; at His second and personal coming at the last day. Then the dead in Christ will rise first and immediately. When this will be no man knows ; yet nothing is more certain than that Christ will come a second time, and His coming will be speedy and sudden. It will be glorious and illustrious, and to the joy and salvation of His people ; since their bodies will then be raised and re-united to their souls, when they, soul and body, shall be for ever with the Lord."

SAMUEL BURFORD.

THE tomb of Samuel Burford, with its slightly detached head-stone, is one row east and two north of John Gill's, the exact position being shown in the photograph.

INSCRIPTION.
(Only a few words of this are decipherable.)

Here lies the Rev. Mr. SAMUEL BURFORD, many years pastor of a church in Goodman's Fields. Died April 16th, 1768.

> His virtues need no stone to show,
> Full well his friends his merits know ;
> While living was by all beloved,
> By all regretted when removed.

THOMAS HUTCHINGS.

THE head-stone of Hutchings is practically in front of Anderson's. It is the nearest to the path of its row, and there are tombs to south-west and south-east of it.

INSCRIPTION.
Rev. THOMAS HUTCHINGS, thirty-two years pastor of the church in Unicorn Yard, Tooley Street, Obt. 1st March, 1827, aged 58 years.

Born at Portsea, Hants, on March 13th, 1768, Thomas Hutchings was in due course apprenticed to his own father as a sail-maker in the Dockyard. In early life he was called by grace, and after his apprenticeship was completed he became a student at Cheshunt College. He preached at Rye, Chipping Ongar and several other places, and was ordained pastor at Unicorn Yard, on July 23rd, 1795. For thirty-two years he devoted his time and talents to this church and practically died in harness. He was in the pulpit on Lord's day, Feb. 25th, 1827, when he was attacked with a fit of apoplexy, which was followed by paralysis of the left side. At the

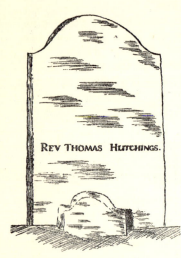

REV THOMAS HUTCHINGS.

particular moment he was in prayer before the sermon, and the last words he spoke in that pulpit which were heard by human ears were, "Lord, we are dying creatures; prepare us for life, prepare us for death, and for eternal glory, for Christ's sake. Amen." His friends rendered all the assistance that was possible, and removed the dying man to his home, where he lingered for a few days. During his last hours he lifted his hand, and said, "All is well;" and when asked if he were happy, replied with marked emphasis, "Yes! Yes!" His end was peace.

GEORGE BURDER.

THE tall head-stone on which is inscribed the name of George Burder practically touches the middle railings, and the inscriptions can be seen best from the path or from the north section of the grounds. There are several persons buried in this family vault, which lies underneath the path made from the City Road to Bunhill Row.

INSCRIPTION.

The Rev. GEORGE BURDER, died 29th May, 1832, aged 86.

In his Memorandum Book Mr. Burder states : " I was born in London, June 5th, 1752, or rather on the 25th of May, which by the alteration of the style in the September following, was accounted June 5th."

He received a good education, but had the great misfortune to lose his mother early in life. She, too, was buried in Bunhill Fields, and Burder writes : " An upright stone is placed at the head of the grave ; and I earnestly desire *my* children and *theirs* to repair or renew that stone, in memory of her." If these lines should be noticed by any of the Burder family, it is to be hoped they will remember their illustrious predecessor's words, and pay some attention to the stone.

SARAH Wife of the Rev.ᵈ G. BURDER,
died 28ᵗʰ February 1821 Aged 70

The Rev.ᵈ GEORGE BURDER
died 29ᵗʰ May, 1832 Aged 80.

" It was," says Burder, "whilst visiting the tombs in Bunhill Fields that I had some affecting thoughts of death, and of the worth of an immortal soul." These feelings were merely transient, but he was only ten years old when, on June 5th, 1762, divine realities were borne in upon his soul. According to his own account, " After tea, and before the family worship, my father was accustomed to catechise me, and examine what I remembered of the sermons of the day. That evening he talked to me very affectionately, and reminded me that it was high time to seek the Lord and to become truly religious. He particularly insisted upon the necessity of an interest in Christ, and shewed me that as a sinner I must perish without it; and recommended to me to begin that night to pray for it.

" After family worship, when my father and mother used to retire to their closets for private devotion, I also went into a chamber (the same room in which I was born) ; and there, I trust, sincerely and earnestly, and, as far as I can recollect for the first time, I poured out my soul to God, beseeching Him to give me an interest in Christ, and desiring, above all things, to be found in Him.

" Reflecting on this evening, I have often been ready to conclude, that surely I was born of God at that time— surely I then was brought to believe in Christ—surely there was something more than nature in all this.

" And yet, when I consider the sad mixture of sin and vanity that prevailed for several years after this, I call it all in question and say, Could this be grace ? Could grace live in such a heart as mine, inmate with so much sin ? And to this hour I cannot decide."

When quite a youth he often used to hear William Romaine, George Whitefield, with other leading ministers, at the Tottenham Court Road Tabernacle.

It was on September 17th, 1775, at seven in the morning, that he for the first time attended the ordinance of the Lord's Supper. The building was the world-famed " Tabernacle," one of the four presiding ministers being Rowland Hill. He records, " I was admitted to the blessed privilege of commemorating the divine love of the dear Redeemer at His table, with the good people of the Tabernacle. My soul cries out, Lord, how great is my unworthiness ! ' Why was I made to hear Thy voice ? ' My soul was greatly overpowered with the solemnity of the ordinance, and I prayed earnestly to the Lord to enable me to honour Him by a strong faith. I hope I had my desire to some measure fulfilled ; for sure I am that Christ was lovely in my eyes—' the Chief among ten thousand, a Sun among ten thousand stars— yea, altogether lovely.' "

As a lad he had been placed under the care and tuition of Mr. Isaac Taylor, who was an artist of some eminence. This, however, was not the path for him, for a long ministerial career lay ahead. His first attempt at speaking was in a private house when on a visit to friends in Shropshire on Lord's Day, June 16th, 1776, and he spoke again the next night in the kitchen of a farm house. His text on this occasion was Luke iv. 18: "The Spirit of the Lord is upon me," &c., and he was greatly helped in speaking. From this time he was much engaged in preaching at various places, and also seized every opportunity to hear such men as Toplady, Rowland Hill, Anthony Crole, Romaine, and Berridge.

One of his early experiences was most striking, and is thus recorded in his diary: "On May 11th, 1777, I preached at Woolwich, at Mr. Percy's chapel. In the afternoon I went in a boat on board the 'Justitia,' the hulk where the convicts were confined. The preachers who visited Woolwich had frequently done so. As we went, the prisoners on board another hulk ('The Taileur') hailed us, and expressed a strong desire for preaching, which they had never yet had. We were doubtful as to the propriety of going, as the captain had not been consulted. We went forward, therefore, to the 'Justitia,' and I preached there on deck. It was a melancholy sight to behold the wretched people in irons. They were generally attentive. As we were coming back, the 'Taileur's' people loudly called upon us again. We rowed to the side of the vessel. They intreated me to give them a sermon. We objected that we had not the captain's leave. But the mate, if I remember, assured us that the captain would not be displeased. I therefore consented. When I first stood up, many seemed very thoughtless, and laughed. But we had no sooner begun prayer than a very visible alteration took place in their behaviour; they fell on their knees unasked (as far as I know), the noise of their irons on deck was tremendous; many were affected so as to weep. I then preached a short sermon, quite extempore; it was, I think, on repentance; but rain coming on, a bustle ensued, which obliged me to stop. The Captain, who came on board while I was speaking, insisted on my coming into his cabin and taking refreshment. I apologised for venturing to preach without his leave; he said he was much pleased, and (sailor-like) swore by his Maker, that 'if *that* would not bring them to repentance, nothing would.' I returned to Woolwich and preached a fourth time, and was unusually weary."

The Independent Church at Lancaster having given him a unanimous call to the pastorate, he felt it his duty to accept, and was ordained on Thursday, October 29th, 1778. Being a Dissenter he was compelled to apply to the local Justices for a license, and this was granted on January 12th, 1779. He remained at Lancaster until the Autumn of 1783, preaching his last sermon on October 12th.

It was during this pastorate in Lancaster that Burder visited a Mr. J. D. Hunt, who was condemned for forgery at Manchester. The penalty in those days was death, and it is strange that Hunt, whose real name was Dalton, had in his youth been a pupil of the remarkable Dr. Dodd,* who had been executed for a similar offence. Hunt was an accomplished man, having, according to Burder's belief, been head constable of Manchester. He received the counsel of Mr. Burder with much attention, and his execution took place on Saturday, April 20th, although it was deferred for several hours in the expectation of a reprieve. On the next day Mr. Burder, at the evening service, preached from Romans vi. 21 : "What fruit had ye then in those things whereof ye are now ashamed? for the end of those things is death."

His next pastorate was at Coventry, where he commenced his ministerial course on November 2nd, 1783, and he resided in this town for nearly twenty years.

It will be well to recount in Mr. Burder's own words certain experiences which happened to him.

"In the month of April, 1784, I attended William Summers, a young man under sentence of death. He was executed on Whitley Common, Wednesday, April 28th. He appeared to be very penitent; and I was not without hope of his having obtained mercy; especially as he felt great concern for others, and desired me to speak to the people just before he was turned off, and to warn them in his name, for he was too weak to speak. I gave notice that I would preach in the Park on the following Sabbath evening, to improve the sad event. The notice of this afforded him great pleasure. On the evening of the day of execution I preached at the meeting on Job xiv. 10, ' Man giveth up the ghost, and where is he?' As proposed, I preached on Sabbath evening, and probably to five thousand

* In the National Portrait Gallery, London, there hangs a beautiful portrait of this Dr. Dodd.

people, from 2 Cor. v. 11 : ' Knowing, therefore, the terror of the Lord, we persuade men.' The people behaved well ; but I believe I could not be well heard, the wind was so high ; and if I recollect aright, rain came on. But I do hope good was done—at least some were brought to attend the ministry of the Gospel.

" On the preceding Monday, April 26th, having exchanged with my worthy friend, that faithful minister, Mr. Moody, of Warwick, I attended the execution of three men ; one a coiner, the other two housebreakers. One circumstance affected me deeply. All the three were on ladders—then the mode of execution—with the ropes about their necks, about to be turned off, when the coiner, endeavouring to fortify his mind in this awful situation, uttered words to this purpose, which I distinctly heard, being at a short distance : ' I never killed anybody, I never hurt anybody—I hope the Lord will have mercy upon me.' This poor creature seemed to die exactly in the spirit of the Pharisee—' I thank God I am not as other men are, or as this publican ;' for I thought he alluded to the two thieves suffering with him, who had robbed the Bull Inn, I think, in Birmingham. I was so deeply affected, that I could scarcely refrain from crying out to the man, ' Do not trust to your own righteousness, look to Christ.' It has often occurred to me as one of the most glaring instances of a self-righteous spirit that I ever knew.

" 1785, March 25th, Good Friday. Preached to the prisoners under sentence, and to a large congregation, in the County Hall. The hall was lent for the purpose by the Mayor, who was present and much impressed ; I hope usefully, as he soon after left the Arian congregation, where he used to attend, and became my constant and serious hearer. It was an affecting season, and I hope good was done.

" March 31st. Preached again to the condemned men at the Gaol Hall, to a very large congregation, from Acts xvi. 30, 31, ' What must I do to be saved ?' &c. Tuesday, April 5th. Preached again at the hall to the malefactors and a great concourse of people from Psalms cxxx. 4, ' But there is forgiveness with Thee that Thou mayest be feared.' The men were respited for ten days.

" April 18th. Monday morning, eight o'clock, preached once more to the condemned men at the hall, from Amos iv. 12 : ' Prepare to meet thy God.' After service they were taken in a mourning coach to Whitley Common, where I attended them with Mr. Wilks. I gave notice from the cart that Mr. Wilks would preach at West Orchard, my chapel ; which he did in the evening, to a vast congregation, from these words : ' And, ye fools, when will ye be wise ? ' "

Mr. Burder was a stalwart Protestant Dissenter, but he could not mix with many others who were endeavouring to obtain the repeal of the Corporation and Test Acts. He was much alarmed and disgusted by the violence displayed by the Socinians, and he made it clear that he could not sanction their proceedings.

During this pastorate Mr. Burder visited many villages and towns on preaching expeditions, and often met with great and brutal opposition from drunken, godless parsons, churchwardens, and their lewd, unruly followers. His discourses were afterwards published as "Village Sermons," and were circulated in tens of thousands, "Early Piety" being perhaps the most popular. He also accomplished much literary work, such as an abridgement of Dr. John Owen's marvellous but ponderous treatise on the Holy Spirit; notes on the "Pilgrim's Progress," and many other sermons and tracts for distribution. He had completed some of the latter when at Lancaster, one being named "The Good Old Way." In this he proved by the Scriptures the Fall and recovery of man, but good use was also made of statements in the Articles and Liturgy of the Prayer Book. Hundreds of thousands were distributed, and Mr. Burder was told of an odd but amusing circumstance which happened at Bolton. The churchwardens only noticing its title came to the conclusion that it had been written against Dissenters generally. Filled with this idea, they purchased and gave away two hundred at the church doors. Well might Burder exclaim, "Sagacious officers!"

Midsummer, 1803, saw the departure of Mr. Burder from Coventry, where he left behind him a large, affectionate, and sorrowing congregation. He, however, felt that he must move to London, where he was to occupy an onerous threefold position, viz., the pastorate of the church at Fetter Lane, the secretaryship of the London Missionary Society, and the editorship of the "Evangelical Magazine." He took a somewhat prominent part in forming the British and Foreign Bible Society, and on March 7th, 1804, he wrote in his diary, "Nations unborn will have cause to bless God for the meeting this day."

His life was an arduous one, as in addition to his stated duties he also engaged in much deputation work. He lost his good wife on February 28th, 1824, and she was laid in the grave at Bunhill on Saturday, March 6th.

His days now caused him weariness, and he seemed to long for his eternal rest. On June 18th, 1826, he wrote :— " It was fifty years yesterday since I preached my first sermon . . . from Luke iv. 18, and this day I have preached to my people at Fetter Lane on the same text. This is a day of humiliation. O what cause have I to lie in the dust of abasement on account of the sins of my ministry ! Enter not into judgment with Thy servant, O Lord, but graciously accept my very imperfect attempts to serve Thy cause ; accept them through Jesus Christ, through Whom alone I can hope for the acceptance either of my person or of my works. This must also be a day of thanksgiving. Half a century I have been spared to serve the Lord in His sanctuary, whilst multitudes of younger ministers have finished their course. I suppose I may have preached nearly ten thousand sermons in that period ; and blessed be God, some of the seed has been productive. To God be all the glory, for ever and ever. Amen."

Owing to failing strength he was compelled to relinquish much of his work, and it should be noted he had served as Secretary of the London Missionary Society for nearly twenty-four years quite gratuitously.

His eyesight became very weak, and he also suffered much bodily pain. The end was nigh, and the bent of his mind can be ascertained by the hymns he wished sung and helped to sing, and the lines which he quoted. Amongst others were :—

" Guide me, O Thou great Jehovah."

" Sons of God by bless'd adoption."

" A feeble saint shall win the day,
    Though death and hell obstruct the way."

" Yet a season and ye know,
        Happy entrance shall be given,
    All your sorrows left below,
        And earth exchanged for heaven."

The aged minister drew his last breath on May 29th, 1832, after a period of intense suffering and anguish.

There was a mighty concourse of people in Bunhill on Tuesday, June 5th, when the body was placed in the tomb, and it is to be wished that the stone on which the name of George Burder is recorded might soon be renovated, and the inscription made quite legible.

It was computed that at the time of his death a million copies of Village Sermons, Sea Sermons, and Sermons to the Aged had been distributed, which was a great record for those days.

The following beautiful hymn was composed by Mr. George Burder :—

> " Come, ye that know and fear the Lord,
>   And lift your souls above ;
> Let every heart and voice accord,
>   To sing that God is love !
>
> This precious truth His Word declares,
>   And all His mercies prove ;
> Jesus, the Gift of gifts, appears,
>   To show that God is love !
>
> Behold His patience lengthened out
>   To those who from Him rove ;
> And calls effectual reach their hearts,
>   To teach them God is love !
>
> The work begun is carried on
>   By power from heaven above ;
> And every step, from first to last,
>   Proclaims that God is love !
>
> O may we all, while here below,
>   This best of blessings prove ;
> Till warmer hearts in brighter worlds
>   Shall shout that God is love ! "

It should also be remembered that not only did he write other hymns, but was the composer of "Luton," the well-known long metre tune.

THOMAS PALMER.

THE head-stone of Thomas Palmer is near the first path, and almost immediately in front of Anderson. There are seven or eight rows of stones and a north-south path between the two. The foot-stone is somewhat large, and the initials, T. P., with those of others buried in the grave, are quite distinct.

INSCRIPTION.

In memory of Mr. THOMAS PALMER, who died after a few days' illness, January 27th, 1840, aged 44 years.

The father of Thomas Palmer was an attendant and pew-holder at the Old Jewry Street Chapel, and the son was taken to the preaching services from his earliest years. It is not now known when Thomas commenced preaching, but in 1830 he was regularly engaged in the work of the ministry at Richmond and Aldersgate Street Chapels. He married in 1831 Elizabeth, second daughter of John Cooper, of Storey Lane, Southwark. In 1836 he published "Palmer's Selection of Hymns,"  the title page stating that the compiler was minister of Founders' Hall Chapel, London. The book was also used at Jewry Street Chapel, where he must have become minister shortly after that year, and where he remained until his death. This took place in January, 1840, after an illness of only four days, which was caused by concussion of the brain following an accident in the street. He left a widow and three children, but his church and congregation kindly collected the sum of £100 to place his only son, Thomas, in the London Clapton Orphan Asylum.

WILLIAM NICOL, D.D.

THE head-stone of Nicol is a very tall one, and to reach it another north-south path must be crossed. A seat is now touching the back of the stone.

The Rev. WILLIAM NICOL, D.D., for nearly twenty-five years minister of the Scots Church in Swallow Street, highly esteemed for his exemplary piety and the faithful discharge of all his ministerial duties, died Feb. 9th, 1821, in the 60th year of his age.

Dr. W. Nicol was born at Roberton, in Lanarkshire, in the year 1761. His parents were godly people, his father being one of the elders of the parish. When he had completed his education he was called to the ministry, and was appointed assistant to Mr. Gillies, at Paisley. Afterwards he acted in the same capacity in the Middle Church, Greenock; but it was at Glasgow where he first came into prominence. Here he was assistant to the aged but famous Dr. Gillies, and the two became very united to each other. Nicol stayed with Gillies until the death of the latter, and then removed to London, where he became co-pastor and ultimately pastor of the Scots Church, Swallow Street. He remained here until his death some twenty-five years later, and during this long period he led a very zealous and useful life. As his end approached he was completely resigned, and continually spoke in such a way as to prove that his mind was at peace.

THOMAS POWELL, Bapt.

THIS head-stone is four rows east from Nicol's, but nearer the middle path.

INSCRIPTION.

Mr. THOMAS POWELL, a faithful minister of Jesus Christ for upwards of fifty-four years; and pastor of the Baptist Church in Mitchell Street upwards of forty-five years. Having fought a good fight, finished his course, and kept the faith, he entered into the joy of his Lord the 18th of November, 1829, in his 80th year.

THOMAS TUTT.

THIS grave is in the same row as Powell's, but two nearer the middle path.

INSCRIPTION.

(A portion of this may be deciphered.)

Sacred to the memory of Mr. THOMAS TUTT, late of Royal Exchange. He had been taught, by the agency of the Holy Spirit, his ruined state as a sinner; his insufficiency as a creature; and the glorious all-sufficiency of the great Redeemer, in His Person, sacrifice, and righteousness. While in health he had the enjoyment of these things, which a gracious God continued unto him in the various stages of languor and disease, until "mortality was swallowed up in life." He departed November 23rd, 1801, aged 49. Resurgam.

JOHN FORD, M.D.

THIS tomb is three rows east from Tutt's grave, but slightly nearer the railings.

INSCRIPTION.
(This is completely obliterated.)

Sacred to the memory of Rev. JOHN FORD, M.D., many years eminent in his profession in the City of London, and a zealous follower of our Lord Jesus Christ. He afterwards became a preacher of the glad tidings of salvation in the extensive connection of the late Countess of Huntingdon till October, 1804; when the principal management of that important trust devolved upon him, which he fulfilled with great zeal and faithfulness; and on the 26th May, 1806, in the 67th year of his age, suddenly fell asleep in Jesus.

> " Firm as the earth Thy gospel stands,
> My God, my hope, my trust;
> Since I am found in Jesu's hands,
> My soul can ne'er be lost."

WILLIAM ALDRIDGE.

THIS tomb is in the next row east from Ford's, but about two rows south. The inscriptions are cut right along the side of the tomb in a somewhat unusual manner.

INSCRIPTION.
Rev. WILLIAM ALDRIDGE, Ob. 28th February, 1797, æt. 60.

Warminster, Wilts, was the birth-place of William Aldridge. After he was called to the ministry he preached at Margate, Dover, and many other places, but settled in 1776 as pastor over the church meeting in

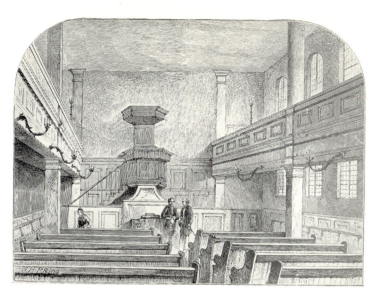

THE MORAVIAN CHAPEL, FETTER LANE.
(See Burder and Hart's accounts.)

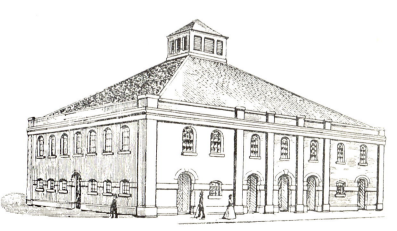

WHITEFIELD'S TABERNACLE. (See page 134.)

WILLIAM ALDRIDGE.   (See page 144.)

THE SUNKEN TOMB AT THE SOUTH-WEST CORNER.
This originally stood on the same level with the other Tombs.

TOMB OF JOHN FORD, M.D.

L

Jewry Street, London. Here he remained until his death, a period of 21 years. During his early ministerial days he was in the Countess of Huntingdon's connection, for he was educated at the Trevecca College. He published a volume of hymns, which passed through several editions, and he was a very popular minister. Anthony Crole preached one of his funeral sermons.

MRS. SUSANNA WESLEY.

THE old head-stone of Mrs. Wesley is now in the Museum at the house opposite the main entrance gates. The grave is in all probability under the path, and the present head-stone stands by the side of it. To reach this from the tomb of Aldridge it is needful to move four or five rows eastward. A tree is now growing at the back of the stone.

INSCRIPTION.

Here lies the body of Mrs. SUSANNA WESLEY, widow of the Rev. Samuel Wesley, M.A., late Rector of Epworth in Lincolnshire, who died July 23rd, 1742, aged 73 years. She was the youngest daughter of the Rev. Samuel Annesley, D.D., ejected by the Act of Uniformity from the Rectory of St. Giles, Cripplegate, Aug. 24th, 1662. She was the mother of nineteen children, of whom the

most eminent were the Revs. John and Charles Wesley,
the former of whom was under God the founder of the
Societies of the people called Methodists.

> In sure and certain hope to rise
> And claim her mansion in the skies,
> A Christian here her flesh laid down,
> Tho cross exchanging for a crown.

Mrs. Susanna Wesley, the youngest daughter of Dr.
Samuel Annesley, was born some seven years after her
father had been ejected from the Church of St. Giles,
Cripplegate. When she was quite young she carefully
examined the great controversy between Dissenters and
the Church of England, and decided that for the future
her place would be in the latter body. Afterwards she
was led to examine more carefully her own personal
experience, and in a letter to her son, Samuel Wesley,
dated October 7th, 1709, she states :—

"There is nothing I now desire to live for, but to do some
small service to my children ; that, as I have brought them
into the world, I may, if it please God, be an instrument of
doing good to their souls. I had been several years collecting
from my little reading, but chiefly from my own observation
and experience, some things which I hoped might be useful to
you all. I had begun to correct and form all into a little
manual ; wherein I designed you should have seen what were
the particular reasons which prevailed on me to believe the
being of a God, and the grounds of natural religion, together
with the motives that induced me to embrace the faith of
Jesus Christ ; under which was comprehended my own private
reasons for the truth of revealed religion. And because I was
educated among the Dissenters, and there was something
remarkable in my leaving them at so early an age, not being
full thirteen, I had drawn up an account of the whole transaction, under which I had included the main of the controversy
between them and the Established Church, as far as it had
come to my knowledge ; and then followed the reasons which
had determined my judgment to the preference of the Church
of England."

This account had been, however, consumed by the fire
which destroyed Epworth Rectory, and from which John
Wesley as a child was rescued.

Previously to this she had made a resolution to spend at

least one hour each morning and evening in private prayer and meditation, and this vow she scrupulously carried out except when sickness or some absolutely necessary business prevented. It was her custom to write her thoughts at such seasons, and some of these are interesting and characteristic.

" Noon.—To know God only as a philosopher; to have the most sublime and curious speculations concerning His essence, attributes, and providence; to be able to demonstrate His Being from all or any of the works of nature, and to discourse with the greatest propriety and eloquence of His existence and operations; will avail us nothing, unless at the same time we know Him experimentally; unless the heart know Him to be its Supreme Good; its only happiness; unless a man feel and acknowledge that he can find no repose, no peace, no joy, but in loving and being beloved by Him, and does accordingly rest in Him as the Centre of his being, the Fountain of his pleasures, the Origin of all virtue and goodness, his Light, his Life, his Strength, his All; in a word, his Lord, his God. Thus let me ever know Thee, O God!"

" Evening.—The mind of man is naturally so corrupted, and all the powers thereof so weakened, that we cannot possibly aspire vigorously towards God, or have any clear perception of spiritual things, without His assistance. Nothing less than the same Almighty power that raised Jesus Christ from the dead can raise our souls from the death of sin to a life of holiness. To know God experimentally is altogether supernatural, and what we can never attain to but by the merits and intercession of Jesus Christ. By virtue of what He has done and suffered, and is now doing in heaven for us, we obtain the Holy Spirit, who is the best Instructor, the most powerful Teacher we can possibly have; without whose agency all other means of grace would be ineffectual. How evidently does the Holy Spirit concur with the means of grace!"

Her life was a very busy one, and she was noted for her good method and arrangement both in her home matters and in her studies. Of her nineteen children ten at least grew up, and were educated, this duty falling on her, as it was practically impossible for the children to have a better instructor than their mother. Although she made no great pretensions to the knowledge of .the Latin and Greek languages, she had acquired some proficiency in these; and she had also studied the human mind, so that she knew how to adapt her words to those who were listening.

As her husband usually attended the sittings of Convocation he was often away from home, and this seriously inconvenienced his wife in financial matters. She, however, faced every trial with a brave spirit, usually acting after mature deliberation and upon real principle.

Her husband's curate, Mr. Inman, was one who simply preached morality, and ignored the fundamentals of the Gospel. On Mr. Wesley's return from London his wife pointed this out, and Mr. Inman was asked by his vicar to preach the next Lord's day. Mr. Wesley remarked, "You could, I suppose, preach a sermon upon any text that I should give you?" The reply was, "By all means, Sir." "Then," said Mr. Wesley, "Preach a sermon on that text, 'Without faith it is impossible to please Him, i.e., God'" (Heb. xi. 6). On the appointed day Inman entered the pulpit and read his text with great solemnity. His opening remarks were, "It must be confessed, friends, that faith is a most excellent virtue; and it produces other virtues also. In particular, it makes a man pay his debts as soon as he can." And thus he went on for about a quarter of an hour, and then concluded. It was quite clear from this experience that Mr. Inman was utterly unfitted to preach the eternal verities of the Gospel, and his services were speedily dispensed with.

In 1735 Mrs. Wesley lost her husband, and then for about four years she divided her time between her children, after which she resided chiefly in London. Just prior to this she was very much concerned with respect to the teaching which her sons John and Charles were giving, and on October 19th, 1738, she wrote to the latter the following letter :—

"It is with much pleasure I find your mind is somewhat easier than formerly, and I heartily thank God for it. 'The spirit of a man may sustain his infirmity, but a wounded spirit who can bear?' If this hath been your case it has been sad indeed. But blessed be God who gave you convictions of the evil of sin as contrary to the purity of the Divine nature, and the perfect goodness of His law! Blessed be God who showed you the necessity you were in of a Saviour to deliver you from the power of sin and Satan (for Christ will be no Saviour to such as see not their need of one), and directed you by faith to lay hold of that stupendous mercy offered us by redeeming love! Jesus is the only Physician of souls ; His blood the only salve which can heal a wounded conscience. It is not in wealth, or honour, or sensual pleasures, to relieve a spirit heavy-laden and weary of the burden of sin. These things have power to increase our guilt by alienating our hearts from God ; but none to make our peace with Him, to reconcile God to man, and man to God,

and to renew the union between the Divine and human nature. No! there is none but Christ, none but Christ, who is sufficient for these things. But, blessed be God, He is an all-sufficient Saviour! And blessed be His holy Name, that thou hast found Him a Saviour to thee, my son. Oh! let us love Him much, for we have much to be forgiven.

"I would gladly know what your notion is of justifying faith, because you speak of it as a thing you have but lately obtained."

She naturally looked upon their movements with motherly pride, although she could not endorse all the teaching and plans of Mr. John Wesley. The latter gives in his diary an account of her death and funeral.

" Friday, July 30th, about three in the afternoon, I went to my mother, and found her change was near. I sat down on the bedside. She was in her last conflict, unable to speak, but, I believe, quite sensible. Her look was calm and serene, and her eyes fixed upward, while we commended her soul to God. From three to four the silver cord was loosening, and the wheel breaking at the cistern; and then, without any struggle, or sigh, or groan, the soul was set at liberty. We stood round the bed, and fulfilled her last request, uttered a little before she lost her speech, 'Children, as soon as I am released, sing a psalm of praise to God.'

"Sunday, August 1st. Almost an innumerable company of people being gathered together, about five in the afternoon, I committed to the earth the body of my mother, to sleep with her fathers. The portion of Scripture from which I afterwards spoke was, 'I saw a great white throne and Him that sat on it; from whose face the earth and the heaven fled away, and there was found no place for them. And I saw the dead, small and great, stand before God, and the books were opened: And the dead were judged out of those things which were written in the books, according to their works.' It was one of the most solemn assemblies I ever saw, or expect to see on this side eternity.

"We set up a plain stone at the head of her grave, inscribed with the following words :—

"Here lies the body of Mrs. Susanna Wesley, the youngest and last surviving daughter of Dr. Samuel Annesley."

JOHN PENNYMAN.

From the grave of Mrs. Wesley the next north-south path must be crossed. The decaying head-stone of John Pennyman is near the middle railings and in the third east-west row from them.

> Here Lyeth the Body of John Pennyman, who was requir'd (by Abraham's God) to offer up (as Abraham did) an unusual Sacrifice at the Royal Exchange in London, upon the 28th day of July, 1670. An Account of which he then caused to be Printed, and hath ordered it to be Reprinted in the Book of his Life. And for a perpetual Memorial of which, he ordered this Inscription to be set in this place. He departed this Life the 2nd Day of July, 1706, in the 78th Year of his Age.

The author regrets that he has been unable to discover what the " unusual sacrifice " was.

CHARLES BUCK.

THIS head-stone is second from the the railings, and four rows east of Pennyman's.

INSCRIPTION.

Sacred to the memory of the Rev. CHARLES BUCK, who departed this life August 11th, 1815, in the 44th year of his age. If an enlarged knowledge of the doctrines of grace, accompanied with unaffected humility of mind; if a tender conscience for sinners at large, and an unremitting attention to his own flock; if a steady attachment to his own principles of religion, and a liberality of sentiment towards other Christians; if an assiduous application of popular talents, and the publication of many useful volumes, be characteristic of an eminent Christian and a faithful minister of Christ—he was one.

SAMUEL STOCKELL.

IN the last row of this section, facing westward, is the head-stone of Samuel Stockell. It is the fifth from Bunyan's tomb.

INSCRIPTION.

Here lies the body of that faithful minister and servant of Jesus Christ, Mr. SAMUEL STOCKELL, pastor of a church near Cripplegate, London, who departed this life May 3rd, 1750, in the 49th year of his age.

REV CHARLES BUCK.

HERE
LYETH THE BODY OF
JOHN PENNYMAN,

IN THE 78TH YEAR OF HIS AGE.

MR SAMUEL STOCKELL
PASTOR OF A CHURCH NEAR
CRIPPLEGATE LONDON.

IN MEMORY OF
THOMAS BLAND

MARY BLAND.

THIS head-stone is adjoining the first path, and is almost opposite the tomb of Henry Cromwell.

INSCRIPTION.

In memory of THOMAS BLAND, son of Thomas and Mary Bland, who departed this life June 18th, 1767, aged 10 months.

Also of Mrs. MARY BLAND, late wife of Mr. Thomas Bland, of the parish of St. Gabriel, Fenchurch, who departed this life on the 15th day of Dec., 1767, in the 26th year of her age.

> Here rests a woman, good without pretence,
> Blest with plain reason, and with sober sense.
> So unaffected, so compos'd a mind ;
> So firm, yet soft ; so strong, yet so resign'd.
> Heaven as its purest gold by tortures try'd,
> The saint sustained it, but the woman dy'd.

This completes the accounts of the most important persons in the southern section of the grounds. The visitor must now cross the middle path and pass through the gateway on the north side.

JOSEPH CARTWRIGHT,

ON the left-hand is a row of head-stones with shrubs growing in front, and the grave of Joseph Cartwright is the seventh from the railings.

In memory of the Rev. JOSEPH CARTWRIGHT, late of Lant Street Chapel, Southwark, died November 5th, 1800, aged 52 years.

What if death my sleep invade,
Should I be of death afraid ?
What if the beams of opening day
Shine around my breathless clay ?
Tender friends awhile may mourn
Me from their embraces torn :
Dearer better friends I have
In the realms beyond the grave.
See the golden gates display'd,
See the crown to grace my head !

ELIZA CROW.

ELIZA CROW'S head-stone is two rows west but directly behind the last one of Cartwright's row.

INSCRIPTION.

ELIZA CROW, wife of Mr. Robert Crow, who died Dec. 23rd, 1757, in the 47th year of her age. Behold the silent grave it doth embrace a loving mother, a most virtuous wife.

Sarah's obedience, Lydia's open heart,
Martha's care, but Mary's better part.

DANIEL DE FOE.

THE splendid statue on which is inscribed the following will easily attract the attention.

INSCRIPTION.

DANIEL DE FOE ; born 1661, died 1731, author of *Robinson Crusoe.*

This monument is the result of an appeal, in the *Christian World* newspaper, to the boys and girls of England for funds to place a suitable memorial upon the grave of Daniel De Foe. It represents the united contributions of seventeen hundred persons. September, 1870.

DANIEL DE FOE was born in the year 1661 in the parish of Cripplegate, London. His father's name was James Foe, and the " De " was assumed by Daniel when he was a man, though it is not clear why he made this addition to his name. James Foe was in business as a butcher, and being a Dissenter, was a member of Dr. Annesley's congregation after the latter had been ejected from the living of St. Giles, Cripplegate.

At the age of fourteen Daniel was sent to a Dissenting Academy at Newington Green, where under the tuition of Charles Morton, he received a good and comprehensive education, especially a thorough training in the use of his mother tongue. He appears to have remained at the Academy until about 1680, and it must be noted that here he had as school fellows, Samuel Wesley, the future father of John and Charles Wesley, and Timothy Crusoe, who later became the famous Presbyterian minister, and whose name was used by De Foe for his island hero. From the scanty evidence obtainable there is every reason to believe that he anticipated becoming a minister, and being in great fear lest Popery should get the upper hand once more and all the printed Bibles should be burned, he copied out the whole of the Pentateuch. Although De Foe remained a Dissenter until the end of his days, he never became a preacher, and there is little doubt that he felt his own ignorance of spiritual religion, and thus his inability for such a sacred position. In those days it was very difficult to become a preacher, as before a man was accepted he had to give very full evidence of his call to the work, and answer questions as to his own personal call by grace.

In 1682 he began his public literary work, and from this time his trenchant pen offended his enemies and wounded his friends, but he was utterly careless of the abuse, misunderstanding and danger to which he exposed himself. He took part in 1685 in the ill-fated Monmouth rebellion, for on all points he was bitterly opposed to James II. It is not certain whether he was present at Sedgemoor, but whatever part he took, by escaping to Portugal he did not suffer the terrible consequences that were the lot of so many. He ventured to return when James was trying to win over to his side the Protestant Dissenters, but De Foe was much clearer-sighted than many of his friends, as he thoroughly understood the duplicity and motives of the false King. When the invasion of the Prince of Orange was imminent, James II. endeavoured to induce the Dissenters by false promises to unite with the Papists in opposition to the Established Church of England. De Foe refers to this in his pamphlet, "An Appeal to Honour and Justice," and a quotation will set forth his principles in a clear light :—

"The first time I had misfortune to differ with my friends was about the year 1683, when the Turks were besieging Vienna, and the Whigs in England, generally speaking, were for the Turks taking it, which I, having read the history of the cruelty and perfidious dealings of the Turks in their wars, and how they had rooted out the name of the Christian religion in about three-score and ten kingdoms, could by no means agree with. And though then but a young man, and a younger author, I opposed it and wrote against it, which was taken very unkindly indeed. The next time I differed with my friends was when King James was wheedling the Dissenters to take off the penal laws and test, which I could by no means come into. And as in the first I used to say, 'I had rather the popish House of Austria should ruin the Protestant in Hungary than the infidel house of Ottoman should ruin both Protestants and Papists by overrunning Germany : so in the other, I told the Dissenters I had rather the Church of England should pull our clothes off by fines and forfeitures than the Papist should fall both upon the Church and the Dissenters, and put our skins off by fire and faggot."

Afterwards when William III. and Mary came to the city they were escorted by " A royal regiment of volunteer horses made up of the chief citizens, who being gallantly mounted and royally accoutred, were led by the Earl of Monmouth, now Earl of Peterborough." Among these troopers, who were for the most part Dissenters, was Daniel De Foe, who was now a hosier in Freeman's Yard, Cornhill.

De Foe was not very successful as a business man, and finally he became insolvent. He, however, acted with much honour, for in the period of thirteen years he says that " with the numerous family, and no helps but his own industry, he had forced his way with undiscouraged diligence through a sea of misfortunes, and reduced his debts, exclusive of composition, from £17,000 to less than £5,000."

He was mixed up in most of the controversies of the day, being particularly severe upon those Dissenters who " in order to obtain Municipal or Government positions occasionally conform to the Church of England." He was always an eager defendant of William III., and commented very severely upon those who spoke of the King as a foreigner. His satire, " The true-born Englishman," which proved that the race was the most mixed upon earth, met with much success, and helped to win a great measure of popularity for William.

In this pamphlet there occur the following well-known and oft-repeated lines :—

> " Wherever God erects a house of prayer,
>   The devil always builds a chapel there ;
>   And 'twill be found upon examination,
>   The latter has the largest congregation."

In May, 1701, there was very great excitement in London as well as in the provinces over the shameful state of public business. The freeholders of Kent presented a petition to the House of Commons, which was couched in strong and forcible language. The members

of the county were afraid to present this, unless they
were backed by a powerful deputation of the principal
memorialists. The plain speaking offended the House,
and it was at once voted to be scandalous, insolent and
seditious, the accompanying deputation being committed
to custody at the Gate House. The excitement grew
when a few days later as the Speaker was entering the
House of Commons, a packet was placed in his hands
which was found to contain a memorial, stating that he
was "commanded by 200,000 Englishmen to deliver to
the House of Commons, and to inform them that it is not
banter, but serious truth, and a serious regard to it is
expected." Although De Foe never owned to the author-
ship, there can be no doubt that the keen, skilful sarcasm,
the clearness, boldness and straightforwardness of the statements, with the air of reality and sincerity that pervaded
the whole, declared him to be the author. Great fear fell
upon the members of the House, some actually fleeing
to their country residences, whilst one member who had
been named in the memorial declared that he stood
in danger of being assassinated. The fear, however,
gradually subsided when it was found that there were not
200,000 Englishmen ready to march upon the Parliament
House, and the flame was allowed to flicker quietly out.

When William died De Foe lost a friend, and he
soon experienced many dangers and penalties. Queen
Anne commenced her reign determined to maintain and
enforce her church principles, and to penalise all Dissenters as much as possible. The "High Church" party
therefore put forward the most extravagant claims, and endeavoured to maintain the most ridiculous and intolerable
principles. In reply, De Foe wrote his celebrated
pamphlet on "The Shortest Way with the Dissenters,"
in which he assumed the character of one of the highest
of High Churchmen, and pretended that he could prove
the shortest and only effectual way to ensure peace. He
declared that the only way to "save many millions of
future souls" was to exterminate the Dissenters, whom
he called the "present race of poisoned spirits." He also
stated :—

"'Tis vain to trifle in this matter; the light, foolish handling of them by mulcts, fines, &c., is their glory and their advantage. If the gallows instead of the counter, and the galleys instead of the fines, were the reward of going to a conventicle to preach or hear, there would not be so many sufferers; the spirit of martyrdom is over; they that will go to church to be chosen sheriffs and mayors would go to forty churches rather than be hanged. If one severe law were made and punctually executed, that whoever should be found at a conventicle should be banished from the nation and the preacher hanged, we should see the end of the tale; they would all come to church, and one age would make us one again. . . . ."

"Moses was a merciful, meek man, and yet with what fury did he run through the camp and cut the throats of three and thirty thousand of his dear Israelites that were fallen into idolatry; and what was the reason? 'Twas mercy to the rest to make these examples, to prevent the destruction of the whole army."

It is remarkable that both parties missed the satire of the whole thing, and it was taken in deadly earnest. The High Churchmen were delighted, the Dissenters dismayed, and all moderate men were overcome with grief and abhorrence. When the truth became known, poor De Foe was in terrible trouble, and he thought it necessary to conceal himself. He published an explanation, but this had no effect, for the violence of his enemies did not slacken in the least. The House of Commons with due gravity resolved that this book, "being full of false and scandalous reflections upon this Parliament, and tending to promote sedition, be burned by the hands of the common hangman in New Palace Yard." A proclamation was issued, offering a reward for the arrest of De Foe. Although this description is not flattering to the celebrated author, it gives some idea of his personal appearance.

"St. James's, Jan. 10th., 1702-3.

"Whereas Daniel De Foe, alias De Fooe, is charged with writing a scandalous and seditious pamphlet, entitled, 'The Shortest Way with the Dissenters;' he is a middle-sized spare man, about forty (forty-two) years old, of a brown complexion, and dark-brown coloured hair, but wears a wig, a hooked nose, a sharp chin, grey eyes, and a large mole near his mouth; was born in London, and for many years was a hose-factor in

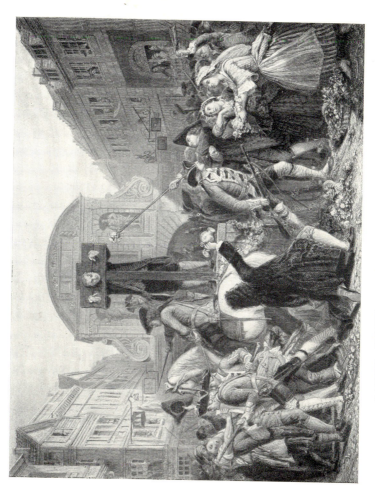

DANIEL DEFOE IN THE PILLORY. (See page 161.)

DANIEL DEFOE.

Freeman's Yard, in Cornhill, and now is owner of the brick and pantile work near Tilbury Fort, in Essex: whoever shall discover the said Daniel De Foe to one of her majesty's principal Secretaries of State, or any of her Majesty's Justices of the Peace, shall have a reward of fifty pounds, which her Majesty has ordered immediately to be paid upon such discovery."

De Foe was captured and tried for libel. The prosecuting Attorney-General treated him with great brutality; his own counsel very poorly defended him, and the result of the trial was that he was found guilty and sentenced to pay a fine of 200 marks to the Queen, to stand three times in the pillory, be imprisoned during the Queen's pleasure, and find sureties for his good behaviour for seven years. He was duly set in the pillory, but this was really a triumph for him, as the crowd looked on with pity, and when he was taken down expressed their sympathy "with loud shouts and acclamations." The feeling was so intense that his persecutors dared not repeat the exhibition. De Foe was no sooner back in his prison than he commenced writing again, and was most merciless in dealing with his opponents. The disgraceful sentence was persevered in until "the high flung party" was driven from office in April, 1704, and Harley, who was now Secretary of State, immediately entered into negotiations with the imprisoned author. De Foe gives a very curious account of the affair in the following words :—

" While I lay friendless and distressed in the prison of Newgate, my family ruined, and myself without hope of deliverance, a message was brought me from a person of honour, who, till that time, I had never had the least acquaintance with, or knowledge of. . . . The message was by word of mouth thus :—' Pray ask that gentleman what I can do for him.' But in return to this kind and generous message, I immediately took up my pen and ink, and wrote the story of the blind man in the Gospel, to whom our Blessed Lord put the question, ' What wilt thou that I should do unto thee ? ' Who, as if he had made it strange that such a question should be asked, or as if that he had said, ' I am blind, and yet they ask me what Thou shalt do for me! My answer is plain in my misery : " Lord, that I may receive my sight." ' "

M

It was, however, four months before De Foe was released, as the Queen declared that " she had left all that matter to a certain person, and did not think he would have used him in that manner." She afterwards gave clear proof of her sincerity, for De Foe writes, she " was pleased particularly to enquire into my circumstances and family, and by my Lord Treasurer Godolphin to send a considerable supply to my wife and family, and to send to me the prison money to pay my fine and the expenses of my discharge." These words were not written until Harley was in disgrace and the Queen dead, so that De Foe could not have been trying to curry favour from those in high places.

He was now employed by the Government in some secret service, but although his pen was not much used, he was still attacked very severely by other writers. Later on, when there was real danger of an invasion by the Pretender, De Foe warned the people what the result would be if they admitted " The French Pensioner." He was once again thrown into prison, but was soon released, as Queen Anne was pleased to issue a patent of pardon. On the death of Anne he was really left without a friend at Court, and was thus exposed to the full malice of his enemies, who wrought him grievous harm. He, however, recovered from a violent fit of apoplexy, and discarding politics wrote several books, including his masterpiece, " Robinson Crusoe." For some time he could not find anyone to publish this, but was at last successful.

The remainder of his life was fully occupied in producing several works, and in combating his enemies. The story of his last days, judging by a letter which he wrote in August, 1730, is a very sad and melancholy one. In this letter, De Foe, who was then at Greenwich, apparently in concealment, said he was " sinking under the weight of an affliction too heavy for my strength, and looking on myself as abandoned of every comfort, every friend, and every relation excepting such only as are able to give me no relief." He also said that he was " weak, having had some fits of a fever that have left me low. But these things much more. I have not seen son or daughter, wife or child, many weeks, and know not which way to see them. They dare not come by water, and my land here has no coach, and I know not what to do." He makes a reference to a son who evidently had been a great trouble.

"I depended upon him, I trusted him, I gave up my two dear unprovided children into his hands ; but he had no compassion, and suffered them and their poor dying mother to beg their bread at his door, and to crave as if it were an alms, what he was bound under hand and seal, beside the most sacred promises, to supply them with ; himself at the same time living in a profusion of plenty. . . . I would say, I hope, with comfort, that it is yet well—I am so near my journey's end, and am hastening to the place where the weary are at rest and the wicked cease to trouble; but that the passage is rough and the day stormy; but what way soever He pleases to bring me to the end of it, I desire to finish life with this temper of soul in all cases. *Te Deum laudamus.*"

He died on 24th April, 1731, in the same parish, and it may have been in the same house, in which he was born. Two days afterwards his body was placed in the tomb in Bunhill Fields, and the entry of his interment in the register is as follows :—"1731, April 26, Mr. Dubow, Cripplegate."

Almost facing De Foe's tomb, and also the head-stone of Eliza Crow, is a garden seat ; JONATHAN FRANKLIN, who was so long the minister at Redcross Street, is buried beneath this. His funeral was attended by Mr. John Kershaw, who gives an account of it on page 212 of C. J. Farncombe & Sons,' Ltd., edition of his Autobiography.

SAMUEL ROSEWELL, M.A.

THE tomb of Samuel Rosewell is in the same row as De Foe's, but five nearer the railings. The inscription is on the top flat stone, and was renewed in 1867 by Geo. H. Cirle, of Edinburgh.

ORIGINAL INSCRIPTION.

In memory of SAMUEL ROSEWELL, minister of the Gospel in this City, whose zeal and labour for God, whose charity and love for men, whose courage and patience under long and acute pain, and whose joyful hope and triumph in death, gave the world a glorious example of Christianity. He died April, 1722, aged 42 years.

Samuel Rosewell was the eldest son of Thomas Rosewell,* and was born when his father was pastor at Rotherhithe in 1679. He was quite a child when his father was tried for treason, and was only twelve years of age when he died. Mr. Rosewell went to Scotland to complete his education, and was called to engage in the public work of the ministry when quite young. The celebrated Puritan, John Howe, honoured him with an invitation to preach to his own congregation in Silver Street, and Mr. Rosewell then became Howe's assistant. He continued in this capacity at the same church with the successor of Howe, Mr. John Spademan. He was also a lecturer on Sunday evenings in conjunction with Dr. Grosvenor.

His health being very indifferent, Mr. Rosewell went to live in Mare Street, Hackney, and it was evident that his mortal life would soon be ended. The last time he administered the Lord's Supper he displayed much bodily weakness, and many of his people, as well as himself, were moved to tears. The words with which he opened the service were as follows :—

"My friends, we are met here once again to see Jesus ; to see Him set forth as crucified before our eyes ; Him who loved us, and gave Himself for us, that He might wash us from our sins in His blood."

Dr. Isaac Watts, being one of his close personal friends, visited him, and gave an account of the solemn scene, and of the words which Rosewell spoke, in the following descriptive manner :—

"Come, my friends, come into the chamber of a dying Christian ; come, approach his pillow and hear his holy language. 'I am going to heaven, and I long to be gone, to be where my Saviour is. Why are His chariot wheels so long

* See page 30.

a-coming ? ' Then, with both arms stretched up to heaven, he exclaimed, ' I desire to be with God. I hope I am a sincere Christian. But I am the meanest and the most unworthy. I know I am a great sinner ; but did not Christ come to save the chief of sinners ? I have trusted in Him, and I have strong consolation. I have been looking into my own heart, and have inquired what are my evidences for heaven. Has not the Scripture said, " He that believeth shall not perish, but have everlasting life " ? (John iii. 16). Now, according to the best knowledge I have of what faith is, I do believe in Christ, and I shall have life everlasting. Does not the Scripture say, " He that hungereth and thirsteth after righteousness shall be satisfied " ? (Matt. v. 6). Surely I hunger and thirst after that ; I desire to be holy ; I long to be conformable to God ; and to be made more like Him ; shall I

not then be satisfied ? I love God. I love Christ ; I desire to love Him, to be more like Him ; to serve Him in heaven without sin. I have faith. I have love. I have repentance ; yet I boast not, for I have nothing of myself ; I speak it to the honour of the grace of God. It is all of grace ! All are nothing without Christ ; it is He makes all acceptable to the Father ; and I trust in Him. My friends, I have built on this only Foundation, Jesus Christ ; this is my hope. Is it not your hope also ? I thank you for all your offices of love ; you have prayed with me, you have refreshed me ; I love and honour you now ; but I shall meet you in heaven. I go to my God, and your God ; to my Saviour, and your Saviour.' "

Dr. Watts also wrote to Mr. Rosewell on the day that he died, and although he was living when the letter reached him, he was unable to read it. It was in the following words :—

"Dear Brother Rosewell,—Your divine conversation two days ago so sweetly overpowered my spirits, and the most affectionate expressions that you so plentifully bestowed on me awakened in me so many pleasing sensations, that I seemed to be a borderer on the heavenly world, when I saw you on the confines of heaven, and conversed with you there. I can hardly ask for your stay on earth, nor wish your services in the sanctuary, after you have been so much within view of the glorious invisibles which the Gospel reveals to us. Our anchor enters within the vail, where Jesus our Forerunner is gone to take our place, Heb. vi. May your pains decrease as your divine joys overpower them! May you never lose sight of the blessed world of glory, and of Jesus the Lord of it, till the storm is passed, and you are safely arrived there. May the same grace prepare me for the same mansions.

" Your affectionate Friend and Brother,

" ISAAC WATTS."

The bodily pains of Rosewell were very severe, but he neither murmured nor repined ; and before he died he enjoyed remarkable peace and confidence. He drew his last breath on April 7th, 1722, in the 42nd year of his age.

JOHN BRINE.

THREE rows west from the tomb of Samuel Rosewell is the head-stone of John Brine. The inscription can be read, but time is working its havoc, and unless attention is paid to it there must in due course be obliteration.

INSCRIPTION.

Here are interred the remains of the Rev. JOHN BRINE, who departed this life, February 21st, 1765, in the 63rd year of his age. His ministerial abilities were very extraordinary, and his zeal and faithfulness in asserting and defending the great truths of religion, equally conspicuous. Not long before his decease he expressed his sentiments in the following words : "I think I am of sinners the chief—of saints the least ; I know that I am nothing, but by the grace of God I am what I am."

It is somewhat surprising to find how little is known

of the life of good old John Brine. Some writers have failed even to mention his name, and it would almost appear as if a conspiracy of silence had been entered into with respect to him. Yet he was one of the ablest and most gracious ministers and writers of his day, two of his works, "A Treatise on Various Subjects," and "The Certain Efficacy of the Death of Christ Asserted," being especially valuable.

John Brine was born at Kettering in 1702, and as his parents were poor people he had not the advantage of an early education. He was, however, a very studious boy, and read all the good works that he could. He was called by grace under his very firm friend and fellow-townsman, John Gill, and he was baptised at Kettering by Mr. Wallis. He was sent forth to preach whilst at Kettering, and in due course received a call to the pastorate of the Baptist Church at Coventry. In 1730 he was invited to become the pastor of the Church at Cripplegate, which position he occupied for 35 years. By this time Gill was also in London, and he gladly welcomed his old companion to the world's metropolis. These two were very fast friends, as their views upon doctrine and practice were in perfect accord.

Brine is described by John Wilson, the historian, as being in his person "Short and thick, and he had rather a strange countenance that was not calculated to possess strangers in his favour; but he was a gentleman." He was a man of considerable attainment, and he excelled in his knowledge of the learned languages. He possessed good ministerial abilities; and was very faithful in the discharge of the pastoral offices.

Brine not only preached to his own congregation, but

he also succeeded Gill as the Wednesday evening lecturer in Great Eastcheap, and took regular services at Devonshire Square Chapel. Indeed, he was considered to be one of the leading ministers of the Baptist Denomination in London, and there were few religious controversies in his day that he took no part in. He left strict injunctions that no funeral sermon was to be preached for him, but these were partially disregarded. Dr. Gill preached to his own people from the text, "By the grace of God I am what I am," and some months afterwards he repeated his discourse when preaching to the Church at St. Albans. It was then published. In it Gill remarks with respect to Brine :

" I am debarred from saying so much of him as otherwise I could do, we being born in the same place, and myself some years older than him, and from his being among the first fruits of my ministry. I might take notice of his natural and acquired abilities, his great understanding and clear light, and sound judgment in the doctrines of the gospel, and the great deep things of God ; of his zeal, skill, and courage in vindicating important truths, published by him to the world, by which ' he being dead yet speaketh.' In fine, I might observe to you that his walk and conversation in the world were honourable and ornamental to the profession which he made, and suitable to the character he sustained as a minister of Jesus Christ, all which endeared him to his friends. But I am forbidden to speak any more."

The number of works which Brine published was stated to be forty, and as most of these only passed through one edition, they are very rare indeed.

It should be noted that the next grave on the north of Brine's is that of JOHN REYNOLDS, M.A., and the second on the south is that of another JOHN REYNOLDS. The inscription of the former is,

To the memory of the Rev. JOHN REYNOLDS, M.A., who after having been many years pastor of a Protestant Dissenting Church, near Cripplegate, with hope of a glorious resurrection, slept in Jesus, Feb. 6th, 1792, in the 63rd year of his age.

" An angel's arm can't snatch me from the grave ;
Legions of angels can't confine me there."

That of the latter is,

In memory of the Rev. JOHN REYNOLDS, late of Hoxton Square, and for thirty years pastor of the Independent Church in Camomile Street. He died Dec. 7th, 1803, aged 64 years.

JOHN SKEPP.

THREE rows west from Brine's head-stone, but nearer the second path, is that of John Skepp. The inscription is decipherable, and next to the grave on the north side is a massive tomb.

The year of the birth of John Skepp is somewhat in dispute, but it probably was 1675. In his early days he became a member of the Independent Church at Cambridge, which was then under the care of the celebrated preacher, Joseph Hussey. When Skepp became a Baptist is not known, but in 1715 he was chosen Pastor of the Baptist Church then meeting in Currier's Hall, Cripplegate, London. In addressing this church, Mr. Skepp said, "Your foundation as to gospel order was skilfully laid in the very beginning of troublesome times by the indefatigable patience and care of that eminent servant of and sufferer for Christ, Mr. Hanserd Knollys; and your walls were beautified by labours of that evangelical son of consolation, Mr. Robert Steed. These two were your chief master builders; by whose ministry you were built upon the foundation of the prophets and apostles; Jesus Christ being the chief Corner-stone."

Mr. Skepp was a very diligent student, and acquired a good knowledge of the original languages of the Scriptures. He excelled as a Hebrew scholar, and Dr. Gill when a young man was much helped by him. Indeed, after Mr. Skepp's death, Gill purchased most of his valuable Rabbinical books, and these were very useful to the future author of the famous Commentary. When Dr. Gill was ordained, Mr. Skepp took part in the services; but his whole ministry was comparatively a short one, for he was only at the Cripplegate Church about seven years. There appears to be no record of his last days; but it may be safely concluded that he made "a good end." Dr. Gill thought most highly of him, and declared that he was "a warm and lively brother of the gospel; a zealous defender of the special and peculiar doctrine of it; whose ministry was blessed to many souls."

In this grave was also buried on April 27th, 1849, the wife of JOHN ANDREW JONES, and previously a son-in-law and a grand-child had been interred there. When writing of the death and burial of his wife, Mr. Jones said, "In this grave the dust of 'Andrew' will also shortly be laid till the morning of the glorious Resurrection—'resurgam.'" It should, however, be noted that Mr. Jones died on July 15th, 1868, when eighty-nine years old, some fourteen years after "Bunhill" was closed, and was buried in Abney Park Cemetery, Stoke Newington.

The author of "Bunhill Fields" would here gladly acknowledge his indebtedness to old J. A. Jones. The latter's work, "Bunhill Memorials," has been invaluable in locating stones and tombs, and also in deciphering inscriptions. In collating facts the author has had recourse to the same standard works as Mr. Jones, viz., Wilson's "History and Antiquities of Dissenting Churches," Ivimey's "History of the Baptists," Palmer's "Nonconformist Memorials," and other records; and he is pleased to testify that, in the main, the ancient patriarch's labours were singularly accurate.

His own personal recollections of Matthew Wilks, Rippon, and many other ministers, enabled Mr. Jones to write some interesting accounts, and thus preserve incidents which otherwise might have been lost. As, however, over sixty-five years have passed away since "Bunhill Memorials" was published, many of the inscriptions which were then decipherable are now completely obliterated, and, on the other hand, some have been recut upon the original head-stones, and new monuments also have been placed in the grounds.

What similarity there is in some of the records contained in "Bunhill Memorials" and "Bunhill Fields" may thus be accounted for easily.

REV. JOSEPH HUGHES.

THE visitor to this grave will need no special directions. It stands a little south-west of John Skepp's head-stone.

INSCRIPTION.

Sacred to the memory of the Rev. JOSEPH HUGHES, A.M., for thirty-seven years pastor of the Baptist Church at Battersea; one of the Founders of the Religious Tract Society; the Originator and one of the Founders of the British and Foreign Bible Society; and one of the Secretaries of each of these Societies for more than thirty years from the time of their formation till his death. He died on the 3rd of Oct., 1833, in his 64th year, and all that was mortal of him was interred in this grave.

This memorial is raised by friends who venerated his excellencies, and honour him as one of the Founders of Societies which have sent the blessed Gospel of Christ to millions abroad and at home.

MDCCCLXXIV.

This striking monument stands out nobly, and the inscriptions give quite a history of the man who lies beneath. The words on the original head-stone were:

Rev. JOSEPH HUGHES, M.A., Secretary to the British and Foreign Bible Society, died October 3rd, 1833, aged 64 years.

When he was only sixteen, Joseph Hughes became a member of the Baptist Church in Little Wild Street, London, and he was sent by this church to the ministry. After a short period as assistant minister at Broadmead, Bristol, he returned to London, ultimately becoming the pastor of a newly-formed church at Battersea. He occupied this position for thirty-seven years, and as he attended to the secretaryships at the same time, his life was a very busy one. Not only did the idea of the British and Foreign Bible Society originate with him, but he drew up the first prospectus. During its early years many difficulties, some of which seemed insuperable, were overcome by his wise counsels and strenuous labours. Although he suffered much in body during the last weeks of his life, he waited with peaceful calmness the hour of his departure.

MATTHEW WILKS.

It is now needful to pass again towards the second path, and three graves from this, and adjoining a north-south path, the tomb of Matthew Wilks will be found. The visitor will be interested in the Fauntleroy family tomb, which is almost at the foot of Wilks. Buried in this with several others is William Fauntleroy, who was executed at Newgate for forgery.

The name of Matthew Wilks is writ large on the religious history of London, as between the years 1775 and 1828 he was one of its leading ministers, and in addition was closely connected with Whitefield and other preachers. He was born at Gibraltar on September 21st, 1746, his father being an officer in the army. During his early years he gave marked evidences that he possessed a singularly acute mind, and it was obvious that he would become a man of great intellect and ability. It was at West Bromwich in 1771 that he heard Mr. Percy, the curate of the parish church, and the word was applied to his heart with power. Through Mr. Percy's influence he was persuaded to enter Trevecca College, and it was while he was a student there that a sermon preached by him was commended to one of Mr. White-field's executors. The result was that he received an invitation to preach in London, and ultimately he was appointed a preacher for the Tabernacle Societies. His ministerial labours were crowned with much success. He was connected with the Tottenham Court Road Chapel and the Moorfields Tabernacle for more than fifty-three years; John Hyatt was one of his colleagues, and when Hyatt died Matthew Wilks mourned as much as anyone. He continued his labours down to the last year of his life, as the infirmities of old age came very gradually upon him. A few weeks before his death a very characteristic and instructive conversation took place between himself and a person who was a Unitarian. Mr. Wilks said, " You cannot be a Socinian ! " and the man replied, " We do not like to be called by that name ! " " But it is your name," said Mr. Wilks, " though you say that you are Unitarians and not Socinians. I am a Unitarian. I worship one Lord Jesus Christ, who is God over all, and blessed for ever ! " But the Unitarian remarking, " Well, Sir, I say let every man be fully persuaded in his own mind," the aged minister exclaimed, " Yes ; but let it be on Scriptural grounds and after much examination and prayer. I, Sir, am an old man, and soon to meet God ; and this is my hope,—

> " ' Jesus, Thy blood and righteousness
> My beauty are, my glorious dress ;
> 'Midst flaming worlds, in these arrayed,
> With joy shall I lift up my head ; '

and more,

> " ' Bold shall I stand in that great day,
> For who aught to my charge shall lay ?
> Fully, through Thee, absolved I am
> From sin and fear, from guilt and shame.'

There, now I have done. I never wish to be always attacking people ; but you are very amiable, very kind, and very clever ; yet all this will not do ; and I wish to do you good as you have done me."

Only twenty-seven days before his death Mr. Wilks drew up his will, of which the following words were the final paragraph :—

REV^D MATTHEW WILKS
died Jan 29TH 1829 aged 81 years.

ERECTED BY HIS GRANDSON
MATTHEW WILKS.

"I conclude by expressing my affection for the managers, congregations, and brother ministers of the Tabernacle and Tottenham Court Chapel; and my gratitude to God for their long attachment to me, their unworthy minister and friend. May God preserve them pure in doctrine and practice, and bless us with a happy meeting in glory."

DANIEL NEAL.

FROM the grave of Matthew Wilks the visitor must move along the north-south path, and the tomb of Daniel Neal is on the left hand.

INSCRIPTION (*now undecipherable*).

The Rev. DANIEL NEAL, M.A., Pastor of a congregation of Protestant Dissenters in London 36 years, and author of the histories of New England, and of the Puritans, as well as several smaller tracts ; who in both characters, as an historian and divine, gave such an unquestionable proof of his diligence, moderation, and prudence, as were honourable to himself and exemplary to others. He was born in London, Dec. 14, 1678, and died, April 4, 1743, in the 65th year of his age.

The fame of Daniel Neal as preacher, but more particularly as author, has spread far and wide. He was born in London on the 14th of December, 1678, and his parents dying when he was quite young, an uncle took charge of the orphan boy and gave him a good education at the Merchant Taylors' School. After becoming head scholar Neal spent three years at the Dissenting Academy conducted by Thomas Rowe,* a further two years at the University of Utrecht, and one year at Leyden. He was now remarkably proficient as a scholar, and after his return to London speedily attracted public notice.

THE REV. DANIEL NEAL M.A.

As a minister he was directly connected with only one church, that meeting at Lorimer's Hall. He was here first as assistant, and then as pastor for thirty-six years, and during the latter period the congregation increased so that a larger building was needed, and a fresh sanctuary was found in Jewin Street.

Mr. Neal's greatest work as an author was "The History of the Puritans," and he will long be gratefully remembered by all who love the memory of those noble and much-suffering people. This work was only completed some five years before his death. The end of his days was clouded by a long, painful illness; and he was compelled in November, 1742, to resign his pastoral

* See page 35.

office. He took a journey to Bath, hoping that the famous waters would give him relief, but after several paralytic strokes he died there, his body being removed to Bunhill Fields for interment.

——— —

In the same grave is buried Nathaniel Lardner, D.D., and on the tomb there was the following inscription :—

NATHANIEL LARDNER, D.D., Presb.

The Rev. Nathaniel Lardner, D.D., author of the Credibility of the Gospel History ; Ancient Jewish and Heathen testimonies to the truth of the Christian religion; and several other smaller pieces ; monuments of his learning, judgment, candour, impartiality, beneficence, and true piety.   He was born at Hawkhurst, in the county of Kent, June 6th, 1684, and died on a visit there, July 24, 1768, in the 85th year of his age.   " An Israelite indeed, in whom there is no guile."

Although considered to be a Presbyterian Dr. Lardner was undoubtedly a Socinian. His name is still to be deciphered at the bottom of the west panel of the tomb.

JOHN HYATT.

———

(Inscription as shown in illustration.)

IN the same row as Wilks and Neal and quite close to middle railings is the head-stone of John Hyatt. Almost immediately in front is a railed monument erected to the memory of the Rev. Henry Hunter, D.D.

On January 21st, 1767, John Hyatt was born at Sherborne, Dorsetshire. His education was very poor, and when fourteen he was apprenticed in his native town to a cabinet-maker. As he advanced in years he indulged freely in sin until he became a terrible profligate. Be-

coming acquainted, however, with a godly young woman
he was led to attend a place of worship, and following a
period of intense conviction of sin he was blessed with
forgiveness and a hope in the mercy of God. He now
had to experience bitter persecution, especially from his
own flesh and blood. Reference was made to this by
his biographer as follows :

"His father beholds the astonishing reverse in his spirit
and conduct; but, instead of rejoicing over his reformed son,
he beholds him with hate-
ful and malicious eyes;
and resolves, if it be possible, to deter him from
pursuing his newly adop-
ted course. The father
vehemently expostulates,
the son meekly replies;
the father is greatly
apprehensive of his son's
derangement, the son is
anxiously concerned for
his father's eternal state!
The father promises, then
threatens; he loves his
child, but he hates his
religion. Ah! ignorant
man! little dost thou
think that thou art
daringly meddling with
God! Forbear, then, from
persisting in thy design;
thy son knows that he
ought to obey God rather
than man."

Nothing could daunt John Hyatt, and he maintained
his profession in spite of threats on the one hand and
tempting offers on the other. After his marriage, at the
age of twenty, doors were opened for him to preach, and
he was regularly engaged at various places round Sherborne. He became pastor of a little cause at Mere, in
Wiltshire, where he was "passing rich on £40 a year";
and then preached for about two years in Zion Chapel,
Frome. Whilst there he was invited occasionally to

N

Moorfields Tabernacle, London, where he ultimately became one of its pastors. Between himself and Matthew Wilks there were feelings of the deepest love, and their friendship has been compared to that of Jonathan and David, or Paul and Timothy. Hyatt's labours as a minister were laborious; and towards the close of his life he was greatly afflicted with asthma. His last sermon was preached on January 8th, 1826, from Eph. iv. 13, and when this was concluded, he attended to the ordinance of the Lord's Supper. A few hours before his end he was visited by Matthew Wilks, who asked, "Well, my brother, if you had a hundred souls, could you commit them all to Christ now?" With his remaining strength the dying man exclaimed, "A million!" As recorded in Mr. J. E. Hazelton's "Inasmuch," John Hyatt was closely connected with that most excellent institution, The Aged Pilgrims' Friend Society; in fact, he drew up the second address that was issued by the committee.

THOMAS GIBBONS, D.D.

FROM the grave of Hyatt to that of Gibbons the north-south path must be crossed. It is almost opposite Neal's tomb, but is in the third row from the path.

INSCRIPTION.

Beneath this stone are interred the remains of the Rev. THOMAS GIBBONS, D.D., whose upright mind, benevolent heart, ardent piety, and successful labours in the cause of Christ, as a minister and tutor, are so well known as not to require a glowing imagination, like that he possessed, to delineate; or those warm feelings which distinguished his character as a friend, to add energy to the description. The affectionate tears which have been found on this tomb are the best tribute that can be offered to his memory. He died Feb. 22, 1785, aged 64.

Multis ille bonis flebilis occidit.

The father of Thomas Gibbons was a minister, who was pastor for several years at Olney, Bucks, and afterwards at Royston, in Hertfordshire. Thomas was born in the little village of Reek, near Cambridge, on May 31st, 1720. When he was fifteen he was placed under the tuition of Dr. Taylor at Deptford, and afterwards studied under the "learned John Eames." Having entered upon the work of the ministry he became in 1742 assistant to Mr. Bures in Silver Street, London, but the following year he was appointed successor to Mr. Wright over the Independent Church which met in the Haberdashers' Hall. In 1754 he became one of the tutors at the Dissenting Academy at Mile End, and five years later he succeeded Mr. William Guyse as an evening lecturer at Monkwell Street.

As noticed in the account of William Cromwell,* Gibbons was closely connected with the descendants of the great Protector, and he compiled a genealogical account of the family. His abilities were of a high quality, and as an orator, preacher, and hymn-writer he occupies a prominent position. In addition to his writings on the Cromwell family, he published "Memoirs of Eminent Women," a life of Dr. Watts, and several other works. Some of his hymns particularly display a striking magnificence.

His end was very sudden, for a few minutes after he had (in answer to a question with respect to his health) replied, "Perfectly well, Madam, I bless God," he was found lying on the floor in a fit. The few remaining days he was quite speechless, but he died without a struggle and apparently in peace. His best known and most loved hymn is the following :—

* See page 107.

Forgiveness! 'tis a joyful sound
   To malefactors doomed to die :
Publish the bliss the world around ;
   Ye seraphs, shout it from the sky !

'Tis the rich gift of love divine ;
   'Tis full, outmeasuring every crime :
Unclouded shall its glories shine,
   And feel no change by changing time.

O'er sins unnumbered as the sand,
   And like the mountains for their size,
The seas of sovereign grace expand,
   The seas of sovereign grace arise.

For this stupendous love of heaven
   What grateful honours shall we show ?
Where much transgression is forgiven
   Let love in equal ardour glow.

By this inspired let all our days
   With various holiness be crown'd ;
Let truth and goodness, prayer and praise,
   In all abide, in all abound.

MR. DAN TAYLOR.

THE head-stone of Dan Taylor, which is in a state of
excellent preservation, is several rows west from Thomas
Gibbons'.

(Inscription as shown on head-stone.)

Dan Taylor was born at Sour-Milk-hall, near Halifax,
Yorkshire, on December 21st, 1738. His early life was
a hard one, as before he was five years old he was
working in a coal-mine, and continued as a miner for
many years. His hours were long and his labours
arduous, and he rarely saw the light of day except on
the Sabbath. Having a real and ardent desire for
knowledge he utilised every spare moment in reading, and
when he was old enough to do so, took a book with him

down into the damp dark mine. Although his opportunities were so limited, and his books few, he gained such a reputation for knowledge that people often applied to him for information. When about twenty years old he joined the Methodists, and soon began to preach; but being unable to accept many of Mr. Wesley's doctrines he severed his connection with this people in 1762. Having been convinced that baptism by immersion was Scriptural he applied to several Baptist ministers, but without success. The Particular Baptists could not receive him on account of his Arminian theology, whilst the Socinians treated him very coldly because of his faith in the doctrines of the Trinity. Hearing, however, of a body of General Baptists at Boston, he with a friend set out in the dead of the winter to walk to the Lincolnshire town, a distance of 120 miles. The first night they slept under a hay-rick; but hearing the next day that there was a Baptist cause at Gamston, in Nottinghamshire, went there instead of to Boston. They were received by the minister, and were baptised in the river on Feb. 16th, 1763.

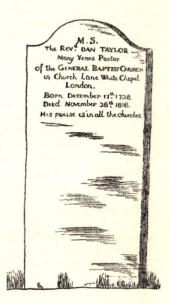

M.S.
The Rev.ᵈ DAN TAYLOR
Many Years Pastor
of the GENERAL BAPTIST CHURCH
in Church Lane White Chapel
London.
BORN December 17ᵗʰ 1738.
DIED November 26ᵗʰ 1816.
HIS PRAISE is in all the churches.

Taylor now entered fully upon the work of the ministry; and after labouring in country places, moved from Halifax to London in 1785. At this period he is described as a man " of extraordinary strength of body; low in stature, but muscular and robust; able to support an unusual degree of corporeal exertion. His mind was active and enterprising; and no difficulties or dangers could move him from the path of duty."

A Baptist academy being opened in January, 1798, Mr. Taylor was appointed president, and occupied this important office for fourteen years. When it is remembered that he worked in a coal-mine from the age of five until he was twenty-four, and that the only teaching he enjoyed was for a short time at Halifax when twenty years old, his industry, perseverance, and ability will be readily understood and appreciated.   His last sermon was preached on November 24th, 1816, from Heb. iv. 9 : "There remaineth therefore a rest for the people of God."   He passed away without a sigh or a groan on the following Tuesday afternoon while sitting in his chair waiting for his tea.   The views of Dan Taylor are well expressed in a letter that he wrote to his friend, Gilbert Boyce :—

" In the last century (the seventeenth) the General Baptists almost universally maintained that the death of Christ for the sins of men was the only foundation of a sinner's hope.   And what was the state of the General Baptist cause then ?   Their churches were numerous, and many of them large ; the zeal and piety of the ministers and people were celebrated, and the pleasure of the Lord prospered in their hands.   Towards the latter end of the century the sentiments of Arius and Socinius were countenanced by some of their leaders.   Others were alarmed at this ; their zeal for the doctrines of the gospel was raised ; they preached and wrote with vigour and earnestness, and in- sisted that Christ atoned for the sins of men, and that none can be saved but through that atonement.   They were cal- umniated and aspersed as defective in charity ; too many of them yielded so far as to trim and temporise, and to treat these fundamental doctrines of the gospel as if they were matters of indifference.   Consequently they were but seldom preached ; and when they were mentioned, even by those who still maintained them, it was rather in a way of controversy, as their opinions ; not as the only foundation on which the ever- lasting all of man depends.   The people too much lost sight of these all-important doctrines, and the relish for them gradually dwindled.   Carnality and conformity to the world prevailed in the then existing members of churches.   The gospel, the great means of conversion, being nearly laid aside, others could not possibly be converted by their ministry.   And thus one church after another came to nothing ; and a great number of their meeting-houses were lost or converted to other uses, in almost every part of the nation.   In a word, they degraded Jesus Christ, and He degraded them."

JOSEPH JENKINS, D.D.

FROM Taylor's grave to that of Jenkins' another north-south path must be crossed. The head-stone is adjoining the path, but only a portion of the inscription can be deciphered, as it is sinking into the ground.

INSCRIPTION.

In memory of the Rev. JOSEPH JENKINS, D.D., who died Feb. 21st, 1819, aged 76 years.

Corruption, earth, and worms
  Shall but refine this flesh;
Till my triumphant spirit comes
  To put it on afresh.

God, my Redeemer, lives,
  And often from the skies
Looks down and watches all my dust
  Till He shall bid it rise.

DAME MARY PAGE.

No directions are needed to find this somewhat extra-ordinary tomb. In the south panel is the following :

" Here lyes Dame Mary Page,
  Relict of Sir Gregory Page, Bart.,
  She departed this life March 11, 1728,
    In the 56 year of her age."

In the north panel may be read :—

" In 67 months she was tap'd 66 times,
  Had taken away 240 gallons of water,
  Without ever repining at her case,
    Or ever fearing the operation."

Dame Mary Page and her husband were persons of considerable wealth and influence, and were members of the old Devonshire Square Church. They befriended distressed Dissenters as much as possible, and after the death of Sir Gregory, Lady Page distributed her wealth with a lavish hand, and by her will bequeathed considerable amounts for the succour and relief of poor fellow members. Her ailment was most painful and distressing, and she was frequently carried into the family pew, as she was always anxious to attend the services. She was an accomplished woman, a kind and affectionate friend, and a lover of Christian people, no matter what their station might be. A short time before her death on being asked whether she had a good prospect of another world, she replied, " I have, I have." She died without a groan or struggle, on March 4th, 1728.

JOSHUA OLDFIELD, D.D.

THIS head-stone is in the third row south from Dame Mary Page.

INSCRIPTION.

Here lyeth the body of the Rev. JOSHUA OLDFIELD, dyed Nov. 8th, 1729, aged 73 years.

Mr. John Oldfield, the father of Joshua, was minister of the church at Carsington, Derbyshire, when his son Joshua was born in 1656. When the Act of Uniformity came into force Mr. Oldfield was ejected for non-conforming. He gave his son a most excellent education during his early years, and afterwards sent him as a student to Christ College, Cambridge. Here Joshua became noted, not only for diligence in his studies, but also for his exemplary life and conduct. On leaving the University Oldfield became chaplain to Sir Philip Gell at his family seat in Derbyshire. Here he became very friendly with a clergyman in the neighbourhood, and they were accustomed to express their views to each other in very frank terms. At this time a good living became vacant, which was in Sir Philip's gift. It was offered to Oldfield. After due consideration he thanked his patron, but told him he could not conform either for that or even a greater living. Sir Philip, being anxious that Oldfield should become vicar of this parish, asked his clergyman friend to press the matter upon him. This he was glad to do, and a great deal of argument took place between the two. Oldfield, however, was immovable; but being mindful of the kindness of his friend, he suggested that as he could not sacrifice his nonconformist principles, and the living was a much better one than the clergyman was then in, he should press his claims upon Sir Philip. The clergyman thanked Oldfield very heartily for his kindness and goodwill, but earnestly begged him not to repeat anything of the kind; he stated that he should have been glad to have drawn Oldfield into the Church in the hope of good being accomplished; but although he himself had no scruple in remaining in the Established Church, his conscience would not allow him to renew his assent and his consent

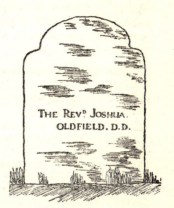

to all that was in the Book of Common Prayer. After leaving Sir Philip Gell, Oldfield took the post of tutor to the son of Mr. Paul Foley, who was Speaker of the House of Commons during the reign of William III., and he travelled with his pupil for a time in Wales and Ireland. He then became assistant to Mr. Samuel Doolittle, and the pastor of a congregation in Tooting, London. Acting upon the advice of several fellow-ministers he next removed to Oxford, where "he had but small auditory and very slender encouragement, but took a great deal of pains." Coventry followed Oxford, and here upon the suspicion of his giving instruction to young people, he was cited to appear before the Ecclesiastical Court on October 14th, 1697. It seemed as if serious trouble were in store for him, but after he had brought the matter to the King's Bench, which put him to great trouble and expense, it was allowed to drop, as William III. gave the Ecclesiastical authorities clearly to understand that he was much displeased with such persecution and prosecution. He again returned to London, where first at Southwark and afterwards at Hoxton he kept an Academy which became world-famous.

During his latter years he met with many sore afflictions, as he was subject to apoplectic fits, but it is recorded that "the Providence of God made the last stage of his life easy and honourable under the disadvantage of his outward circumstances; of which he entertained a high sense of gratitude." His last illness was a short one, an account of which is given by his friend, Dr. Harris, who preached the funeral sermon.

"The day before he died," said the preacher, "I asked him whether all was easy and comfortable within. He said he had a judicious satisfaction and peace of mind, though by reason of present weakness and lowness of spirits he was dull and heavy. He was sensible his life was drawing to an end, and continued sensible to the minute, without any violent shock of dissolving nature, and with an undisturbed tranquillity of mind. He said, 'That nature must submit,' and 'that all was well, and all was easy within.' This," added Dr. Harris, "was an honourable testimony to religion, after so long a trial, and from so wise, sedate, and upright a person."

AN EPITAPH.

Here lyeth the Body of Francis Smith, Bookseller, who in his youth was settled in a separate Congregation, where he sustained, between the Years 1659 and 1688, great persecution by Imprisonments, Exile, and large Fines laid on Ministers and Meeting Houses, and for Printing and Promoting Petitions for calling of a Parliament, with several things against Popery, and after nearly 40 Imprisonments, he was fined £500 for printing and selling the Speech of a Noble Peer, and Three Times Corporeal Punishment. For the said Fine, he was 5 Years Prisoner in the King's Bench: His hard Duress there utterly impaired his Health. He dyed Housekeeper in the Custom-House, December the 22nd, 1691.

SAMUEL STENNETT, D.D.

THE somewhat peculiar tomb of Stennett is several rows west from Oldfield's grave. One north-south path must be crossed, and the tomb stands on the west edge of another.

The great-grandfather Edward, the grandfather Joseph, and the father of Samuel Stennett, whose name was also Joseph, were noted ministers and citizens in their day.

Edward Stennett, in addition to his preaching, was a celebrated doctor, and meeting with great success in the medical profession, amassed a considerable fortune. He, in common with other Dissenters, suffered persecution and imprisonment after the Restoration, his home at this time being in Wallingford Castle. About the year 1686 he became pastor of the Sabbatarian Baptist Church, then meeting in Pinner's Hall, London, but as he continued to reside in his palatial home his visits to the metropolis were comparatively few, yet he held the position until his death in 1689. He thus witnessed the complete overthrow of James II. and the triumph of the Protestant cause under William III.

His son Joseph, who had been born at Abingdon in 1663, became pastor in 1690, and held this office until he too was gathered to his fathers in 1713. During his pastorate a dreadful passion for war and a lust for killing had taken a firm hold upon the English and the French people. The great General Marlborough was winning his notable victories upon the Continent, and when the news reached England of the marvellous victory over the French at Blenheim and of the capture of Gibraltar from the Spaniards, there were extraordinary rejoicings, and Joseph Stennett, with other ministers, made public reference to the events. The drowning French soldiers in the Danube were compared by Stennett to the Canaanites in the river Kishon and the Egyptians in the Red Sea, whilst he exulted in the complete humiliation of the French King and people. His sermon being published, thousands of copies were sold, and Queen Anne was so pleased that she made a grant from her privy purse for Stennett, this being the more remarkable because she was always most ungracious to Dissenters. In the early part of 1713 Stennett went to Knaphill because of his failing health, and he died in this Surrey village in the 49th year of his age, and was buried in Hickenden churchyard.

After being minister for a period at Exeter, Joseph his son moved to London in 1737, and became the pastor of the Baptist Church in Little Wild Street, Lincoln's Inn Fields. Samuel, who had been born in Devonshire's county town in 1727, was thus a lad of ten years, and he was still a youth when he was baptised by his father, and admitted a member of his church. He had been brought into serious concern through the singing of the hymn :—

> " Come, ye that fear the Lord,
>   And listen while I tell
> How narrowly my feet escaped
>   The snares of death and hell."

After a period of conviction he was led into the liberty of the Gospel, and was in communion with the church at Little Wild Street for more than fifty years, during forty-seven of which he held office, first as assistant to his father and afterwards as pastor.

Soon after Samuel Stennett joined his father's church, news reached the Metropolis that the Pretender had landed in Scotland, and after marshalling his forces, but meeting with little success, was marching into England. The people were greatly alarmed, especially the Dissenters, who had every reason to dread the House of Stuart's again being in the ascendency. The church now became very militant, and it was quite a common thing for a chapel to be turned into a place for drill. The Protestant Associations presented an address to the King assuring him of their loyalty, and styling the Invader, "The Popish Pretender and traitor." Mr. Joseph Stennett preached a sermon which aroused such enthusiasm in his congregation, that men rose in their seats drawing and waving their swords, and declaring their intention of taking their places by the side of the King when he led the army into the field. It is a matter of history that after the Pretender had reached Derby he retired, ultimately to meet with the disastrous defeat at Culloden.

Joseph Stennett was pastor of the church in Little Wild Street for upwards of twenty years, and was noted for his loyalty to the House of Hanover. He was much esteemed by George II., and was also on terms of close friendship with some of the leading men of the day. He wrote to a friend concerning an interview with the Bishop of London, and said, " I told his Lordship that I more than ever saw the usefulness of the Book of Common Prayer ; for, considering how little the Scriptures are read by the common people and how little the Gospel preached by the clergy, if it were not for what is said of Christ in the Prayer Book, multitudes would forget there was any such person. He heartily joined in my observation, and told me that he had lately heard a sermon by an eminent preacher, who seemed to labour to keep the name of Christ out of it. ' For my part,' added he, ' my time is now short, and therefore my charge to all my clergy is short too. I say to all of them that come to me : " See to it that you preach Jesus Christ ; don't preach Seneca, nor Plato, but preach Jesus Christ." ' "

Samuel Stennett, after being assistant to his father, succeeded him in the pastoral office in 1758. The well-known prison Reformer, John Howard, was a great friend of his, and when in London was accustomed to attend his ministry. On one occasion Howard wrote to Stennett from Smyrna, the letter being dated August 11th, 1786.

" With unabated pleasure I have attended your ministry ; no man ever entered more into my religious sentiments, or more happily expressed them. It was some little disappointment when anyone occupied your pulpit. Oh, Sir, how many Sabbaths have I ardently longed to spend in Wild Street ; on those days I generally rest, or, if at sea, keep retired in my little cabin. It is you that preach, and I bless God that I attend with renewed pleasure. God in Christ is my Rock, the portion of my soul. I have little more to add—but accept my renewed thanks. I bless God for your ministry ; I pray God reward you a thousand fold."

The death of Stennett's wife was a very great blow, for although she had been unwell for some time, she was only confined to her bed for one week.

From this period he was more earnest than ever in his ministry, and his two last sermons were remembered long afterwards by his church and congregation. The subject of one was Christ as a High Priest, who is "touched with the feeling of our infirmities." Stennett said "that during a sleepless night, the preceding week, this subject had been upon his mind, and although in a physical sense it was so distressing, in every other way he had never enjoyed a night so much in his life." He spoke of the perfect knowledge the Lord Jesus had of all His people's wants, of His tender care for every one of them, and the sufferings He underwent for them, and how He exhorted them to "Come boldly to the throne of grace, that they might obtain mercy, and find grace to help in time of need." He prayed earnestly that God might give him an easy passage out of life, and this petition was heard and granted. During his illness vinegar being given him as a throat gargle, he tasted it and said with great emotion, "In His thirst they gave Him vinegar to drink." "When I reflect upon the sufferings of Christ, I am ready to say, 'What have I been thinking of all my life?' What He did and suffered are now my only support! 'He is able to keep that which I have committed to Him against that day.'" He repeated upon another occasion a verse of his own composing :—

"Father, at Thy call I come,
In Thy bosom there is room
For a guilty soul to hide,
Press'd with grief on every side."

To his son he exclaimed, "My son, God hath done great things for us. He is very gracious to me; and I can leave myself and my family in His hands." One of his last sentences was, "Christ is to me the chief among ten thousand, and the altogether lovely."

He died on August 25th, 1795, in the 68th year of his age, and his body was placed in the same grave as that of his wife, who had predeceased him only a few months. The tomb and the head-stone are quite striking, and the long Latin inscription is partly discernible. Several of Stennett's hymns are still sung, the following being perhaps one of the best known :—

How soft the words my Saviour speaks,
How kind the promises He makes!
A bruised reed He never breaks,
Nor will He quench the smoking flax.

The humble poor He'll not despise,
Nor on the contrite sinner frown :
His ear is open to their cries,
And quickly sends salvation down.

He sees the struggles that prevail
Between the powers of grace and sin ;
He kindly listens while they tell
The bitter pangs they feel within.

Though press'd with fears on every side,
They know not how the strife may end ;
Yet He will soon the cause decide,
And judgment unto victory send.

THOMAS BRADBURY

THIS tomb is two or three rows west from Samuel
Stennett's, but nearer middle railings. Only a very few
words are now readable upon this substantial tomb, but
they are all worthy of being read by everyone who visits
Bunhill.

INSCRIPTION.

In this vault is deposited the body of the Rev. Mr.
THOMAS BRADBURY, a very eminent dissenting minister
of this City. He was greatly distinguished for his zealous
defence, both from the pulpit and the press, of the fundamental principles of religion ; nor was he less remarkable
for his hearty affection and firm attachment to the Protestant succession in the illustrious House of Hanover ;
particularly in the alarming and perilous crisis at the
close of the reign of Queen Anne. Full of the expectation
of a better and eternal life, he departed from our world
September 9th, 1759, in the 82nd year of his age, and in

the 64th of his ministry. Reader! Go thy way and consider that, if the vivacity of genius, or the charms of eloquence, could have prevented the stroke of Death, this monument had not been erected. Remember, also, that as surely as night succeeds the longest day, so surely will death conclude the longest life. Work, therefore, while it is day.

The best known incident in the life of Bradbury was connected with the death of Queen Anne. The Dissenters were greatly alarmed at the prospects before them in consequence of the passing of the Schism Bill. When walking along Smithfield on Lord's day morning, August 1st, 1714, Bradbury was passed by Bishop Burnett, who stopped his carriage and called him to his side. He asked what was the cause of Bradbury's seriousness, and the reply was, "I am thinking whether I shall have the constancy and resolution of that noble army of martyrs who were burned to ashes in this place; for I most assuredly expect to see similar times of persecution, and that I shall be called to suffer in a like manner." The Bishop, who had been such a friend of William III., and who was a very staunch Protestant, did what he could to quiet Bradbury's fears; and he told him that the Queen was very ill, and was not expected to recover. He also said that he was going to the Palace, and would despatch a messenger to him with the earliest intelligence of the Queen's death. If it should happen that Bradbury was in his pulpit the messenger would be instructed to drop a handkerchief from the gallery, as a token of the event. Bradbury had not long to wait, for whilst he was preaching the handkerchief was dropped, and he knew that the Queen, who had so long and bitterly persecuted Dissenters, was no more. He completely suppressed his feelings of emotion whilst preaching, but during his closing prayer he returned thanks to God for the deliverance of these kingdoms from the evil counsels and designs of their enemies; and implored the divine blessing "upon His Majesty King George and the House of Hanover." Mr. Bradbury always maintained that he was the first man who proclaimed King George I.

The South Panel of Tomb of DAME MARY PAGE.
(See page 183.)

The North Panel of Tomb of DAME MARY PAGE.

SAMUEL STENNETT, D.D.
(See page 187.)

The Tomb of THOMAS BRADBURY.
The head-stone near the railings is that of RICHARD and ROBERT WINTER.
(See pages 191 and 194.)

Bradbury was for many years minister of New Court, Carey Street, London, and was an outstanding man in his advocacy of civil and religious liberty. He was ill-treated again and again by Popish mobs, and on one occasion his meeting-house was burned down. He spoke bravely and strongly against allowing the Pretender to come to the throne, for he knew that this would mean the re-establishment of the Papacy. His opposition to persecuting measures was so successful that Queen Anne endeavoured to buy him over by offering him a bishopric, but her efforts were in vain. The Queen died quite suddenly, and by the accession of King George I. Protestant Dissenters obtained considerable relief and protection.

At one time Bradbury was very friendly with Dr. Isaac Watts, but through serious disputes concerning the doctrine of the Trinity they were much estranged. Indeed, on one occasion Bradbury startled a clerk, who was in the act of giving out a hymn, by telling him in stentorian tones to "let us have none of Mr. Watts' whims." He also spoke of some of Watts' hymns as "garblings, manglings, and transformings."

Isaac Watts, however, certainly paid him back in his own coin on one occasion, for while addressing a company of ministers his voice showing signs of weakness, Bradbury called out, "Brother Watts, shall I speak for you?" and the poet replied, "Brother Bradbury, you have often spoken against me."

When going to present an address to King George on his accession to the throne on September 28th, 1714, as the head of a Nonconformist deputation, a nobleman, referring to the sombre-looking cloaks which were then worn by Dissenting ministers, asked with a sneer, "Pray, Sir, is this a funeral procession?" "Yes, my Lord," was Bradbury's quick response; "it is the funeral of the Schism Bill, and the resurrection of Liberty."

The last sermon preached by Mr. Bradbury was on August 12th, 1759. In his dying moments he was succoured and cheered by the presence of God with him, and his daily prayer was, "Come, Lord Jesus, come, come quickly."

o

RICHARD WINTER, D.D., and ROBERT WINTER, D.D.

THIS head-stone stands between the tomb of Bradbury and railings of middle path.

RICHARD WINTER, D.D.

In memory of the Rev. RICHARD WINTER, D.D., for near 40 years the able and faithful pastor of the Protestant Dissenters in New Court, Carey Street. The co-pastor and successor of the Rev. Thomas Bradbury. He was a considerable Biblical scholar; an able supporter of the doctrines of grace; a judicious instructor, and practical preacher; and, in the whole of his deportment, a consistent and exemplary character. He died in cheerful hope, March 29th, 1799, in the 79th year of his age.

ROBERT WINTER, D.D.

Here waits the resurrection in glory, the remains of the Rev. ROBERT WINTER, D.D., the third son of John Winter, Esq.; and who presided with eminent fidelity, honour, and usefulness, over the same church of Christ that had enjoyed the ministry of his distinguished grandfather, the Rev. Thomas Bradbury. He died on the 9th day of August, 1833, aged 71 years.

" Whose faith follow."

WILLIAM LANGFORD, D.D.

FROM Bradbury's tomb a move must be made in a northwest direction. The head-stone of Langford is on the north side of the path, and the inscription is quite legible.

INSCRIPTION.

The remains of the Rev. WILLIAM LANGFORD, D.D., are here deposited, who, beloved by his family, and the churches of which he was successively pastor, departed this life, April 23rd, 1775, aged 71.

William Langford, who was born on September 29th, 1704, at Westfield, in Sussex, lost his father when only three or four years old. He received his early education at Tenterden, whither his mother had moved; and he went from the Kentish village to the University at Glasgow, leaving the College in May, 1727. Upon returning to England Mr. Langford became pastor of the church at Gravesend, where he remained about seven years. In 1734 he became co-pastor with Thomas Bures at Silver Street, and in 1736 was appointed assistant to Mr. Wood at the celebrated Weigh-house Chapel.

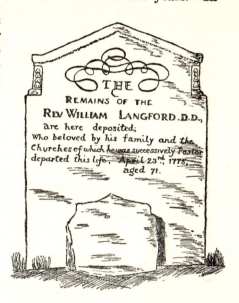

The name Weigh-house is derived from the original use of the building, which stood in Cornhill, but after the Great Fire it occupied the ground of one of the consumed churches. In the early days it was an institution of considerable importance, and the man who obtained the appointment as the chief weigher also became a member of the Court of Aldermen. The business consisted in weighing and marking packages brought from vessels in the river; fees varying from 2d. to 2s. a draught being charged, although for "a bagg of hopps" there was a uniform charge of 6d. A chief weigher was employed for special officials, and these in turn had charge of many subordinates, the whole establishment being governed by the Grocers' Company. The Parliament exercised control over the Weigh-house, passing many Acts for regulating weights and measures. All foreign mechandise was weighed at the King's Beam, and in the presence of sworn officials. These men were disqualified from any other business ; and if there was found to be any deviation from strict morality and rectitude there was a punishment of imprisonment for a year and a day. As new conditions were introduced the custom of weighing was gradually relinquished, and it was quite abolished in the seventeenth century, for mathematicians then provided their own measures. Many quaint sayings arose owing to peculiar things connected with the weighing, one being, "A pint's a pound all the year round ; " this was owing to the fact that 32 grains of wheat were always the legal weight of the English silver penny.

The first congregation at the Weigh-house was Presbyterian, Samuel Slatter and Thomas Kent, who had been ejected from the Established Church by the Act of Uniformity, being the first ministers. Mr. Langford very ably discharged his duties as a minister until his 70th year, when he was disabled by many infirmities. His departure was gentle and peaceful, for as one expressed it, he for some time seemed to be on the " borders of heaven." He retired to bed at a friend's house in Croydon on Saturday, April 22nd, 1775, about four o'clock. The following morning he was apparently struck with death. He murmured in the night, little thinking that anyone overheard him, "I have been in pain through fear and unbelief ; but now all is removed by faith." At six o'clock he breathed his last, and "the same day was the Sabbath." The address at the graveside was delivered by Dr. Gibbons, whose opening remarks were as follows :—

"In what a solemn spot are we here assembled ? Golgotha, the place of a skull ? What graves clustered upon graves ! What tombs rising upon tombs ! How is human earth ejected to make way for human earth ! The valley of dry bones, the valley of the shadow of death ! Here the ghastly tyrant has erected his throne, has planted his banners, and reigns in wide devastation, while he daily sees fresh numbers added to his conquests, and enlarging his tremendous dominion ! "

The funeral sermon at the Weigh-house was also preached by Dr. Gibbons, the text being, "Blessed are the dead which die in the Lord " (Rev. xiv. 13).

WILLIAM JONES.

THIS head-stone is north of Langford's—i.e., nearer buildings, but one row west.

INSCRIPTION.

WILLIAM JONES, A.M., died 21st Jan., 1846, in his 84th year.

The ancestors of William Jones were farmers in the village of Poulton, near Chester, and it was at this place in the year 1762 that the future minister was born. He early showed traces of marked ability, and was sent to Chester to be educated by a clergyman for the Established Church. Whilst in the Cathedral City he read the writings of Mr. Archibald McLean, and according to a phrase which he used himself, they gave his mind "such a twist that always remained." About the year 1786 he was baptised by Mr. McLean, and joined the church at Chester. He afterwards removed to Liverpool, his daily occupation being that of a book-seller, and whilst in the seaport town he was chosen pastor by a people whom he had been instrumental in gathering together. Somewhere about 1809 he moved once more, making his future and final home in London.

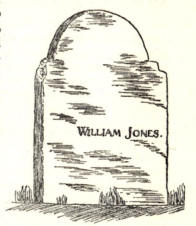

He now appeared as an author, many of his works being quite valuable, especially his "History of the Waldenses." He also became Elder of a Scotch Baptist Church which met in Windmill Street, Finsbury.

One day on going out of his house to the chapel his foot slipped, and he fell, breaking one of his thigh-bones. It was hoped that he would recover, but about 17 days after the accident the person with whom he was living went into his room and found him looking very ill and weak. In less than ten minutes the good old man was dead, his last audible expression being that he hoped God would take compassion upon him, a guilty sinner.

There is a very extraordinary circumstance connected with Mr. Jones' last days, which causes his character to shine as an honourable Protestant Dissenter. When he had reached the great age of 82, and was afflicted with the loss of sight in one eye, and also with chronic rheumatism, he received a letter which had been written him by command of Queen Victoria. The editor of "Bunhill Memorials" records this as well as the answer that Mr. Jones gave. They are as follows:—

         " Windsor Castle, Oct. 22nd, 1843.

" Sir,—Her Majesty has been informed of the situation to which you are reduced : and is sorry to find that an author to whom the public is so considerably indebted should arrive at the state in which Her Majesty understands you are now placed ; and I am commanded to write to you to ascertain whether it would be agreeable to you to avail yourself of the benefit of a charitable institution for decayed persons who have formerly seen better days, to which Her Majesty could nominate you. The appointment in question is—a poor brothership of the Charter-House ; the qualifications for it are, that he must be a bachelor, or a widower, a British subject, a member of the Church of England, and not under fifty when admitted. The advantages derived from it are as follows : each poor brother has a separate apartment, with table, chair, bed and bedding, kept in repair and clean ; fifty-four bushels of coals, and 13lbs. of candles yearly ; room kept clean, and bed made, and fire lighted by a nurse, with such extra attendance as sickness and infirmity may render necessary ; dinner in the hall when in health, at other times in his room ; bread and butter daily for breakfast and supper ; advice and medicine in sickness ; a cloak once in two years, worn in chapel and hall ; a yearly allowance of £26 10s. in money, paid quarterly. Should it suit you to accept this appointment the Queen has much pleasure in offering it to you, and will nominate you forthwith.

         "I am, Sir, your obedient servant,

                   " G. E. ANSON."

" To Mr. William Jones, A.M."

Mr. Jones' reply to the above was very long; but the reader shall have nearly the whole, verbatim; not a sentence of the least importance being omitted.

"London, 25th October, 1843.

"Much-honoured Sir,—The receipt and perusal of the communication with which I was yesterday favoured from you, Sir, by Her Majesty's gracious command, was so wholly unexpected, and so completely a matter of surprise to me, that I found myself quite overpowered by the royal condescension, and incapacitated for the task of making any immediate reply.

"I have attentively read your letter, Sir, and perceive, with unbounded gratitude, the provision which the royal mind has contemplated for the solace and accommodation of her old and faithful, but very unworthy subject; the very offer of which has penetrated me with sentiments of profound gratitude to Her Majesty which no language that I can command is adequate to express. As you, Sir, have kindly undertaken to be the medium of conveying to me her most gracious Majesty's pleasure on this occasion, I beg to return my very sincere thanks for the handsome manner in which you have, so far, executed your commission. And now let me intreat the favour of your completing what remains, by making known to our gracious Sovereign the high sense of gratitude with which I am impressed, and also my unfeigned regret at being compelled to decline her munificent offer! In the detail of the qualifications indispensable to the participation of the Charter House grant, there is *one item* which forms an insurmountable barrier to my availing myself of Her Majesty's intended munificence. I am not a member of the Church of England, and, in consequence, am disqualified. I am a Dissenter upon principle, as is well known to all who are conversant with my writings, whether historical or theological. Permit me to intreat the favour of you, Sir, to cast an eye over the enclosed paragraph, and you will instantly perceive how impossible it is for me to avail myself of Her Majesty's nomination to the Charter House Institution without a shameful sacrifice of principle, such as I hope never to be guilty of. It is true I was educated with a view to the ministry in the Church of England; but, when it pleased the Most High to open my understanding, and favour me with some little knowledge of the Holy Scriptures, and especially of the import of our Saviour's good confession concerning His kingdom, when (in answer to Pilate's interrogation) He said, 'My kingdom is not of this world,' I bade adieu to all national establishments, and took my lot among the Dissenters; which, after an interval of three-score years, I have never seen just cause to regret, though persecution and the offence of the cross have been my constant companions. I hope, Sir, you will pardon this prolixity; you know that one of the infirmities of old age is garrulity.

" Have the kindness to assure Her Majesty that my declining to accept her gracious offer arises from purely conscientious motives, from deference to the authority of our great Master in heaven, to whom we must all shortly render in our account! I hope you will be successful in prevailing on our most gracious Sovereign to put a favourable construction on my motives in this instance; and, if afterwards she should feel disposed to extend her sympathy towards one that is worn down by age and its usual concomitants, she may possibly avail herself of some other plan of carrying into effect her benevolent intention. But should the case turn out otherwise, I shall, to my latest moments, continue to indulge an honourable pride in reflecting that I have not been thought altogether unworthy of Her Majesty's notice and regard; nor ever cease to pray that the choicest blessings which heaven has to bestow, may rest upon the Royal Family.

" With every sentiment of respect and gratitude I remain, Sir, your very obedient and obliged servant,

" WILLIAM JONES."

" To G. E. Anson, Esq., Windsor Castle."

It is impossible not to admire this noble old man, and it should be added that Her Majesty directed the sum of £60 from the Royal Bounty Fund to be paid to Mr. Jones in annual instalments of £20 each. This was far short of what he would have received in the Charter House; but the principles of William Jones were not up for sale. As he died in 1846 he lived to receive about two-thirds of Her Majesty's grant.

It is only a few steps from the grave of old William Jones to that of Ann Davis. The latter is almost in a line with William Langford's, and, like his, adjoins the path.

MISS ANN DAVIS.

To the memory of Miss ANN DAVIS, who died Feb. 27th, 1803, aged 21 years.

" Go! Spotless Honor and unsullied Truth,
Go! smiling Innocence and blooming Youth;
Go! Female softness joined with manly sense,
Go! winning Wit that never gave Offence ;
Go! soft Humanity that blessed the Poor,
Go! Saint-eyed Patience from Affection's Door ;
Go! Modesty that never wore a Frown,
Go! Virtue, and receive thy Heavenly Crown.

These virtues could never merit a heavenly crown; we can only hope that Miss Ann Davis trusted not in these, but in the righteousness of the Spotless One to give it to her.

ALEXANDER WAUGH, D.D.

THE peculiar tomb with this inscription is east of Jones,' and with the new head-stone stands at the corner of the second and of a north-south path.

INSCRIPTION.

In this grave are deposited the mortal remains of the Rev. ALEXANDER WAUGH, D.D., Pastor of the Scots' Secession Church, in Wells Street, Oxford Street; where for nearly forty-six years he laboured as the Peacemaker, the Friend, and the Father of his people. He was one of the earliest promoters of the London Missionary Society, in 1795, on the behalf of which, and of the numerous charities in this City, he was enabled by his God to exhibit, in no common measure, the varied gifts of a powerful and eloquent advocate. This plain stone is raised not to eulogize his name, or to delineate his character, but to record the solemn and grateful testimony of his widow and children to the many Christian graces which adorned her husband, and their father. He was born at East Gordon, Berwickshire, August 16th, 1754; educated at the Universities of Edinburgh and Aberdeen; ordained at New Town, in the parish of Melrose, N.B., August 30th, 1780; translated to the pastoral charge of Wells Street Chapel, London, May 9th, 1782; died December 14th, 1827, in the 74th year of his age.

"Thou shalt come to thy grave in a full age, like as a shock of corn cometh in in his season" (Job v. 26).

To go from the tomb of Alexander Waugh to that of Joseph Hart is only a few steps. In moving to it, how- ever, so as to read the inscription on the south side, the head-stones of Timothy Priestley—on the left hand—and of his wife facing it must be passed. The inscription on the former can still be partially deciphered, and is the following:—

Sacred to the memory of the late Rev. TIMOTHY PRIESTLEY, who for more than half a century preached with fidelity and success the unsearchable riches of Christ; twenty-five years of which he was Pastor of the Independent Church in Jewin Street, London. Born June 19, 1734; died April 23, 1814.

That on the latter is:—

To the memory of Mrs. ANN PRIESTLEY, who died March 2nd, 1793, aged 47 years.

"Her worth unknown to ages yet unborn,
Shall be disclos'd at that triumphant morn,
When this dear dust in brilliant form shall rise
And join with raptur'd saints above the skies.

Before those millions shall it then be prov'd
How highly this dear child of God was lov'd;
The assembled world her character will see;
Will thine, O Reader, thus admired be?"

Readers of William Huntington's works will remember that the celebrated Coal-heaver dealt very sharply with Priestley in "The Barber Shaved."

JOSEPH HART.

INSCRIPTION.

In memory of the Rev. JOSEPH HART, late minister of the Gospel in Jewin Street, who died May 24th, 1768, aged 56 years.

THE above inscription was upon the original stone which marked the resting-place of Joseph Hart. This can still be seen, for it stands just at the back, but slightly to the north of the present memorial. In 1875 there was placed on the spot a red granite obelisk, which is one of the most striking features of Bunhill. On the front, which is the east side, there is this inscription :—

" Erected by lovers of Hart's hymns, published in 1759, and still highly prized by the Church of God. The author's remains were interred in this spot, as the original stone yet remains to show." JOSEPH HART, Minister of the Gospel, died May 24th, 1765, aged 56.

On the south side are the words :—

JOSEPH HART was by the free and sovereign Grace and Spirit of God raised up from the depths of sin, and delivered from the bonds of mere profession and self-righteousness, and led to rest entirely for salvation in the finished atonement and perfect obedience of Christ.

" Mercy is welcome news indeed
    To those who guilty stand ;
Wretches who feel what help they need,
    Will bless the helping Hand."

On the north side appear the following lines :—

"Though I am a stranger to others and a wonder to myself, yet I know Him (Christ), or rather am known of Him. Where sin abounded Grace did much more abound."

" O ! bring no price !
God's grace is free
To Paul, to Magdalene and me."

. . . .

" None but Jesus
Can do helpless sinners good."

With perhaps the one exception of John Bunyan's
tomb, there are more pilgrimages to that of Joseph Hart
than to any other in Bunhill. This may be explained by
the fact that in hundreds of villages as well as in the
towns and cities of this and other countries, Hart's Hymns
are loved and sung by godly persons of all ages and
classes. It is quite certain that there is no other hymn-
writer who has so fully entered into the various experiences of God's living family, and his hymns on the
sufferings of Christ are particularly so descriptive and
accurate that, when applied by the Spirit of God, they
have brought true repentance and godly sorrow to the
hearts of multitudes.

From Australia, America, Canada, India, China, indeed
from the ends of the earth, people have made their way to
the world's metropolis, determining that at the earliest
possible moment they would go to Bunhill to "see Hart's
stone." Bunyan is remembered with much affection and
sympathy—Gill, Owen, and Goodwin with respectful
admiration—Stennett and Swain with sweet gratitude,
but Hart is loved with an intensity that is wonderful, and
no grave draws tears from the eyes like that in which is
reposing the dust of the author of

"Come ye sinners, poor and wretched,
Weak and wounded, sick and sore."

It is difficult to say anything new concerning this
great and good man, for in "The Life of Joseph Hart,"
by Mr. Thomas Wright,* an accurate record of his life
is preserved. And have we not his spiritual experience
recorded by his own pen? Yet it seems needful to present
our readers and visitors to Bunhill Fields with a short
sketch of his career.

He was born in the year 1712, "within the sound of
Bow Bells," and being blessed with godly parents, he was
favoured to hear good preaching, and the glorious doctrines of the Gospel set forth in all their fulness from his
earliest years. At times there were tears in his eyes and
remorse in his heart, but when he was about twenty-one
years of age, he became seriously distressed and anxious

* See "Life of Joseph Hart," C. J. Farncombe & Sons, Ltd., 30
Imperial Buildings, Ludgate Circus, E.C.

concerning his soul. Thinking that he could please God by a due and close observance of His holy law, he became most strict in his attendance at preaching services, hoping thereby that he was making peace with God and working out a way to heaven. His was the spirit of the Pharisee, which ultimately led him into a state of gross carelessness and even sin, for it is evident that he went some distance along the paths of outward wickedness. But let him speak for himself in his autobiographical hymn !

Come hither, ye that fear the Lord,
  Disciples of God's suffering Son ;
Let me relate, and you record,
  What He for my poor soul has done.

The way of truth I quickly miss'd,
  And further stray'd, and further still ;
Expected to be saved by Christ ;
  But to be holy had no will.

The road of death with rash career
  I ran, and gloried in my shame :
Abus'd His grace ; despis'd His fear ;
  And others taught to do the same.

Far, far from home, on husks I fed,
  Puft up with each fantastic whim.
With swine a beastly life I led ;
  And serv'd God's foe instead of Him.

A forward fool, a willing drudge,
  I acted for the prince of hell ;
Did all he bid without a grudge ;
  And boasted I could sin so well.

Bold blasphemies employed my tongue,
  I heeded not my heart unclean ;
Lost all regard of right or wrong ;
  In thought, in word, in act obscene.

My body was with lust defil'd :
  My soul I pamper'd up with pride :
Could sit and hear the Lord revil'd ;
  The Saviour of mankind deny'd.

I strove to make my flesh decay
  With foul disease, and wasting pain.
I strove to fling my life away,
  And damn my soul—but strove in vain.

The Lord, from whom I long backslid,
   First check'd me with some gentle **stings**;
Turn'd on me, look'd and softly chid;
   And bid me hope for greater things.

Soon to His bar He made me come;
   Arraign'd, convicted, cast, I stood;
Expecting from His mouth the doom
   Of those who trample on His blood.

Pangs of remorse my conscience tore;
   Hell open'd hideous to my view;
And what I only heard before,
   I found by sad experience true.

Oh! what a dismal state is this!
   What horrors shook my feeble **frame**!
But, brethren, surely you can guess:
   For you, perhaps, have felt the **same**.

But O, the goodness of our God!
   What pity melts His tender heart!
He saw me welt'ring in my blood,
   And came and eas'd me of my **smart**.

While I was yet a great way off,
   He ran, and on my neck He fell:
My short distress He judg'd enough;
   And snatch'd me from the brink of hell.

What an amazing change was here!
   I looked for hell, He brought me heav'n.
"Cheer up," said He; "dismiss thy fear:
   Cheer up; thy sins are all forgiv'n."

I would object; but faster much
   He answ'd, "Peace." What, me?—"Yes, **thee**."
But my enormous crimes are such—
   "I give thee pardon full and free."

But for the future, Lord—"I am
   Thy great salvation, perfect, whole.
Behold, thy bad works shall not damn;
   Nor can thy good works save thy soul."

"Renounce them both. Myself alone
   Will *for* thee work, and *in* thee too.
Henceforth I make thy cause My own;
   And undertake to bring thee thro'."

He said. I took the full release.
  The Lord hath sign'd it with His blood.
My horrors fled; and perfect peace,
  And joy unspeakable ensu'd.

I only begg'd one humble boon;
  (Nor did the Lord offended seem)
Some service might by me be done
  To souls that truly trust in Him.

Thus I, who lately had been cast,
  And fear'd a just but heavy doom,
Received a pardon for the past;
  A promise for the time to come.

This promise oft I call to mind,
  As thro' some painful paths I go;
And secret consolation find,
  And strength to fight with ev'ry foe.

And oft-times, when the tempter sly
  Affirms it fancied, forg'd, or vain,
Jesus appears; disproves the lie;
  And kindly makes it o'er again.

When about forty-five years of age, he heard in the
Moravian Chapel, Fetter Lane,* a sermon from Rev. iii.
10, which greatly moved him. He had intended to pro-
ceed to the Tottenham Court Chapel on leaving Fetter
Lane, but instead, he felt compelled to return to his
home. He had no sooner entered the house "when,"
says he, "I felt myself melting away into a strange softness of affection, which made me fling myself on my knees
before God. My horrors were immediately dispelled, and
such light and comfort flowed into my heart as no words
can express. The alteration I felt in my soul was as that
which is experienced by a person almost sinking under a
heavy burden, when it is immediately removed from his
shoulders. Tears ran in streams from my eyes, and I was
so swallowed up in joy and thankfulness that I hardly
knew where I was. I threw myself willingly into
my Saviour's hands; I lay weeping at His feet wholly
resigned to His will; and only begged that I might, if He
was graciously pleased to permit it, be of some service to
His Church and people."

* See illustration.

It is given to very few to have such a deep experience as this of the grace and mercy of God, and the conversion of Joseph Hart was, in its way, quite as remarkable as that of Saul of Tarsus. He almost immediately began to write hymns, but did not commence to preach until about 1760 ; it is supposed that his first sermon was preached at the old Meeting House in St. John's Court, Bloomsbury. It is worth noting that in 1760 he became minister of the Independent Chapel in Jewin Street, which was erected in 1672 for William Jenkyn.* This was a very large building, and was constantly crowded. Sad to say only one of his sermons has been preserved, but there is great cause for rejoicing that his hymns have not been allowed to sink into oblivion.

In his family circle, Mr. Hart met with many afflictions, and he suffered very severely in his own body. He was minister of Jewin Street for the short period of eight years, as he died on May 24th, 1768, at the comparatively early age of 56. It is estimated that 20,000 persons attended his funeral, and the service was conducted by Mr. Andrew Kinsman, of Plymouth, who gave out the hymn commencing,

> " Sons of God by blest adoption,
> View the dead with steady eyes."

When this had been sung, the voice of Mr. Kinsman rang forth as he quoted the words from Isaiah xl., " The voice said, Cry. What shall I cry ? All flesh is grass." It was a solemn occasion, and Mr. Kinsman gave a most touching address. The funeral sermon was preached by Mr. John Hughes, and it contains a graphic and true character sketch of Hart, both as a man and a minister.

As a preacher and a hymn-writer, Joseph Hart was quite in a class by himself, whilst as a father, a husband and a friend, he was kind, faithful and true. His hymns will be valued as long as there are those who desire to have fellowship with Christ in His sufferings ; as long as His righteousness, His Name and His doctrines are prized and loved.

The hymn to which we have already referred, and which is mentioned on his tomb, " Come, ye sinners, poor

* See page 49.

JOSEPH HART'S MEMORIAL.

$\times$ This marks the original headstone.

(See page 203.)

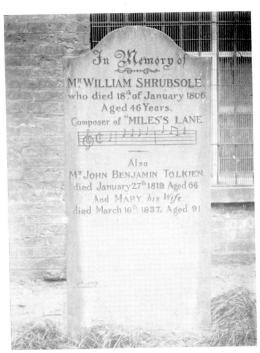

(See page 210.)

LADY ANN ERSKINE.

(See page 211.)

and wretched," is in all evangelical hymn-books, and is so
well known that it is hardly necessary to insert it. Of
the others, it is somewhat difficult to select one, but the
author has chosen the following as a particular favourite
of his own. This should be sung to the tune " Evening
Hymn" (Bristol 589), for the two blend most beautifully.

When the chosen tribes debated
'Gainst their God, as hardly treated,
   And complain'd their hopes were spilt,
God, for murm'ring to requite them,
Fiery serpents sent to bite them ;
   Lively type of deadly guilt.

Stung by these they soon repented ;
And their God as soon relented ;
   Moses prayed ; He answer gave ;
" Serpents are the beasts that strike them,
Make of brass a serpent like them;
   That's the way I choose to save."

Vain was bandage, oil, or plaister :
Rankling venom kill'd the faster ;
   'Till the serpent Moses took,
Rear'd it high, that all might view it,
Bid the bitten look up to it :
   Life attended ev'ry look.

Jesus thus, for sinners smitten,
Wounded, bruised, serpent-bitten,
   To His cross directs their faith.
Why should I then poison cherish ?
Why despair of cure, and perish ?
   Look, my soul, tho' stung to death.

Thine's (alas !) a lost condition.
Works can not work thee remission ;
   Nor thy goodness do thee good.
Death's within thee, all about thee ;
But the remedy's without thee :
   See it in thy Saviour's blood.

See the Lord of glory dying !
See Him gasping ! Hear Him crying !
   See His burden'd bosom heave !
Look, ye sinners, ye that hung Him ;
Look, how deep your sins have stung Him ;
   Dying sinners, look and live.

P

WILLIAM SHRUBSOLE (1).

The head-stone of William Shrubsole is to the north of Hart's tomb. It is, however, in the row nearest the buildings, and opposite the number 106, which is on the wall. The inscription is so plain upon the stone that only the illustration is needed.

William Shrubsole, the youngest son of Thomas Shrubsole, was born at Canterbury in January, 1760. Thomas was a farmer, but perceiving that his young son was musical, obtained in 1770 an appointment for him as an alto chorister in the famous cathedral choir. He remained there until 1777, and became organist at Bangor Cathedral in 1782. During the interim he is supposed to have sung both at Drury Lane and in Westminster Abbey. In 1784 he got into serious trouble at Bangor because he attended worship at a conventicle. The records of the cathedral speak of this in the following terms :—

"October, 1783. Mr. William Shrubsole, the organist of the Church, having given great offence to the Dean and Chapter by his close connexion with one Abbot, late of this place, as by his frequenting conventicles, that Mr. Dean be impowered to discharge the said William Shrubsole from his place as organist, if the said Abbot (who is supposed to have gone to reside in Dublin) shall at any time hereafter return in order to abide in the town of Bangor, or the neighbourhood thereof, or if the said William Shrubsole shall be found to frequent any conventicle or religious assembly where anything is taught which is contrary to the doctrine or discipline of the Church of England."

"December, 1783. That William Shrubsole be employed to play on the organ of our Cathedral till Lady-day next and no longer ; that in case it should not be convenient for him to continue in that employment till Lady-day next he shall be at liberty to leave it before that time, and shall be paid the full allowance to Lady-day next notwithstanding."

He then became organist at Spa Fields Chapel, London, and continued in this office until his death. Several celebrated organists were trained by him, one of whom

is buried in Bunhill. Close to Abraham Hume's* tomb is
a head-stone marking the resting-place of "Benjamin
Jacob, Organist of Surry Chapel," and Jacob was one of
Shrubsole's pupils.

Whilst at Canterbury Shrubsole was very friendly with
Perronet, who was the author of that universally favourite
hymn, "All hail the power of Jesus' Name," and for
which the musician composed "Miles' Lane." Indeed,
Perronet appointed Shrubsole his executor, and in addition left him a considerable sum of money.

LADY ANN AGNES ERSKINE.

THE tomb of Lady Ann Erskine stands in a row three
east and fourteen north of Shrubsole's. The number on
the west building will therefore be 120. This long
inscription is now completely obliterated, but as shown in
the photograph the name stands out quite boldly in the
east panel of the tomb.

INSCRIPTION.

Beneath are deposited the mortal remains of The Right
Hon. LADY ANN AGNES ERSKINE, eldest Daughter of
the late Earl of Buchan; who departed this transitory life
October 5th, 1804, Aged 65. Being appointed by the late
Countess Dowager of Huntingdon, one of her Trustees,
for the care and management of her Chapels, after her
decease; she executed the Trust with great wisdom,
assiduity, and zeal, during a period of more than thirteen
years. She was affable and condescending in her
deportment; kind and generous to the poor; and com-
passionate to the afflicted. Her piety was sincere and
unaffected, her life honourably useful, and her death easy
and happy.

Lady Ann was the daughter of the Earl of Buchan,
and came of a distinguished family. Her great grandfather suffered severely in the persecuting days of

* See page 109.

Charles II. The famous preachers, Ralph and Ebenezer Erskine, were also of the same family. As a child of seven or eight, her mind received a deep impression when her nurse was reading to her certain books. She early learned the value of prayer, for her mother, Lady Buchan, when on a visit to Edinburgh, bought her a guitar as a present, the very thing for which the child had been praying during her mother's absence.

She found, like many others, that early impressions of religion often wear off, and she mixed much with the world and went into pleasure as far as she could. There is a generally accepted incident in her life, which is very singular and striking. It appears that the eccentric Rowland Hill was preaching in the open air to a vast company of people at Moorfields, when he saw a gaudy equipage approach, a stylishly dressed lady being the occupant of the chariot. The text was, " I am black, but comely" (Cant. i. 5), and the preacher was stating that he regarded it to mean that the Church was "black as the tents of Kedar" in the estimation of the world, but " comely as the curtains of Solomon " in the eyes of her Bridegroom. As he was proceeding with his sermon, Lady Ann, for it was she, left her attendants and took a position at the back of Rowland Hill, and by so doing, drew considerable attention to herself. Noticing that the eyes of his audience were turned towards the new comer, Hill paused in his discourse, and leaving the subject upon which he was engaged, entered upon a fresh one, which compelled the undivided notice of the auditory. To the wonder of the people and the alarm of Lady Ann, he imagined an auction sale. There were three bidders, viz., the world, the devil, and Jesus Christ, and the article offered was the soul of Lady Ann. According to Hill's sensational presentation of the case, the world offered " riches, honours, and pleasure;" the devil, "all the kingdoms of the earth and the glory of them;" and the Lord Jesus Christ, " grace here and glory hereafter." This is supposed to have had a very solemn effect upon Lady Ann, but doubtless the incident itself has been greatly exaggerated. It is difficult to believe that even such an impulsive visionary and at times irresponsible man as

Rowland Hill could go to such lengths as he is stated to have done. The idea of putting the Lord of life and glory into competition with the world and the devil, is decidedly repulsive to a well-instructed mind.

Shortly after, the whole family moved to Bath, and there they met the good Lady Huntingdon, who was destined to be such a friend to Lady Ann. Indeed, the Countess invited her at once to remain with her as a companion, and from this time they were most intimate and constant friends. The Countess consulted her upon most of her projects, and when the venerable lady died on June 17th, 1791, Lady Ann became a very prominent person, as she was appointed one of the Trustees and Executors of the will. Her position was most difficult, as she had only very slight means of her own, and the income of the Countess died with her. The position was rendered more trying by the fact that Lady Huntingdon had been somewhat rash in opening chapels and incurring debts, although she spent very little upon herself. The Trustees arranged that Lady Ann should occupy part of Lady Huntingdon's house in Spafields, there to carry on the immense correspondence and give an oversight to the affairs of the connection.

For some time Lady Ann had suffered much physical ill-health, and as she could not take sufficient exercise, the dropsical tendency to which she had been for some time liable, very much increased. Her respiration was laborious, and she was troubled with asthma. Her spirits, however, were bright and cheerful, and her mind seemed quite prepared to meet death. Two or three mornings before her departure she came much refreshed from her room and said to a friend, " The Lord hath met me this morning with so much sweetness of mind that I seemed as if surrounded by God." She added with fervour, "My Lord and my God." She went out for a drive the day before her death, conversing as usual, and in the evening when a friend visited her, she said, " I have no presentiment of death upon my mind ; " but she also added, " Be that as it may, God is faithful, and I feel unshaken confidence in Him." On retiring to rest she said to her maid, " The Lord will reveal Himself to me to-

morrow." When asked if there were any outward matters
to make her uneasy, she replied, " No ; in those respects I
am perfectly easy." Her voice was never heard again by
any human ear, for when her attendant went to her
room at six o'clock the next morning, she found her mis-
tress in the sleep of death. Of her sixty-five years, more
than forty had been spent in the work of faith and
labour of love. The day of her death was Friday, October
5th, 1804.

On the Saturday week the body was taken to Bunhill ;
Mr. Kirkham reading the burial service, and Mr. Clark
delivering the address.

FROM Lady Ann Erskine's tomb a return is necessary
almost to Hart's tomb, and the path running eastwards
must be taken. On the right hand at the top is the
head-stone of THOMAS POWELL, JUNR., and the same
side at the bottom is the tomb of GEORGE DURRANT.
The former is the son of Thomas Powell, Senr. (see page
143) ; and on the latter, in addition to what is showing
in the illustration, there are the following lines :—

> " That grace which oft the rebel heart subdues,
>   A kind and early conquest made of thine ;
> 'Midst prosp'rous trade thou couldst not long refuse
>   To publish loud a Saviour all benign.
> He freely gave—thou freely gav'st again ;
>   Nor was thy preaching found to be in vain."

HERE LIE THE REMAINS OF
Mr GEORGE DURRANT.
WHO DIED 25TH MARCH 1802 AGED 61 YEARS.

WILLIAM SHRUBSOLE (2).

AFTER leaving Durrant's tomb the visitor must pass along the path towards the buildings. This head-stone is several rows distant from but almost in a line with Lady Ann Erskine's.

This William Shrubsole was the son of W. Shrubsole, who was the author of "Christian Memoirs" and other books. Having been bitten by a mad dog and fearing hydrophobia, he took to literary work in order to divert his attention.

William the son was born at Sheerness, November 21st, 1759, and in due course became a shipwright and a clerk in the dockyard. He moved to London in 1785, having been appointed to a clerkship in the Bank of England. His service with the Bank lasted until his death, his final position being that of Secretary to the Committee of Treasury.

He was one of the first secretaries of the London Missionary Society, and he also wrote several hymns. As stated on the head-stone, he died August 23, 1829.

The best known and most popular of his hymns is the one on Isa. li. 9, of which three verses are given below. It should be remembered that there are at least two other hymns commencing with the same words.

> " Arm of the Lord, awake! awake!
> Put on Thy strength, the nations shake;
> And let the world, adoring, see
> Triumphs of mercy wrought by Thee.

O send ten thousand heralds forth,
From east to west, from south to north,
To blow the trump of jubilee,
And peace proclaim from sea to sea !

Thus may the gospel's joyful sound
Reach to the earth's remotest bound ;
Until Messiah's kingdom come,
And the elect be gathered home."

DAVID BRADBERRY.

A FEW rows east from William Shrubsole's, and nearer the path, is the head-stone of David Bradberry.

INSCRIPTION.

In memory of KATHERINE BRADBERRY, the daughter of the Rev. David Bradberry & Dorothy C. his wife, who departed this life December 29th, 1795, aged 23 years.

Here lies, alas ! the Florist and the Flower,
Death grudged the World her Worth, and urg'd his Power,
Nor Skill Botanick could the Florist save ;
Yet Piety is fragrant in the Grave :
How sweet her Memry ; and her Dust shall rise,
Faith—Prudence—Prayer—shall blossom in the Skies.

The Rev'd. DAVID BRAD-BERRY, father of the above, departed this life Jany 13th, 1803, aged 67, having been a preacher of the Gospel forty-two years.

David Bradberry was not only a minister but he was also a hymn-writer. The place of his birth was Reek, in Yorkshire, and the date November 12th, 1735. The ministry of Whitefield was made a blessing to him, and after he became a preacher he held pastorates at Alnwick,

THE REV° DAVID BRADBERRY.

Ramsgate, Manchester, and Kennington, London. He
was pastor of the last-named church at the time of his
death. Just before his last breath was drawn, in answer
to a friend's question as to his feelings, he replied, " I am
very near heaven ; I am prepared to meet my God
through Christ."

ANTHONY CROLE.

THE broken head-stone of Anthony Crole will not be
difficult to discover. It is two rows east of Bradberry's,
but close to buildings. The top half of the stone is placed
in front of the next one, and is sunk so much in the
ground that the inscription is almost out of sight.

INSCRIPTION.

The Rev. ANTHONY CROLE, who closed a laborious and
useful life, July 3rd, 1803, aged 63 years ; having been
upwards of twenty-six years pastor of a church of Christ
in this city.

Anthony Crole was born in Scotland in the year 1740.
As a youth he was highly favoured in having conferred
upon him a good education. This was not of the godless
character in which so many now delight, but was perme-
ated with true religious teaching and feeling. As a
young man of twenty-two years he made his home in
the great metropolis, and chiefly attended the ministry
of Mr. William Cruden, who preached at the Crown-
court Chapel.

There is ample evidence to prove that Mr. Crole
possessed abilities quite out of the ordinary, and having
a desire to be fully engaged as a minister he relinquished
his business and entered Lady Huntingdon's College at
Trevecca. He soon became noted for " the unaffected
simplicity, seriousness, and ability with which he delivered his sentiments on religious subjects ; the humility
and fervour with which he poured forth his soul in
devotional exercises ; the sanctity of his life and the

affectionate concern which he always expressed for the souls of his fellow-men."

During his stay at the College he became deeply exercised as to his own spiritual standing, but although his darkness of mind was great he was much used in giving consolation to other weary and heavy-laden souls. Light at last broke in upon him, and he was then favoured with a sweet and firm assurance of his interest in the work, life and death of Christ.

When his term at the College was completed he was sent with Mr. Clayton to the Tabernacle at Norwich, where Mr. Shirley had previously laboured so successfully.

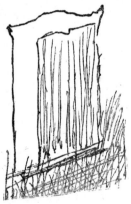

After serving as co-pastor with Mr. Clayton at Norwich, Mr. Crole became minister of the Independent Church meeting in Cumberland Street, Curtain Road, about 1776, and although in 1797 they removed to Pinner's Hall, and afterwards to Founder's Hall, he continued with this people until his death. He took a very prominent part in the opening of Cheshunt College in July, 1792, delivering a charge to the students in English, to the president in Latin, and finally to the trustees in English.

THE BROKEN HEAD-STONE.

His mind is clearly shown in a letter that he wrote to his dear friend, Mr. George Burder; it is evident that he had no sympathy with sensational preaching, or with anything unusual in the worship of God.

" Hoxton Square, Dec. 17th, 1779.

" Very dear Sir,—My neglect will not admit of an apology, therefore I shall not attempt the hypocrite in making one. Ten thousand circumstances conspire to convict me of ingratitude, and to lay me low at the feet both of God and His people. I must know but this, that He is ever and superabundantly merciful, and that I am ever and most unnaturally forgetful of Him, in comparison of what I ought to be. Jesus

I have proved, and do now find to be, an overflowing Fountain
of all kinds of goodness ; my prayers have come up before
Him, and been presented by Him with freedom of access, and
most gracious acceptance in ten thousand instances ; His
blood, His righteousness, His adorable Person are everlastingly prevalent before the throne of the Majesty on high ;
and it is the grandest boast of Satan when he can tempt us to
leave out, or but sparingly to introduce, these in preaching.
These topics God always has blessed, now does, and ever will
bless to spiritual hearers ; and nothing else but these to any
kind of hearers whatever. A neighbour of yours last time
he was in town grieved many of us sadly in the choice of
his texts and manner of treating them ; such words and
phrases as these were singled out : ' Him,' ' nothing,' ' who
can tell ? ' etc., etc. Then the ingenuity of the preacher was
put on the stretch to torture these words through I do not
know how many fancies, and into a corresponding number of
ludicrous shapes. Such essays of skill please a certain congregation far better than a solid and well-digested discourse ;
and I am well persuaded that the good man was overcome by
a temptation to please ; and that upon mature reflection he
will blush for his levity. We hope, if his voice is restored,
that he will use it to better purposes than when in town last.
Perhaps you may think it proper to give him a hint. Our
time is short ; souls are precious ; death and judgment are at
the door ; who, then, should trifle or be idle ? Popery increases, blasphemy is bold, and damnable errors like the
waters are out almost everywhere. Is this a time for amuse-
ment ? We have ten thousand thanks to render to our God
for His mercies manifested in Pinner's Hall ; we are tolerably
well-attended, and are translated into quite a new climate.
No greater blessings can there be to a minister than to be
connected with spiritual, upright, and honest men. God's
presence must not be expected to consecrate hypocrisy ; nor
His power to promote, under the mask of religion, a worldly
plan. We had need to be cautious of our company ; some
men to serve themselves will not stick at ruining a minister's
character or family ; and to cover a selfish end (as Mr. Hilder-
sham says), would have him so heavenly as not to need the
institution of marriage ; so strong in faith as to coin money
for all his supplies ; and so holy as to be without even an infirmity ; and if he fails in all or either of these then he is
' earthly, sensual, and devilish.' Upon the whole, I think
Christ grows more precious to me every day. O what a
shame that ever our love should abate, or our zeal suffer one

moment's eclipse! I love and admire Ryland for this; his honest zeal glows and shines in every page : we have few such men ; our ministers here are almost half dead ; nothing will rouse us but the trump of God ; all the alarms of war, Popish bills, and declining grace, have little affected us yet. Lord, have mercy on this ungrateful and unfeeling land !

"I have one favour to beg of you before I conclude, and that is, to help me to praise the God of all grace. My dear wife this morning was safely delivered of another daughter, and both are doing exceedingly well. The words of the psalmist, by Dr. Watts, are well adapted to my case :

> "'Give to our God immortal praise,
> Mercy and truth are all His ways.
> Wonders of grace to God belong,
> Repeat His mercies in your song.'

"Time forbids my saying any more, than that I am sincerely yours, in all Christian and brotherly love,

"A. CROLE."

As a minister Mr. Crole was most diligent in his study of the Scriptures, and fearless in proclaiming the truth. No labour was counted too great and no fear of consequences was ever before his eyes. He suffered long and severely, but his death was quite sudden and peaceful.

GARNET TERRY.

ALMOST in front of Anthony Crole's head-stone is the railed tomb of Garnet Terry.

INSCRIPTION.

In this vault are deposited the remains of GARNET TERRY, Esq., of Artillery Place, Finsbury Square; many years Engraver to the Governor and Company of the Bank of England; who departed this life 31st July, 1817, aged 73. He built at his own expense a Meeting in Curtain Road, Shoreditch ; where he preached the Gospel for several years without any emolument; and as a token of his affectionate regard, bequeathed £6,000 to be equally divided amongst the members of the church belonging to that place. He also left £500 to a society for visiting the sick, which he had also established. "Inasmuch as ye did it to the least of these My brethren, ye did it unto Me."

Garnet Terry was at one time a great friend of William Huntington, but being taken to task very severely by the "Coalheaver" on points of doctrine they became estranged.

———————

THREE rows east from Terry's tomb, but nearer to the path, is the head-stone of ESTHER BENNET, and five farther east, but much closer to the buildings, is that of W. JOHNSON.

JOHN CONDER, D.D.

THE visitor must return westwards and pass a few steps along the first path on the left hand. The head-stone of John Conder is on the right, and three or four rows from the path. The stone was renewed and the present inscription placed upon it in 1867, but the original one was in Latin.

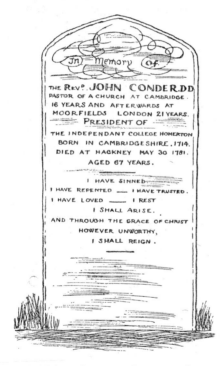

IN MEMORY OF

THE Revᵈ. JOHN CONDER.DD.
PASTOR OF A CHURCH AT CAMBRIDGE.
16 YEARS AND AFTERWARDS AT
MOORFIELDS LONDON 21 YEARS.
PRESIDENT OF
THE INDEPENDANT COLLEGE HOMERTON
BORN IN CAMBRIDGESHIRE. 1714.
DIED AT HACKNEY MAY 30 1781.
AGED 67 YEARS.

I HAVE SINNED
I HAVE REPENTED ___ I HAVE TRUSTED.
I HAVE LOVED ___ I REST
I SHALL ARISE.
AND THROUGH THE GRACE OF CHRIST
HOWEVER UNWORTHY,
I SHALL REIGN.

The place of Dr. Conder's birth was Wimpole, in Cambridgeshire, the date being June 3rd, 1714. At the time of his birth the Nonconformists were in great fear because of the Schism Bill, but with Queen Anne's death and the accession of King George I. much brighter days followed.

Dr. Conder has stated that his grandfather, kissing him when a babe, said with tears in his eyes, "Who knows what sad days these little eyes are likely to see?" but in referring to this circumstance Dr. Conder remarked, "These eyes have for more than 60 years seen nothing but goodness and mercy follow me, and the churches of Christ, even to this day." His first sermon was preached in 1738, the text being, "I am not ashamed of the Gospel of Christ" (Rom. i. 16); and as stated in the inscription he then became pastor of a church at Cambridge. By doctrine and practice he was an Independent; and after a successful and acceptable ministry at Cambridge he became the President of the Independent College, Homerton, in 1754. In 1762 he was accepted as pastor of the church meeting in Moorfields, and he continued there for twenty-one years. He was an eminently skilful and gracious minister. In his last illness he said, "I bless God that I can say that I have no doubt that all things are rightly settled between me and my Master." The latter part of the inscription was composed by himself; in fact, he was a writer of repute, the following hymn being a good specimen of his powers in this direction:

"Blessed are the dead which die in the Lord" (Rev. xiv. 13).

> Christ watches o'er the embers
>   Of all His faithful dead;
> There's life for all the members
>   In Him, the living Head;
> Their dust He weighs and measures,
> Their every atom treasures.
>
> He, once a Victor bleeding,
>   Slew Death, destroy'd the grave;
> Now throned, yet interceding,
>   He lives, the soul to save:
> He comes, O day of wonder!
> The graves are rent asunder!
>
> But, oh, that vast transition!
>   How shall a creature dare
> Gaze on the awful vision,
>   To find a Saviour there?
> They whom He deigns to cherish
> Shall never, never perish!
>
> Their Saviour shall receive them,
>   From sin and death released;
> He shall Himself present them
>   Before the Father, dress'd
> In robes of spotless whiteness,
> All beauty, joy, and brightness.

JOHN CONDER, D.D.

JOHN MARTIN.

THE north-south path must be crossed, and the head-stone of John Martin is four rows on the grass and slightly south.

John Martin was born at Spalding, in Lincolnshire, March 15th, 1741. As a lad he was apprenticed to a man at Stamford, whom he afterwards described as " a confectioner, china and glass man, mustard-maker, brick-maker, maltster, a considerable dealer in tiles, slates, free-stone, and I know not what besides." Mr. Martin has told how he was first brought under conviction of sin, but the account is too long for insertion. It appears, however, that he was travelling with his em-ployer, and they were compelled to spend the night at a village called Claynorth. Being told a religious service was to take place during the evening, he attended this, which was held in a large room. There were about twenty or thirty persons present, and the preacher was a grave-looking man, who took for his text, " They shall ask the way to Zion, with their faces thitherwards " (Jer. l. 5). No impression was made until, as the service was drawing to a close, the preacher said, " Some, instead of asking their way to Zion, with their faces thither-wards, are asking the way to hell, with their faces thitherwards." This caused young Martin much trouble, and he tried to reform himself, but in vain. After many distressing experiences he was brought to see that God had made Christ, who knew no sin, to be sin, that they who believe might be made the righteousness of God in Him.

In 1765 he was baptized, and joined the little Baptist Church in the Cambridgeshire village of Gamlingay, and he was soon after called to the ministry. Until 1774 he laboured in the country, and then removed to London, becoming pastor of the church meeting in Grafton Street, Soho. At his ordination Abraham Booth gave the charge to the minister, and John Macgowan preached to the Church. The old building being unsuitable a new one was opened in Keppel Street, Bedford Square, in

JOHN MACGOWAN, V.D.M., and × JOHN STEVENS

(See pages 225 and 228.)

The marked head-stone is JOSEPH SWAIN'S.   In the distance
between the trees the tomb of JOSEPH HART is seen, and JOHN
MACGOWAN'S is on the left in front of the first tree.

(See page 229.)

WATTS WILKINSON, A.B.

(See page 237.)

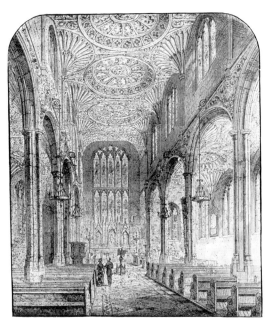

ST. MARY, ALDERMARY.

(See page 238.)

1795. One of the deacons, William Ashlin,* undertook all responsibility for the work, telling the church that after all was completed they might give him what they were able towards the expenses. The sum of £1,700 was subscribed, which left Mr. Ashlin £1,775 to pay.

It is not a little remarkable that in one of his last discourses Mr. Martin imagines a preacher falling under terrible trials. He loses first his physical and then his mental powers, until he is as helpless and as foolish as a babe; yet through it all he

The Reverend JOHN MARTIN.

feels he is not cut off from the love of God. This described literally the condition into which he himself was brought, and in which he remained for six years.

INSCRIPTION.

Here are laid the remains of the Rev. JOHN MARTIN, who, after having honourably filled the office of Pastor over the Church of Christ in Keppel Street for more than forty years, and being prevented by disease from continuing his labours for nearly six years, was removed from an earthly to an heavenly sabbath on Lord's Day, April 23rd, 1820, in the 80th year of his age.

JOHN MACGOWAN.

THE head-stone of John Macgowan stands by the side of the second path, and almost in a line with John Skepp's. It therefore lies in a south-east direction from Martin's.

---

* Mr. Ashlin is also buried in Bunhill Fields. The fine large tomb may be seen in the north-east corner, but will crumble away, as so many others have done, unless attention is paid to it.

Q

INSCRIPTION.

Here lies JOHN MACGOWAN, U.D.M.,* who at the hand
of God merited nothing but final destruction, yet, through
grace, was enabled to hope in a finished salvation. He
died Nov. 25th, 1780, aged 54 years. "For by grace are
ye saved, through faith, and that not of yourselves, it is
the gift of God."—Eph. ii. 8.

This famous minister and author was born in Edinburgh
about the year 1726. There is very little information
obtainable with respect to his early life, but it appears that
owing to the poverty of his parents he only received a very
ordinary education and was apprenticed to the weaving
trade when still young. His early religious experience
was amongst the Wesleyan Methodists, and for a time
he was one of their itinerant preachers. Being convinced, however, that their doctrines were not in keeping
with the Scriptures, he became connected with the
Calvinistic Independents and afterwards with the Particular Baptists. His first pastorate was at Bridgnorth
in Shropshire, but very poor success attended his labours.
This discouraged him greatly, but having been invited to
preach at the Devonshire Square Baptist Church as a
supply, his ministry met with so much acceptance that
he was appointed pastor there. The ordination took
place on July 29th, 1767, the ministers taking part being
Dr. Gill and Dr. Stennett, with Mr. Burford and Mr.
Wallin. The three first named ministers are, of course,
buried in Bunhill. During his ministry at Devonshire
Square Macgowan obtained a high reputation for his
literary work, his best known book being "The Dialogue
of Devils." A sermon, however, that he published entitled, "The Shaver, or, Priestcraft Defended," at the
time of the expulsion of the seven young men from
Oxford for indulging in private worship, is a most powerful
piece of satire mingled with shrewd wit. The action of
the authorities at the University called forth the strongest
condemnation of George Whitefield, the Countess of
Huntingdon and many others, but no one was quite so
effective in protesting as John Macgowan. His "Life of
Joseph" is an extraordinary piece of allegory, but when
Macgowan dealt in this kind of thing he was really

* This stands for *Verbum Dei Minister*, i.e., Minister of the Word of God.

inclined to go beyond legitimate bounds. His pastorate at Devonshire Square lasted for nearly fifteen years, and death at last severed the divinely appointed relationship. Mr. John Reynolds, M.A.,* who was then pastor at Cripplegate, wrote a preface to Macgowan's "Boaz and Ruth," and gave in it the following account of his last days.

"I frequently visited him in his last sickness, when he took occasion, as opportunity offered, of opening to me his whole heart. At one time he was in great darkness of soul, and lamented exceedingly the withdrawings of the presence of God. Two things, he said, had deeply exercised his thoughts. The one was how these heavy and complicated afflictions which God had seen fit to lay upon him could work so as to promote his real good. And the other was, that God, his best Friend, should keep at a distance from his soul, when He knew how much his mind was distressed for the light of His countenance. 'Oh!' said he, turning to me and speaking with great earnestness, 'my soul longeth and panteth for God, for the living God; His love visits would cheer my soul, and make this heavy affliction sit light upon me. The wonted presence of Jesus, my Redeemer, I cannot do without. I trust He will return to me soon—yea, I know He will in His own good time: for He knows how much I need the influence of His grace.' In this conversation, he often mentioned the depravity of his nature, and what a burden he found it. 'My heart,' said he, 'is more and more vile—every day I have such humiliating views of heart-corruption as weigh me down. I wonder whether any of the Lord's people see things in the same light as I do?' And then turning to me, he said, 'And do you find it so, my brother?' Upon my answering in the affirmative, he replied, 'I am glad of that.'

"The next time, which was the last of my conversing with him, I found him in a sweet and heavenly frame; his countenance indicated the serenity of his mind. On my entering the room, he exclaimed, 'O my dear brother, how rejoiced am I to see you! Sit down, and hear of the lovingkindness of my God. You see me as ill as I can be in this world, and as well as I can be whilst in the body. Methinks I have as much of heaven as I can hold.' Then tears of joy like a river flowed from his eyes; and his inward pleasurable frame interrupted his speech for a time. He broke silence with saying: 'The work will soon be over—you see what you must soon experience. But death, to me, has nothing terrific in it—I have not an anxious thought. . . . We are to part here; but we shall meet again. You cannot conceive the pleasure I feel in this reflection, viz., that I have not shunned to declare (according to my light and ability) the whole counsel of God. I can die on the doctrines which I have preached—they are true—I found them so. Go on to preach the Gospel of Christ, and mind not what the world may say of you.' All the while I sat silent ; and rising up to take my leave, fearing he would spend his strength too much, he immediately took me by the hand, and weeping over each other, we wished mutual blessings. Upon parting, he said, 'My dear brother, farewell—I shall see you no more.' Thus I left my esteemed friend and brother ; and the next news I heard of him was, that on the Saturday evening his immortal spirit left the body, to go to the world of bliss, and keep an eternal Sabbath with God, angels and saints."

The funeral sermon was preached by Mr. Wallin on a text which had been chosen for the occasion by Macgowan himself : "Is not this a brand plucked out of the fire?" Zec. iii. 2. As a preacher and writer Mr. Macgowan would give no quarter to priestcraft in any form, nor to Socinianism, Arianism or Arminianism.

As shown in the illustration, just at the back of Macgowan's head-stone is that of JOHN STEVENS. The inscription is practically obliterated, which is a great pity.

Sacred to the memory of the Rev. JOHN STEVENS, who exchanged mortality for immortal vigour, and for a crown of life ; after a long affliction of excruciating pain from the stone, &c., under which he enjoyed great supports, lively joys, and strong comforts ; composedly and resignedly waiting and wishing for the uninterrupted enjoyment of his covenant God, whom living he delighted to proclaim ; whom dying he glorified, October 17, 1778, aged 56. Rev. xiv. 13 : "Blessed are the dead which die in the Lord from henceforth : yea, saith the Spirit, that they may rest from their labours ; and their works do follow them."

> "Look up, my friends, pant towards the eternal hills,
>   Those heavens are fairer than they seem ;
> There pleasures all sincere glide on in crystal rills ;
>   There not a dreg of guilt defiles,
>   Nor grief disturbs the stream.
> That Canaan knows no noxious thing,
> No curséd soil, no tainted spring,
> No roses grow on thorns, no honey wears a sting."

JOSEPH SWAIN.

THE head-stone of Joseph Swain is a few rows north-west of Macgowan's. It stands on the south side of a fast breaking-down tomb.

In memory of the Rev. J. SWAIN, of Walworth, *Obt.* April 14, 1796, *æt* 35.

The above portion of the inscription is practically obliterated, but the words, " Susannah, his wife, and their three children," are still quite distinct upon the head-stone.

This saintly hymn-writer was born at Birmingham in the year 1761, and his father and mother died when he was very young. He was apprenticed to an engraver, but did not complete his full time, coming to London in order to be with his elder brother. For a time he lived a very gay life, and as he was always bright and cheerful his company was much desired and greatly sought for. In the midst of his gaiety the thought came to his mind that he was completely neglecting the Holy Scriptures, that he was going to destruction, and that his end would be most terrible. These things led him to purchase a Bible, and through reading this his convictions of sin increased. He describes his feelings in his diary under the date of April 2nd, 1782.

" I was followed, for about six months or more, with dreadful torments, particularly in the night season ; fearing lest by fire, or sickness, or some other means, I might be removed into the endless fire of hell. These things, however, were insufficient to wean me from my worldly acquaintances and sinful practices, for I still found that I loved my sins, and was not able to give them up ; though I feared the punishment due to them. After a long succession of these things, together with many legal workings, and various attempts to make my own peace with God, on the day before mentioned, as I was going with my companions in sin to a place of entertainment, I felt my heart gradually melted into love of being : into love of my own being : and desired that everybody might be made happy. I then attempted to seek to God by prayer ; and was assisted with such a spirit of supplication as till then I was a stranger to. I then had many passages of scripture brought to my remembrance, wherein I saw myself as a sinner, and Christ as a Saviour. Yea, I saw and believed that He died for me, and that I should soon be with Him in glory, at the right hand of God. And oh! how did my enraptured soul rejoice in this great salvation at this time! So great were the peace and satisfaction I enjoyed, that I thought I could bear to be confined in the darkest dungeon for ever, provided I might always feel what I then felt of the presence of God in my soul: and so much did I fear getting back into the world again, that I was ready to pray that I might never eat, drink, or be employed about earthly things, any more for ever. But ah! the heavenly vision was not to continue always, as I soon found by experience. For in about two hours from the time I went into the place (of entertainment), a kind of coldness seized my frame; and, almost on a sudden, the heavenly scene was snatched away, and I was left with little more than the remembrance of it; except that in my heart I felt an aching void, which I was persuaded all things else could never fill."

Early in 1783 he went to hear Dr. Rippon, and was publicly baptized by him on May 11th of that year. It appeared to his friends that his ecstasy of spiritual joy was so great that he was fast ripening for heaven, and once after hearing Mr. Berridge preach, he said to his wife, "My dear, I do think I shall die with joy." An extract from his diary will give real indication of his almost unique experience.

"July 17, 1783. Bitterness of soul inexpressible! Much relief from private prayer. Surprising deliverance in meditation, and ejaculation of thought to God! yet more blessed in prayer. This day the Valley of Achor was a door of hope to thee, O my soul! Remember this, and always cast thy burden on the Lord, who careth for thee. The goodness and condescension of the heart of God are astonishing beyond measure; and can only be felt, but not expressed, by man. Oh the height, depth, length, and breadth of the love of God! Who can measure it? Such deep distress, and such amazing liberty of soul, in one day, I never remember to have felt before! 'Wait on the Lord,' O my soul; wait on the Lord, 'and forget not all His benefits.' Note, that it is good, it is very profitable, though it be never so bitter, to have one's wounds probed to the quick."

In the early part of the year 1784 he commenced holding services at his house for prayer and Christian fellow-

ship. He would frequently expound the Scriptures there,
and also at a small meeting in another place; his friends
and the church, after hearing him preach, and noting his
excellent gifts for the ministry, gave him an invitation to
become the pastor at East Lane, Walworth. He commenced his labours in 1791, and he also delivered an
evening lecture each Lord's Day in Devonshire Square
Chapel. The building at Walworth soon became too
small to hold the congregations, and had to be enlarged
on two separate occasions. When he commenced his
ministry the church consisted of 27 members, but within
four years it increased to upwards of 200. Mr. Swain
suffered much from bodily weakness, but he would not
relax his efforts in any way, as he felt the work of the
ministry to be deeply important.

During this period he was continually writing hymns,
poems and essays, and there were thousands who hoped
he would be long spared to preach the Gospel. This,
however, was not to be, for he was struck down with a
fatal illness, when he was only about half-way to the
allotted span of man's life. His friend, Mr. Upton, when
preaching his funeral sermon, gave some particulars of his
last days, from which the following extract is taken :—

"On the Saturday night before his death, for about three
hours, he was favoured with the full use of his reason, and conversed as a dying man. He said to Mrs. Swain, 'Oh, my dear, I
perceive I have been under a mistake; I thought I was getting
better, but I now feel I am very bad. I have been seeking the
Lord about my case, and can get no other answer but this—
'Set thine house in order, for thou shalt die, and not live.'
On seeing her much affected, he said, 'Oh, my dear, don't
grieve; the Lord can make you a happy widow. You were
happy in the Lord before you knew me, and He can make you
happy when I am gone.' He reminded her also of a Christian
friend, who had been greatly supported and comforted under
the loss of a valuable husband. He then exclaimed; 'Oh, my
dear Redeemer! Am I coming to Thee so soon? Is my work
done? It is just fourteen years since I first knew Thee, Lord!
If it were Thy will, I should rejoice to labour a little longer
with the dear people; yet not my will, but Thine be done!'

"He then took his wife by the hand, and prayed very
fervently for her, and for the dear children; also for his church
at Walworth, and on behalf of those who attended his lecture

near Devonshire Square. After this he conversed about temporal concerns, and then returned to the solemn subject of death. He said, 'I am not afraid to die; I have not the shadow of doubt; I know that I shall receive my crown. Yet I should be glad to be engaged in my Lord's work a little longer, if it were His will.' He then exhorted those around him to aim at living near to God, and to wrestle with Him in prayer for the fulfilment of His gracious promises.

"On the Lord's day morning he was much in prayer for the church, and proceeded as regularly as though he had been in public. The minister who was to supply his place at Walworth that morning, called to see him, and engaged in prayer with him. But he could not attend long. The delirium came on so violently that he was not able to converse many minutes together, but often seemed to be engaged in ejaculatory prayer."

After suffering great afflictions for nearly a fortnight, Joseph Swain went to that heaven of which he had himself often written so beautifully. He was buried in Bunhill Fields on Friday, April 22nd, and many thousands of people were present. Mr. Abraham Booth delivered the address, and multitudes were overcome by emotion.

The poem chosen for insertion here, is entitled, "Conversion and Death of Poor Joseph," and the story which led to Swain's writing it is as follows:

"A poor, half-witted man named Joseph, whose employment was to go on errands and carry parcels, passing through London streets one day heard psalm-singing in the house of God. He went into it, having a large parcel of yarn hanging over his shoulders. It was Dr. Calamy's church, St. Mary's, Aldermanbury. A very well-dressed audience surrounded the Doctor. He read his text from 1 Tim. i. 15: 'This is a faithful saying, and worthy of all acceptation, that Christ Jesus came into the world to save sinners, of whom I am chief.' . . . Joseph, in rags, gazing with astonishment, never took his eyes from the preacher, but drank in with eagerness all he said, and, trudging homeward, he was heard thus muttering to himself: 'Joseph never heard this before; Christ Jesus, the God who made all things, came into the world to save sinners like Joseph; and this is true, and it is a "faithful saying."'"

Joseph soon after was taken ill, and in his delirium said some wonderfully touching things. One of the watchers fetched Dr. Calamy, who, as stated in the poem, received from dying Joseph's hand a purse of gold, which contained five guineas.

CONVERSION AND DEATH OF POOR JOSEPH.

Was it a chance; or the unerring hand
Which (holding all things at supreme command)
Gives the bright sun to cheer a world with light,
And clothes in black'ning shades the dreary night;
That bid the event recorded here revolve?
Christian, thy heart can soon this query solve!
A poor man, clothed in rags and short of wit,
Was one day strolling careless through the street:
A knot of yarn across his shoulders hung,
And trailed behind him as he walked along:
Little he thought that he possessed a soul,
Or whose the power that bids the seasons roll:
When sent on simple errands he could go;
Nought else he knew, or aught desired to know:
Alike of things in heaven, or things on earth,
Of what begets events, or gives them birth,
Listless, he trudged along till, with the sound
Of music roused, he starts, and gazes round—
Where he perceives a full assembled place,
And enters, gaping with unmeaning face. . . .
Above the rest, a servant of the Lord
Stood to proclaim the everlasting Word;
Who, with a pause, opened the sacred book;
Then, with a voice profound and speaking look,
Pronounced that faithful word—that Christ came down
From heaven's bright mansions and His Father's throne,
And put on mortal flesh, that He might save
A sinking world from an eternal grave;
Yea, how He for the chief of sinners died,
And every claim of justice satisfied.
Poor Joseph trembled, while he heard him speak
Of wrath to come, as if his heart would break:
Till through his soul he felt the silver sound
Of sweet salvation and a ransom found.
Struck with astonishment, he fix'd his eyes
Full on the preacher; and with glad surprise
Drank down the joyful news with greedy ears,
Which reached his heart, and filled his eyes with tears.
The service ended, Joseph trudged away,
And thus within himself was heard to say—
" Joseph was never told of this before!"

Did Jesus Christ, the mighty God, whose power
Made heaven and earth and all things, come and die
To save poor helpless sinners, such as I ?
Why this is brave !   And, if all this be true,
Who knows but Jesus died for Joseph too ? "
   Soon after this a message from on high
Was sent to warn poor Joseph he must die :
A burning fever raged through all his veins,
And racked his body with a thousand pains.
Ye who delight the paths of sin to tread,
Attend poor Joseph to his dying bed,
And listen to the language of his heart,
When soul and body were about to part.
No rich variety of speech he knew,
Heart-sprung and simple were his words, though few :
Jesus, and Jesus' love, was all his theme—
Sufficient proof that Jesus had loved him !
And while with pain from side to side he rolled,
He these great things in little accents told :
" Joseph's so vile, there cannot be a worse,
Joseph deserves God's everlasting curse.
The chief of sinners, Joseph is indeed ;
But did not Jesus for such sinners bleed ?
I heard one say that Jesus was a friend
To poor, lost sinners, whom He would defend
From God's just vengeance and the pit of hell ;
And, if a friend of sinners, who can tell
But Joseph may be one whom Jesus loves ? "
   But while poor Joseph thus his interest proves,
One standing by, with cautious tone, replies :
" But, Joseph, we are told by One that's wise,
That nothing's so deceitful as the heart ;
How do you find yourself about that part ?
Remember what the word is to all men,
None can be saved but who are born again :
Have you no token thereabout for good ?
No relish, no desire for heavenly food ?
Have you no inward evidence to prove
That you are loved with everlasting love ?
'Tis a great thing to be an heir of heaven—
To see your sins, and see them all forgiven ;
To have your soul redeemed with precious blood,
And as a pilgrim walk the heavenly road ;
To tread the path of holiness below,
And drink the streams from Zion's Rock that flow ;

To live by faith upon the Son of God,
To own His sceptre and to kiss His rod;
To die to sin and live to righteousness;
To be possessed of covenanted peace;
To trust for life in Christ, and Christ alone:
And none but such shall sing around His throne."
  Poor Joseph listened, and with artless tongue
Resumed the burden of his former song:
" Joseph has nothing for himself to say;
He's deep in debt, and nothing has to pay.
Joseph's a sinner—Jesus came from heaven,
And shed His blood, that sins might be forgiven.
Jesus did die to set poor sinners free,
And who can tell but Jesus died for me?
Joseph desires to love Him for this love,
And why not Joseph sing His praise above?" . . .
  Meanwhile, in came that servant of the Lord
Who first in Joseph's ears proclaimed the Word.
Ghastly and pale, between the jaws of death,
Just ready to resign his feeble breath,
Upwards he looked, and trembling with surprise,
The briny moisture starting in his eyes:
" Sir, is it you?" with quivering lips he cried;
" 'Twas you that told me first how Jesus died
For sinners such as Joseph, weak and poor,
That seek the bread of life at Mercy's door.
Oh, pray for Joseph to that loving Lord!
Tell Him that Joseph trusts His faithful Word;
And loves Him as the sinner's only Friend,
Who died His chosen people to defend."
  He prayed; poor Joseph held his hand the while,
Pressed it, and thanked him with a peaceful smile;
Then from his pillow took a purse of gold:
" This was," said he, " to keep me when grown old;
Which for the poor beloved of Jesus take,
And tell 'em Joseph loved them for His sake."
Then calmly met the uplifted hand of death,
Blessed the kind Saviour with his fleeting breath,
And died! With tears the preacher left the place,
And Joseph's gone to sing redeeming grace!

Ought not the head-stone of Joseph Swain to be refaced? Surely the resting-place of such a poet, hymn-writer and preacher might be remembered.

MARY LILBURN'S head-stone is standing almost at the corner of the buildings. There are several rows of head-stones,and a north-south path separating it from Swain's. A few words of the inscription can with great difficulty be made out.

MEMENTO MORI.
Here lyes interr'd the Body of MARY LILBURN, the wife of Nathaniel Lilburn, of Cripple-gate Parish, who departed this Life Nov. 12, 1713. Aged 38.

"Lo here she lies interr'd, who humbly gave
Her Soul to God, her Body to the Grave.
Throughout her Passage to a better Life,
She prov'd a pious, virtuous, loving Wife.
She dy'd to live, and humbly liv'd to dye;
So God remov'd her to compleat her Joy:
And her surviving Spouse in Christ doth trust
To mix his Ashes with her sacred Dust."

WESTFIELD LILLEY,

A FEW rows east and three from the path is Westfield Lilley's head-stone.

In memory of WESTFIELD LILLEY, son of Westfield and Sarah Lilley, who died June 2nd, 1798, aged one year and ten months.

"Bold Infidelity, turn pale and die,
Under this stone an Infant's ashes lie.
Say, Is it Lost or Saved?

If Death's by sin, it sinned, for it lies here ;
If Heaven's by works, in Heaven it can't appear.
    Ah, reason, how deprav'd !
Revere the Bible ! (sacred page) the knot's unty'd ;
It died, through Adam's sin ; it lives, for Jesus died."

The above lines were written by the Rev. David
Brown, of Calcutta, on the death of his infant son David.
The child was born at sea on Feb. 1st, 1786, and died at
the Orphan Home, Bengal, April 20th, 1787. The lines
have been a good deal altered at various times, and are
to be found in a number of burying grounds.

WATTS WILKINSON, A.B.

THE tall head-stone of Watts Wilkinson is east of
Lilley's, but nearer the buildings.

> The Rev. WATTS WILKINSON, A.B., Lecturer of the
> united parishes of St. Mary Aldermary, and St. Thomas
> the Apostle, Bow Lane ; Tuesday morning Lecturer at St.
> Bartholomew's Exchange ; and late Chaplain to Aske's
> Hospital ; died December 14th, 1840, in the 86th year of
> his age, and in the 62nd year of his ministry. "They
> that be wise shall shine as the brightness of the firma-
> ment ; and they that turn many to righteousness as the
> stars for ever and ever."

Watts Wilkinson was born in London, November 14th,
1755, and his father, Robert Wilkinson, was a fervent
Protestant Dissenter. Although at the outset Wilkinson
was strenuously opposed to the Established Church he
ultimately entered it as a minister, but although his
opinions of Church Government and discipline were
changed he held strenuously to the vital truths of the
gospel. Before he left school he attended a Friday evening Lecture at St. Antholin's Church, to hear Henry
Foster. This was to him a memorable evening, for during the preaching real and lasting good was received.

In due course he went to Worcester College, Oxford,
and was ordained a deacon in the Chapel Royal on

February 17th, 1779. The same day he preached in the Church of St. Ann, Blackfriars, taking for his subject, the conversion of Manasseh. At the close of this year he was elected to the Lectureship of St. Mary and St. Thomas, and some two months later was appointed Chaplain of Aske's Hospital, Hoxton. He was also Lecturer at St. Antholin's, Watling Street, but he resigned this post when he obtained the "Golden Lecture" at St. Bartholomew's, close to the Royal Exchange. The word "Golden" was applied because of the endowment connected with it. Mr. Wilkinson retained this Lectureship for upwards of 37 years. Large congregations attended his ministry, and he preached the last sermon here on April 28th, 1840, the building then being demolished.*

Wilkinson preached his last sermon from the words, "Ye are no more strangers and foreigners, but fellow citizens with the saints, and of the household of God" (Eph. ii. 19), and as he was much distressed by a racking cough he finished his discourse earlier than usual. When he reached home he expressed his conviction that he should never preach again, and it was soon clear that his work was done. It was fourteen weeks later that he drew his last breath, and during this period he gave utterance to many solemn words, some of which have been preserved by his son. He frequently said, "Glory be to His name. I am fixed upon the Rock; a firm foundation is beneath me." He also said, "I find it very delightful to look back upon all the way by which the Lord has been leading me these twice forty years in the wilderness. Under mysterious dispensations of providence I have often derived great consolation from that text, 'What I do thou knowest not now, but thou shalt know hereafter.' Never did I expect on earth to have the 'need be' for every trial so clearly revealed to me, as I have of late. I now feel and know that I have not only been led by a right way to a City of habitation,

---

*Nearly 300 years previously the remains of Miles Coverdale, the man who had the honour of giving to the English Nation the first complete Bible in their own tongue, had been buried near to the Communion Table. Coverdale died on May 20th, 1567, when 81 years of age, and his remains were re-interred at St. Magnus, London Bridge.

but by the only right way that could have led me there."

He once observed with emotion, " I have been trying to read a little in my Bible, but I cannot do that now without fatigue ; that blessed Book has been my constant study for above sixty years ; I can still feed upon it ; it seems as fresh in my memory as ever ; I believe I could quote any part of it as well as ever. Oh! the mercy and lovingkindness of the Lord to me is unbounded ! Cleave closely to Jesus ; cleave closely to Jesus ! The truths I have been preaching all my life are my support and comfort now." When referring to the doctrines which he had so long and faithfully preached, he stated, " I wish to leave this as my dying testimony, that these alone were the doctrines which supported me when I was first convinced of sin, without which I never could have found peace ; and with this experience of a preciousness in my soul, how could I withhold them from others ? They have been my support and comfort all my life, and now in the near approach of an opening eternity, I still find them sufficient to bear me up, as a firm foundation beneath my feet."

The night before he died he was heard to say, "Christ is worth more than ten thousand worlds. I do desire to depart, I do desire to depart."

> "Oh ! let me catch one glimpse of Thee !
> Then drop into eternity."

Only one other word was he heard to speak, and this he repeated three times,—" Name, name, name." And there can be no doubt that this name was the name of Jesus, which had so long been sweet in his ears.

The day of his death was December 14th, 1840. He was one of the few Episcopalians buried in Bunhill

Fields, and his stone is in need of immediate attention. There are several other members of the family buried in the same grave.

Mr. Wilkinson was a generous and most enthusiastic supporter of the " Aged Pilgrims' Friend Society," and also of many other religious and philanthropic agencies.

BETWEEN the grave of Wilkinson and the path there is the splendid tomb of DANIEL WILLIAMS, D.D. It is railed round, but the original inscription, which is a long and complex one, cannot be read. On the north side of Williams' tomb is that of BENJAMIN GROSVENOR, who was in his day a minister of some repute.

WILLIAM DOWARS.

THE head-stone of William Dowars is several rows east, and adjoins the path. The ' reader ' will have to very 'attentively survey this stone' to make out any of the inscription now, as it is for the most part undecipherable.

INSCRIPTION.

In memory of the Rev. Mr. WILLIAM DOWARS, minister thirty-eight years of the Church of Christ in Little Alie Street, Goodman's Fields. *Obit.* July 1st, 1795, *ætatis* 75.

" Reader, attentively survey this stone ;
Here lies a minister whose work is done ;
A workman in the temple of the Lord,
Who sweetly quoted portions of His Word,
Exalted Christ, and laid the creature low :
The Church this commendation must bestow."

ISAAC WATTS, D.D.

(See page 241.)

THE SPIKED GATE. (See page 7.)

ISAAC WATTS.

THE tomb of Watts will already have attracted the visitor's attention. It must be pointed out that across the path on the east side is the head-stone of Samuel Say, who was a fellow student of Watts, and who also became a preacher. Almost in a line with Say's head-stone there is quite a cluster of tombs of noted people, amongst them being the learned John Eames and Mr. William Cruden—not Alexander of Concordance fame.

HEAD-STONE INSCRIPTION.

ISAAC WATTS, D.D., Pastor of a Church of Christ in London; successor of the Rev. Mr. Joseph Caryl, Dr. John Owen, Mr. David Clarkson, and Dr. Isaac Chauncey: after 50 years of feeble labours in the Gospel, interrupted by 4 years of tiresome sickness, was at last dismissed to rest, Nov. 25, A.D. 1748, age 75. 2 Cor. 5, 8, "Absent from the body, present with the Lord." Col. 3, 4, "When Christ who is our life shall appear, I shall also appear with Him in Glory."

In Uno Jesus Omnia.

Who better known than Isaac Watts? His hymns are sung in every professed Christian body, although it is to be feared many know not the meaning of the words they sing. When advanced in years he is described as a "little feeble old man, shy in manner yet rich in speech. . . . Wherever he goes he is regarded with veneration and love, for his mind is stored with knowledge and his heart is alive with tender sympathies."

The date of his birth was July 17th, 1674, and thus he came into the world in the stormiest days of Nonconformity. His father kept a boarding-school at Southampton, but being a stedfast Dissenter and a deacon at a chapel in the seaport town he was often called upon to suffer. On more than one occasion he was placed in a prison-cell whilst his property was sequestrated. The sorrowing mother of Isaac often took her little child and sat on a cold stone by the prison walls, and one cannot wonder that the principles of

R

Dissent soon became very dear to the future poet. His father was never a time-server, but stood firmly amidst sore tribulations, counting it a joy to suffer for righteousness' sake, and scorning the respectability and social standing which a connection with the Established Church would have brought him.

It is recorded that almost as soon as Isaac could lisp a word his oft-repeated request was for " A book! a book! Buy a book ! " His early years must be passed over with a few words. The school which he attended was one where he was well instructed, and had he been willing to forsake the conventicle he would have been sent to one of the Universities, as several wealthy people were anxious to find the necessary money for this purpose. While quite a child Watts showed much skill in writing rhymes, and when this gift was developed and sanctified he penned the hymns which are so valued by the Church of God. To complete his education he was placed under the care of Thomas Rowe, who in addition to his duties as pastor of the Independent Church in Girdlers Hall, London, kept an academy in which he trained many who became famous in their day and generation. On the return of Watts to his home his abilities were put to good use. It appears that the hymns sung at his father's chapel, whilst sound in doc- trine, were very poor from a poetical point of view, and each time gave offence to at least one member of the congregation. The young man was at last constrained to mention the matter to his preacher-father, who very sensibly invited him to try his own hand and endeavour to produce more pleasing lyrics. Isaac was not slow in acting upon this suggestion, and before long there were enough hymns to fill a volume.

The country around Southampton is well watered, and river and stream evidently inspired the poet, as is plainly seen in many of his hymns. It is quite easy to imagine the sweet singer roaming along the beautiful banks of the Itchen, which rises some twenty miles north of the famous port. At the old-fashioned village of Bishops Sutton the clear water gushes forth from the chalky earth. The brook soon increases in size owing to the many springs, and taking the form of a small river runs into a lake or large pond at Alresford. When it has forced its way through this it passes on towards Winchester and becomes full of trout and other fish. After leaving the ancient capital of England it grows larger still, and finally empties itself into Southampton Water. Think on this river, and then read:—

> " There is a land of pure delight,
>   Where saints immortal reign ;
> Infinite day excludes the night,
>   And pleasures banish pain.
>
> There everlasting spring abides,
>   And never-withering flowers ;
> Death, like a narrow sea, divides
>   This heavenly land from ours.
>
> Sweet fields beyond the swelling flood
>   Stand dress'd in living green :
> So to the Jews old Canaan stood,
>   While Jordan roll'd between.
>
> But timorous mortals start and shrink
>   To cross this narrow sea ;
> And linger shivering on the brink,
>   And fear to launch away.
>
> Oh ! could we make our doubts remove,
>   Those gloomy doubts that rise,
> And see the Canaan that we love
>   With unbeclouded eyes !
>
> Could we but climb where Moses stood,
>   And view the landscape o'er,
> Not Jordan's stream, nor death's cold flood,
>   Should fright us from the shore." *

It is very interesting to note what frequent references Watts makes in his hymns to water, tide, springs, sea, etc., and in these may be clearly traced the influence of the scenes of his boyhood.

When about 22 years of age he was invited by Sir John Hartopp to take up his residence at Stoke Newington, in the north of London, and act as tutor to his son.

* When the author asked his friend, Mr. John Newton, who has been so long the beloved minister of Hanover Chapel, Tunbridge Wells, which hymn of Dr. Watts' he loved the most, the reply was, " There is a land of pure delight."

To readers of Puritan literature, especially of the works of John Owen, the name of Hartopp will be familar. This godly man, with his family, befriended the Lord's people as much as possible, and often incurred considerable risk and expense. Whilst with Sir John, Watts preached his first sermon, and he was soon chosen assistant-minister to Dr. Chauncey. The Church was Independent, and met for worship in Mark Lane; after some time had elapsed Watts was appointed pastor. This position he held for the long period of 46 years, although he was not able to preach regularly owing to grievous bodily affliction. His nervous system was in a shattered condition, and this entailed insomnia. For nights he was utterly unable to sleep, and the most powerful drugs had no more good effect upon him than water, whilst, on the contrary, they helped to wreck and shatter his poor body. Humanly speaking, he could not have lived but for the unremitting and loving care bestowed upon him by Lady Abney and her daughter.

In his own words, as spoken to the Countess of Huntingdon, he expressed his feelings: "I came to the house of my good friend, Sir Thomas Abney, intending to spend a single week beneath his roof, and I have extended my visit to thirty years." "I consider your visit, my dear Sir, as the shortest my family ever received," replied Lady Abney in the courtly style used at that period. Sir Thomas died eight years after Watts became a resident under his roof, but Lady Abney survived the poet for some twelve months. In the Abney Park Cemetery there is a monument to Watts, but his dust is resting in Bunhill Fields.

In addition to the Abneys and Hartopps, the poet was favoured to have many choice friends. Lady Huntingdon loved him for the truth's sake, and amongst others, introduced him to the godly Col. Gardiner, who was afterwards slain at Prestonpans. The Colonel was a tall, stately man, making a noble figure in his regimentals, whilst at this time Watts was feeble and palsied, and in addition was sadly wasted.

Col. Gardiner's regard for Dr. Watts may be easily gauged from a letter which he wrote to Doddridge :

"I have long been in pain lest that excellent person, Dr. Watts, should be called to heaven before I had an opportunity of letting him know how much his works have been blessed to me, and, of course, of returning to him my hearty thanks. I must beg the favour of you to let him know that I intended to have waited on him in the beginning of last May when I was in London, but was informed, and that to my great sorrow, that he was extremely ill, and therefore I did not think a visit would be seasonable. I am well acquainted with his works, especially with the psalms, hymns, and lyrics. How often by singing some of these to myself, on horseback and elsewhere, has the wild spirit been made to flee away,

> "'Where'er my heart in tune was found,
> Like David's harp of solemn sound.'

I desire to bless God for the good news of his recovery; and entreat you to tell him that although I cannot keep pace with him here in celebrating the high praises of our glorious Redeemer, which is the great grief of my heart, yet I am persuaded when I join the glorious company above, where there will be no drawbacks, that none will out-sing me there, because I shall not find any that has been more indebted to the wonderful riches of divine grace than I :—

> "'Give me a place at Thy saints' feet,
> On some fallen angel's vacant seat ;
> I'll strive to sing as loud as they
> Who sit above in brighter day.'"

In his young days Watts was frequently in the company of a homely old man who gave little or no sign that he had been the most exalted person in the land, or that he had been a fugitive from his mother country and often in deep poverty for the long period of twenty years. This was none other than Richard Cromwell, who succeeded his famous father, Oliver, as Protector, but who, after seven months and twenty-eight days, retired from his honourable but dangerous position, and hastened away to France. Here he lived at various places, and under assumed names—it being his custom to change his name each time he moved his home—for twenty years, during which time his much loved wife and daughter Dorothy died. He had lived with the former only a few years, whilst the latter was the only Cromwell "born in the purple," but through this long period poor Richard

dared not place himself within the reach of Charles II.
He, however, ventured to return to England in 1680,
and died after much family trouble and strife in 1712,
at the age of 85. To the end of his days he enjoyed
remarkable health, and at the age of eighty could
gallop a horse several miles with keen enjoyment. He
was tall and fair-haired, making quite a striking contrast
to his diminutive friend, Isaac Watts. The latter testi-
fied that Richard Cromwell was a man of much ability,
and he missed no opportunity of being in the company of
the old soldier and ex-Protector. It is probable that the
influence of Cromwell may be seen in the numerous
and various descriptions which he gives in his hymns
of battles, fighting, armies, marching, and conflicts.

Watts died trusting alone in the merits, righteousness,
and blood of Christ, of which he had so often written.
One sentence from his death-bed was: " I remember an
aged minister say that the most learned and knowing
Christians when they come to die have only the same
plain promises of the Gospel for their support as the
common and unlearned of the people of God; and so I
find it. They are the plain promises which do not
require labour or pains to understand them ; for I can do
nothing now but look into my Bible for some promise to
support me, and live upon that."

His earthly course ended peacefully on November 25th,
1748, in the 75th year of his age, and his ransomed
spirit went to the land of which he had written so many
times, even " To mansions in the skies." When his
terrible sleeplessness is remembered we see a special and
pathetic meaning in this verse :—

> " There shall I bathe my weary soul
> In seas of heavenly rest,
> And not a wave of trouble roll
> Across my peaceful breast."

His poor " weary " body often longed for " rest." Oceans
of " trouble," physical, mental, and spiritual, rolled over
him here, and there was no freedom from pain. But
when he reached his home there was not even a "wave,"
and all was " peace."

When Dr. Watts quitted the devotional and the

practical for the speculative, he was away from home and dealing with things too high for him. He failed to ascend the heights to which he repaired, and it would have been more to the credit of his prudence if he had never tried.

Perhaps this is hardly the place to go fully into those doctrines held by him, which caused so many debates and disputes. It is, however, important to state that some things believed and preached by the " seraphic doctor " are entirely opposed to the Scriptures, and invariably have been looked upon with abhorrence by all who insist on dividing the true from the false and the precious from the vile. He sought to re-adjust the doctrine of the Trinity, and fell into error with respect to the Person and work of the Lord Jesus Christ and the personality and operations of the Holy Spirit, expressing notions which the Scriptures denounce and the experiences of God's people contradict. How far his aberrations from truth may be attributed to his shattered bodily and mental faculties will probably never be known, and the matter must therefore be left. The author, however, having read carefully most of the available writings upon the subject, feels compelled to record his conviction that, whilst Watts sadly erred upon some fundamental doctrines, the claim of Belsham and other Socinian ministers, that he died believing in their pernicious teachings, cannot be maintained.

As there are over three hundred ministers of religion buried in Bunhill, it has only been possible to mention a few of these.

The graves of some of the most gracious and famous cannot now be found, and preference has been given to those whose tombs or head-stones are still standing. If space had permitted, a short account of each one would have been given, and should there be a general desire for another volume, this may be complied with.

The following list contains the names of some of those whose particular resting-places are not known :—

Abbott, Mordecai	Kiffin, William	Palmer, Anthony
Clarke, Matthew	Knollys, Hanserd	Powell, Vavasour
Cole, Thomas	Lambert, James	Ridgley, Thomas
Doolittle, Thomas	Lobb, Theophilus	Robinson, Benjamin
Dyke, Daniel	Loder, John	Stretter, Richard
Evans, John	Maisters, Joseph	Stubbs, Henry
Faldo, John	Mather, Nathaniel	Towers, John
Gosnold, John	May, Samuel	Vincent, Nathaniel
Jacob, Joseph	Ness, Christopher	West, Edward
Jessey, Henry	Newman, John	Wilson, Samuel.
Key, Mark	Newman, Samuel	

The graves of the following ministers have been found, but no space was available for accounts of them :—

Barber, Joseph	Hunter, H.	Saunders, Thos.
Bradford, John	Jerment, G.	Simpson, R.
Clayton, John	Kello, John	Spilsbury, F.
Clayton, William	King, W.	Towle, John
Hall, Christopher	Lawson, Robert	Townsend, John
Hardcastle, Joseph	Platt, W. F.	Upton, James
Harris, Joseph	Savage, S. M.	Wilton, S.
Hockly, W.		